PLANETARY PROJECT

PLANETARY PROJECT
FROM SUSTAINABLE DEVELOPMENT TO MANAGED HARMONY

ALEKSANDR V. BEZGODOV

Copyright © 2015 by Aleksandr V. Bezgodov.

Library of Congress Control Number: 2015919761
ISBN: Hardcover 978-1-5144-4715-4
Softcover 978-1-5144-4714-7
eBook 978-1-5144-4713-0

All rights reserved. No part of this book may be reproduced or transmitted in any form or by any means, electronic or mechanical, including photocopying, recording, or by any information storage and retrieval system, without permission in writing from the copyright owner.

Author:
Dr Aleksandr Bezgodov, Doctor of Economics

Editors:
Prof. Dmitry Gavra, Doctor of Sociology
Dr Konstantin Barezhev, Ph.D. in Philosophy

Translators:
Dr Vadim Golubev, Ph.D. in Philology
Mr Peter Ellis, BSc in Engineering

Any people depicted in stock imagery provided by Thinkstock are models, and such images are being used for illustrative purposes only. Certain stock imagery © Thinkstock.

Print information available on the last page.

Rev. date: 12/04/2015

To order additional copies of this book, contact:
Xlibris
800-056-3182
www.Xlibrispublishing.co.uk
Orders@Xlibrispublishing.co.uk
727877

CONTENTS

Preface vii

Introduction ix

Chapter 1 Global World: Inevitability, Risks, and Needs 1

Chapter 2 Unification of Humanity: Utopia or an Alternative 31

Chapter 3 Criticism of the Concept of Sustainable Development 61

Chapter 4 Planetary Project: Premises, Basis, and Definitions 94

Chapter 5 Planetary Project Design: Goals, Specific Objectives, and Methodology 118

Chapter 6 Planetary Resource Base 141

Chapter 7 Planetary Property and World Income ... 166

Chapter 8 Industrial and Financial Foundations and Mechanisms of the Planetary Economy 187

Chapter 9 Planetary Governance Institutions 210

Chapter 10 Concept of Managed Harmony 233

Chapter 11 Planetary Ethics 257

Chapter 12 Planetary Project Implementation
             Results 278

Conclusions... 307

PREFACE

The author of this research monograph, *Planetary Project: From Sustainable Development to Managed Harmony*, is Aleksandr Vasilyevich Bezgodov. He is a serious scholar, whose interdisciplinary research focuses on global macroeconomic and social issues. Dr Bezgodov is not only a theoretician, but also a practical researcher and research administrator. He is involved in both developing and implementing research-based technologies. His economic and sociological solutions to business administration are extremely valuable.

His *Planetary Project* is a scholarly approach to solving current global problems involving global human unification with the intention to save our planet for present and future generations. The Planetary Project Concept proposes a harmonious global development model based on integrated economic and rent revenues from the use of resources held in planetary ownership. The Planetary Project implies removing contradictions resulting from globalisation and its consequences. These include unrestrained economic growth and the unbalanced development of a few countries. The Planetary Project argues for creating and implementing a just system of world income distribution, including the revenue from the use of globally-owned resources. Such a system could serve the interests of all nations including Asian and African countries, many of which are now experiencing serious socio-economic problems. New planetary resources and economic mechanisms will enable us to: save the Earth's biosphere; improve the health of the environment; eradicate starvation and epidemics; alleviate the threat of a Third World War; and help humanity to unite around the universal values of life and harmony between civilisation and nature, for present and future generations.

I find the Planetary Project ideas very timely and necessary in our crisis-ridden time. Developing them could generate a whole new field of research, and a wide social life-affirming and peace-making movement. The Planetary Project ideology does not contradict Islamic values; it promotes respect for the humanistic principles of religion, and sees spirituality as one of the genuine bases for human unification. In this regard, the Planetary Project philosophy can be organically integrated into the cultural, ideological and value universe of the Arab world, and the worldview based on Islamic beliefs.

Professor Mikhail Zalikhanov
Full Member of the Russian Academy of Sciences
Fellow of the Islamic World Academy of Sciences

INTRODUCTION

Our ideas about the evolutionary and historical age of people and humanity are as different from each other as our beliefs about the rationality of our species, our morality, culture, and civilisation. Some people count the age from the Day of Creation, the birth of Christ or Hegira, while other people rely on archaeological data or spectral analysis of previous life forms. Today, it is not all that important that periodisation and anthropogenesis mechanisms are at the heart of scientific or philosophical debate. What is of utmost importance is that, at the beginning of the twenty-first century, people feel united as never before but also, paradoxically, they feel disunited at the same time! Our thinking is ambivalent. Having found ourselves on the brink of self-destruction, we perceive with a varying degree of conscious awareness the need to unite in the face of unseen threats. At the same time, we are divided by serious disagreements based on divergent interests, values, and ambitions. Today's challenges are the most large-scale and significant that people have ever had to face.

The significance of the challenges derives from the fact that the reasons and basis of global problems, risks, and catastrophic events, can be traced to the side effects and consequences of our own activity, and our treatment of the environment and each other. Over the last hundred odd years, human reason and the products of its activity have shown qualities that are more destructive than beneficial. This might have occurred because, possessed by an illusion of omnipotence, we began to claim boundless superiority over the natural state of things. Perhaps, the cause is that some ideas on which we used to base our goals and life assessment have proven to be not only false, but also dangerous. But whatever the real cause, we have now found ourselves in a dramatic situation that can result either in the death of all life (a fast or slow death depending on the factors creating it), or in a *real unification of people* in order to survive. The latter is not only the most important condition for solving global problems, by removing threats and alleviating contradictions, but also the first step on the road to the spiritual and technological–in the long run–evolutionary transformation of humanity.

It is important to note that the goal of this book is not to propagate globalisation. On the contrary, the subsequent chapters contain critical analysis of many aspects of the process and ideology of globalisation. Moreover, underlying the proposed Planetary Project is the philosophy of re-globalisation as a mobilisation movement that is meant to remove the asymmetry of a unipolar world on a parity basis for different countries and cultures. We believe that *self-preservation*, the basic need of people as an organic part of the biosphere, can be the basis of this movement. It is sufficient alone to form integration motivation for a cause, for whose sake it is worthwhile to reduce and agree interests, as well as to combine values into a single universal system based on compromise between people. In this monograph, it will be referred to as the World Spiritual Synthesis. However, before we formulate it, we must outline the designs of economic and organisational mechanisms making global salvation processes realistic.

Today, when humanity is feeling on the brink of extinction, a new paradigm of existence and development is needed, a new *philosophy* of salvation common and clear to anyone, and, most importantly, built on a strong foundation of the natural and spiritual needs of people as a species. Previous models of life, civilisation concepts, and development scenarios taken alone with a prospect of absolutisation of one of them, are neither fit for the role nor can they fulfill this most important mission in the historic destiny of man. They will not be able to integrate humanity, unify it in the face of global threats, and put it on the right course to optimal solutions of pressing issues primarily because they are not universal. They contain values that contradict each other or even negate the very idea of the unity of humanity. At the same time, a number of ideas, principles, and sacred values of most metaphysical teachings, scientific theories, and religious systems, are so close in meaning, and so compatible with each other, that they invoke a conclusion that people living in different countries of the world have common value systems. Thus, positive, productive, humanistic ideas, irrespective of their origin, can be synthesized in order to serve a foundation of a new worldview. These ideas include, for instance, the notions of *life, justice, common good, order and harmony*.

New goals, motivation, arguments, and ideas are required to radically change the thinking of our contemporaries from the priority of the split of private interests to the superiority of the unity of common needs. Not less important are concrete models, mechanisms and technologies for the practical steps to unify humanity to resolve global problems and save all life. If we are to avoid involving ourselves in empty, utopian or sci-fi projects, and if we want to develop the genuinely effective measures needed today to save the biosphere and our civilisation, then we must understand that such measures can only be born out of the *planetary purpose*. This planetary purpose is: to defeat the narrowness of the globalist worldview according to which the future belongs to the so-called "golden billion;" to see contemporary humanity as a planetary community of people with equal rights and opportunities; and to see future humanity as a key planetary agent, who co-creates with nature and actively explores outer space.

Today, we live in an exciting and unique moment of our history, which, because of many factors, could be considered the eve and pre-cursor of a new *axis time* (Karl Jaspers) ushering in a qualitative leap in the development of nations. The Axial Age is characterised by fundamental changes in the primary mode of production and a high level of civilisation infrastructure growth. During this age new cultures, sciences, and spiritual movements emerge, and most importantly, *alternative social practices* emerge such as non-violent conflict resolution and institutionalised forms of political-economic compromises. A *new rationality* is expected during this age, which is more tolerant, humanised, and spiritualised than classical or post-classical. It may help create a harmoniously meaningful image of planetary unity "man – society – nature". It is important that the emergence of new growth points lead to a new stage of integration in all its dimensions: economic, political, cultural, and social.

Moreover, on the eve of the Sixth Techno-economic Paradigm, we can forecast considerable changes in human reason. In the age of informatics, cybernetics and nanotechnologies, it does not only become an object of labour but also a driver of a future civilisation. We say that reason could undertake the role of managing a further historical process and the responsibility for the mission, providing it is renewed, humanised, and collective, and placed in the framework of new rationality and universal spiritual synthesis. We believe strongly that the initiative and start of this large-scale movement should belong to the scientists of the world, whose efforts are intended to be united in the Planetary Project. The Planetary Project key ideas will be described in this monograph.

The reasoning presented in this book is not the fruit of the author's imagination. The monograph contains a concise overview of some of the principal results of original research conducted over a ten-year period, which has focused on the analysis and rethinking of *the theory of sustainable development*, *noospheric theory* and *innovation economics*. We have taken upon ourselves the task of thoroughly and critically examining the current world condition; bearing in mind that the main task of contemporary humanity is to preserve itself, and to survive in a situation of historically unseen risks and threats of self-destruction of humans as a species, and Earth as the planet that can generate life. We have generalised the ideas of outstanding scholars, and natural and social scientists; and we have formulated a number of points systemically connected to the concept of managed development and process harmonisation. Thus, the goal of the monograph "Planetary Project: From Sustainable Development to Managed Harmony" is mobilising the world's intellectual potential for solving global problems of contemporary humanity and harmonising world development.

CHAPTER 1

Global World: Inevitability, Risks, and Needs

Globalisation, anti-globalists, and the global world. Its incompleteness and transition character. Global problems and threats. Criticism of globalisation and the global world. The necessity for global unification as the global and most pertinent task of humanity.

The world has become global, whether we want it or not. It is a *fait accompli* that has its advantages and disadvantages but, notwithstanding, they do not make it less natural, inevitable, and obvious. Despite its great scale and serious content, the criticism of globalisation both scientific and purely ideological has not been able to undermine the naturalness of globalisation as a process or expose it as a "false" scenario of the development of society.

The interdisciplinary term *globalisation* literally means "spreading across the world", "of the whole world", and it derives from the two English words "globe" and "global". A French term *mondialisation* is also in use. It is derived from the two French words "le monde" and "mondial".

The study of the phenomenon of *globality* is said to have started even before the term "globalisation" came into use, namely as early as the 1960s. The theoretical foundations of the theory can be found in the ideas of Vladimir Vernadsky, Edouard LeRoy and Pierre Teilhard de Chardin whose development by the early 1970s had led to the creation of an analytic methodology of studying global processes and global issues. By the second half of the 1970s a whole new scholarly field emerges in the USA and Western Europe that receives the name of Global Studies. Its main schools are technocratic, environmental-demographic, existential-cultural, and evolutionary-deterministic.

In the 1980s, the concept of globalisation acquires a more extended and systemic character. The same period saw the term "globalisation" used for the first time by the American scholars, sociologist Jason MacLean (1981), economist Theodore Levitt (1983) and sociologist Roland Robertson (1985).

However, Karl Marx first used the word "globalisation" in a letter to Friedrich Engels at the end of 1850 when he emphasized the global importance of California and Japan entering the world market.

The following scholars made major contributions to globalisation research in the twentieth century: Immanuel Wallerstein, Anthony Giddens, Manuel Castells, Ulrich Beck, Alvin Toffler, Yoshihiro Francis Fukuyama, George Soros, Karl Popper, and Anatoly Utkin. However, as of today there is no unified, generally accepted approach to understanding globalisation. From the social science perspective, globalisation is interpreted with a focus on its various aspects:

- History treats it as the most mature stage of capitalism in which this formation reveals features initially untypical of it: multifacetedness (e.g. combination of private, state and public ownership of means of production); and a wide social redistribution of capital (to a great extent resembling that which is characteristic of *socialism*);
- Economics looks at globalisation processes from the point of view of transnational financial, commodity and resource markets, as well as the translocation of production forces;
- Political science focuses on the spread of democratic institutions and practices, liberalisation of political cultures, and as a reaction the strengthening of fundamentalist regimes in national-state organisms of the so-called traditional, closed type;
- Cultural studies see the essence of globalisation in the westernisation of culture, "pan-Americanism" (American economic and cultural expansion), dissolution of the ethno-cultural identity of nations in the most convertible and competitive – *Western* – cultural code;
- Sociology reveals the nature of globalisation through the transformation of a person's "lifeworld" on a societal level: when all previous forms of social organisation lose their dominant role the individual becomes freer; and when horizontal connections in society acquire larger importance for people and become more effective than vertical ones;
- Theory and history of science are interested in globalisation as a social science and humanities

field of the second half of the twentieth century, whose essence is the paradigm of civilisation;
- Philosophy analyses globalisation as a new form of social relations, a new form of dominance and power, as well as corresponding types of thinking operating such categories as "global necessity", "global conditions", "global interests", "global contradictions", "global goals and objectives", etc.

Also, as already noted, a specialised field of global studies emerged in the West during the second half of the 1970s. It integrated methods of different sciences using their research findings.

As far as popular reference literature is concerned, globalisation is treated essentially as the interconnected world processes of:

- Economic, political and cultural integration and unification, which saw a dramatic upsurge in the twentieth century;
- Increased impact of various international factors on the life of states, countries and communities;
- Changing world economic structure and the formation of a unified network market economy;
- Increased dependence of nation-states and their political systems on the commercial activity and power ambitions of transnational corporations;
- Increased openness of national economies, trade regime and capital flow liberalization, and the emergence of the world financial market;
- Internationalisation and totalisation of media and mass communication media, the spread of the Internet and its transformation into a global information and communication instrument;

- Creating a "mega-community", a global world whose important functions and relationships also take place in "virtual reality;"
- The increasing prominence of universal human values such as information, time economy, individualism and consumption.

In any case, the economic factor, backed up by the increasing capacity of electronic computing machines and communication networks, is universally considered the driver of globalisation. The most vivid example of this factor is seen at the level of transnational corporations that can operate simultaneously in a number of countries using new historical conditions in their interests and largely creating them themselves. International trade plays a leading role, primarily trade in energy and other raw resources, especially strategic ones, which are fundamental for industry.

Today, a number of directions of the most dynamic globalisation can be identified:

- financial institutions, lobbyist organisations in different industries, cross-industry international organisations;
- software, global communication networks, the information market;
- human rights and environmental associations.

To understand and accept the fact of the naturalness and inevitability of globalisation, it is enough to view it as a certain historical stage in the development of fundamental economic relations, production, distribution and consumption, as well as division of labour. Indeed, a consequence of economic specialisation and consumption standardisation on the interregional and continental levels, globalisation stimulated a further evolution of these practices and took them to an international and global level. Current economics encourages network co-operation dependent on such factors as the price of labour and distribution of production forces as well as regional specialisation, which in turn depends on resource bases and possibilities. In this sense, globalisation is a natural stage in the development of humanity. Certain society types correspond to it, to be more exact, an ongoing dynamic of hybrid types: *post-industrial society – information society – knowledge society*. The development seems to be clearly progressive. However, if it is the case in theory, is it the case in actuality?

In actuality, i.e., at least in the practice of forming public opinion, the anti-globalists set the current trend in understanding and assessing globalisation, and not the qualified specialists in economics, political science, sociology and the arts, or representatives of global institutes. From the outset, their movement become an internationally fashionable phenomenon whose popularity surpassed even that of all the agents of globalisation put together.

Anti-globalism is an international social-political and countercultural movement uniting those who oppose both globalisation and westernisation and global financial, commercial and industrial organisations. Anti-globalists believe that globalisation leads to human rights violations in specific countries, infringes their national interests, and undermines their sovereignty. According to them, the spread of western (primarily, American) values and way of life threatens the ethno-cultural identity of Old and New World countries. They view the exploitation of the majority of the Earth's population by the so-called "golden billion" as the biggest danger; it creates inequality in wealth and deepening discrimination vis-à-vis the consumption of natural and artificially created products.

A Mexican humanitarian, known as Subcomandante Insurgente Markos (his real name is apparently Rafael Sebastián Guillén Vicente), is believed to be the founder of anti-globalism. While 1994 is considered to be the year of the movement's inception, when the Maya guerrilla movement led by Markos took power in the Mexican state of Chiapas.

In Europe, anti-globalism made its debut a year later with a scandal when a French farmer, José Bové, destroyed a McDonald's restaurant in Paris. Later, the left-wing writer Susan George joined the scandalous farmer, and they launched the radical organisation ATTAC. It targeted global institutions such as the World Trade Organization, the International Monetary Fund, and transnational corporations, which are together dubbed the Devil's Troika.

It is interesting to know that the term "anti-globalism" itself was coined and started to be widely used slightly later, namely between 1999 and 2000 in the USA.

The ideological precursors of anti-globalism are: the ideology of the New Left, existential philosophy and the Frankfurt school, and of course, neo-Marxism. While the American scholar and activist Lyndon LaRouche is a key theoretician of anti-globalism, anti-globalists hold in higher esteem the Slovenian philosopher and publicist Slavoj Žižek.

It can be said that even if the anti-globalist movement did not exist, it would have been invented – it can be seen how convenient it has proved to be as a cheap form of transport for various types of conservative ideas ranging from Eurasianism to neo-Nazism. On the one hand, it is absolutely obvious that anti-globalism is a destructive force. First, in their pronouncements, anti-globalists often use clearly extremist methods of expressing interests; and as with any extremist movement, they destabilise a complicated situation in itself, and create a threat to public order. Second, we cannot say that all anti-globalists in all countries and at all times (especially at the height of their activity) were well organised. As with any amorphous community, whose negative energy is kick-started by an aggressive stimulus, a more organised and more disciplined community that has centralised and systemic interests can use them. These interests can include: unfair competition with transnational companies; discrediting political regimes in the world's leading countries; and those that propagate the ideology of globalisation, as well as profanation of global institutions and practices. Local elites and economic entities, political radicals and ultra-right opposition, foreign agents or unfriendly powers, can all become the invisible puppeteers of anti-globalists, and masterminds of their illegal acts.

Zapatistas, the so-called Mexican "guerrillas", conducted the first international *anti-globalist event* in 1996. Two years later, anti-globalist coordinated events took place in different European countries. One of the rallies took place in Cologne in 1999.

The year 1999 also saw the biggest anti-globalist protest in the New World that came to be known as the Battle of Seattle. Over 50,000 people turned out on the streets of the city during a WTO conference under the slogan "Mobilization against Globalisation". This provoked a number of demonstrations in many countries involving anti-globalists, nationalists, leftists, anarchists, and other protest movements, which boosted the mass creation of anti-globalist organisations in those countries.

The year 2000 saw the launch of the anti-globalist information network IndyMedia. In 2001, between 120 and 200 thousand people came out on the streets of Genoa attempting to disrupt the G-8 meeting being held there. By 2003, the number of anti-globalist organisations worldwide was estimated to be over 2,500.

On the other hand, there are clear reasons why anti-globalism, as a movement and ideology, is a natural development: it would be strange not to have such a reaction to some of the controversial ideas of the philosophy of globalisation, and dubious practices of its institutions. The fact is that the current global world is unjust to many people on the planet Earth! This finds objective manifestation in such negative processes as poverty, hunger, pandemics, exploitation of cheap hired labour, cultural and social backwardness, and the asymmetric and unequal processes of development in the Third World countries. Nevertheless, we should not share an illusion that attempts to stop globalisation will lead to a positive result for the whole of humanity and each nation. As if the good old world of "separate" sovereign cultures could replace the global world; everybody could live in isolation and happiness, with their own value universe and at their own level of development. In this sense, a return to an idealized past is impossible; and even a "soft" degradation to a barbaric stage cannot happen in an idyllic manner. Only *something even more global* can replace the global world if we intend, of course, positive and productive changes.

Whether globalisation is true or false from a historical perspective, it is important to note that it has brought about this *global world.* It has reached a stage when it does not need termination, slowing down, or reduction; but rather transformation, and bringing it to a new level of integration and development of its agents, objects, and processes. It needs new goals and vectors of development to help it to both relieve its own internal contradictions, and to reproduce a progressive scenario of world history. Thus, this monograph will discuss the global world rather than globalisation. Not even the global world per se, because its own value already seems dubious due to a number of considerations and estimates from economic to moral-ethical, but because it is a transition state to a new format of human life organisation on the planet. The world order of the global world cannot be considered the best of all possible ones and the final version, but it deserves to be viewed as suitable for transformation and development in the right direction that is yet to be determined.

What is the global world today? We understand it as a product of globalisation, and at the same time the form in which it is becoming possible for a more mature globalisation phase to continue.

Historically, globalisation conditions began forming in the 1830s to 1850s (the so-called *proto-globalisation*), and were completed by the first half of the twentieth century. They resulted from macroeconomic factors including intensified world trade, transnational capital flow, and financial protectionism policies. The beginning of its development can be albeit indirectly traced back to the world wars when international coalitions began to create a political-economic agenda. Born into the imperialism of the beginning of the twentieth century, globalisation had largely transformed it by the end of the century; and we are now living the reality of a digital age and cognitive capitalism.

The Global World, according to some thinkers, is different from all of the previous ideological-practical constructs of social being of people with its compactness and torsion. According to Pierre Teilhard de Chardin, it has experienced "convolution onto itself" ("reploument sur lui-meme"). Paradoxically, in terms of living time and space, the world has not widened or grown larger with each new discovery starting with Alexander the Great's campaigns and the arrival of Europeans in the American Continent, to the emergence of the World Wide Web entangling humanity. On the contrary, it has shrunk as if it has become smaller than it was before! Today, due to global communication systems, aviation, weapons of mass destruction, and diseases of civilisation, the world is totally bonded by human connections and dependent on all its subjects. It has become more fragile and vulnerable than ever before in its history.

Compactness, torsion, and convolution are primarily mentioned in relation to space and time, movement and communications, decision-making, and choice variability. The ability to make contact practically in every point of the world without having to leave one's house or office, as well as to transport oneself to a new place within hours however far it might be, allow people to perceive borders and distances, as well as their own resources, needs and objectives, differently. The plane-based system of reference characteristic of the *optical metaphor worldview* is replaced by a spherical reference system typical of the *digital worldview*. The spherical universe is characterised by a different temporality, which is much more intensive than that of the plane one. Time is increasing in value and becoming more easily convertible to money, both in the direct and indirect sense of the word. The whole social metabolism is becoming faster: information exchange, reception and acquisition of knowledge, socialisation, interaction and feedback. This dynamic results in social existence itself being transformed: it is becoming more condensed and homogenous, the private and the public interpenetrate, and so do the virtual and the real.

The essence of *social defragmentation* of traditional social structures in the global world is in the fact that vertical hierarchies are less important than horizontal cluster links, which form not by historical inertia but by interests and free will of people. At least, it is a characteristic feature of open societies where the state needs public approval to acquire and maintain its authority. Moreover, national states have national sovereignty within their borders quite conditionally now in terms of self-sufficiency: their citizens can be considered neither their property nor the sole owners of their state. Connected by the common fate of humanity at the level of global problems and prospects, they are also participants of global co-operation at the level of users, agents, and distributors.

The global world is also an ideology based on the principles of cosmopolitism, liberalism, perception digitalisation, consumption, horizontal connections, self-realisation and personal rights. In the format of global worldview, our contemporaries, especially the so-called "Generation Y", tend to converge beliefs, needs and values, including common understanding of the main principles of life structure manifested in specific forms of social practice.

It is fair to say that in the new millennium the global world has not made much progress for over 15 years; more and more it is sliding down to the chaos of its own contradictions, not able to abandon some atavisms of previous eras and formations. The reason is that at the stage of the global world globalisation itself loses its value in the historical sense and must– to ensure the progress of evolution and complexity of collective biosocial life and noosphere–transform itself to the processes of *planetisation* and *cosmisation* of man. They, in turn, will be different from globalisation not only by increasing scales, but also qualitatively by a higher degree of organisation and management of agents, objects, and processes. The problem is that it has not gone beyond disparate scholarly studies and progressive modelling.

Today, we characterise the global world through features such as: the global economy (or geoeconomy) and global business; global communication networks and communication functional languages; global institutions (first of all, financial-economic and human rights); global society; and even in some sense global culture built on the foundation of universal human values and consumption standards. However, besides the institutions, the global world is perfectly characterised by an appropriate type of thinking, which is very pertinent to the context of our reasoning. Underlying the *global worldview* is the image of people as active agents of current civilisation, who have access to all its wealth because they act both in the role of user, and in the role of producer and co-creator. The image of a perceived collectivity of *people as humanity* and *humanity as a unity* is no less formidable. Indeed, the global world only gave people, who initially represented the populations of specific countries, the opportunity to feel one humanity in the sense of unity of their biosocial species, in which species and populations different by their race, culture and way of life are actually not essentially different at all. Awareness of global threats and challenges must also contribute to humanist belonging. So at least due to the above circumstances, we can say that the contemporary global world is not irreparable: the world cannot only preserve itself and develop further, but also transfer itself to a qualitatively higher state. This is due to the current level of scientific knowledge and its popularisation, technologies and economic practices, as well as legal systems. However, humanity's consolidated good will have to be added to this; and life-sustenance and social development mechanisms will have to be boosted. They provided humanity's complete and organic integration, which will later be analysed and established as *planetary*.

Global problems, which largely are considered deriving from globalisation and being global world symptoms, are direct indicators for the need of such integration.

It is believed that problems become *global* not so much on the basis of what caused them (environment, economics, politics, health, demographics, etc.), as on the basis of meeting the following criteria serving as sense making, systemic and representative in relation to the global level of objectification:

- encompassing the interests of the whole of humanity in the present and future;
- total and world character in relation to the nature of man, society and ecosystem on the whole and in principle;
- ability to influence historically and evolutionary on the level of social and planetary existence and development;
- large-scale risk potential, and a high level of threat in the event that they are not resolved;
- absolute impossibility to resolve global problems on a local or regional scale using local resources, private instruments and mechanisms.

Therefore, global problems present both a threat of a planetary scale and a factor of planetary unification. Global problems can be ranked in the following way:

- increasing environmental harm and the risk of environmental catastrophe;
- asymmetric development of humanity and social-economic disparity between people and nations;

- demographic problem: uncontrolled growth in the poorest countries and birth rate decrease in developed countries;
- international terrorist threats;
- a threat of a Third World War;
- food crisis and famine;
- resource and energy crisis and a deficient hydrocarbon energy sector as a current economic basis;
- socio-cultural and religious conflicts and *conflicts of civilisations*;
- regional separatism as a form of countering globalisation;
- latent class struggle, the deepening of classical capitalist contradictions and the emergence of new ones;
- pandemics in Third World countries and "diseases of civilisation" in developed countries;
- decrease in the general human intellectual level;
- the advent of the Sixth Techno-economic Paradigm and economic risks caused by the unequal levels of development in different economic and production sectors as well as unequal consumption markets.

Features of the Portrait of Global Problems

Environmental Damage

The following processes indicate a global increase in environmental damage caused by anthropogenic impact:

- increased CO_2, methane and halocarbon concentrations in the atmosphere;

- contamination of inland water bodies and parts of shore waters of the World Ocean with nitrogen, phosphorus and other chemicals;
- soil degradation in 60% of global landmass;
- the planet's fauna and flora reduction: 63% of landmass are destroyed as a result of human economic activity;
- increase of the industrial production of hazardous waste amounting to from 0.1 to 0.5 tonnes per capita.

Standard of Living Asymmetry

The "golden billion" countries (the USA, Canada, Australia, EU countries, Japan, Israel and South Korea), whose population is only about 20% of that of the planet, spend about 86% of the world's resources and produce 75% of the economically-generated waste. Meanwhile, the poorest countries, which are categorised as developing countries: have 20% of the world's population; produce only 1% of the world's GDP; are plagued by poverty and destitution; and have clear signs of degradation of society and the environment. The majority of countries, which have 60% of the Earth's population, consume 13% of the world's GDP.

Demographic Problem

The population growth is slowing down in developed countries (the demographic outsiders are Scandinavian countries, Germany, Italy and Japan), whereas it is accelerating in developing countries (the demographic leaders include China, India, Indonesia, Pakistan, Bangladesh, Brazil, Mexico, Nigeria and Ethiopia). The fastest population growth is characteristic of the 50 least developed countries of the world. This includes the populations of Afghanistan, Burkina Faso, Burundi, Guinea-Bissau, Congo, Mali, Nigeria and a number of other countries.

Terrorism

The number of terrorist attacks has experienced a steady growth since the 2010s, while terrorism itself has become more aggressive, large-scale, technological, and sophisticated. The following countries have seen the most terrorist attacks that happen on a regular basis: Iraq, Pakistan, Afghanistan, India, Yemen, Somali, Nigeria, Thailand, and Russia.

Threat of a Third World War

The aggregate explosive power of the world's weapons currently stands at roughly 18 billion tonnes in TNT equivalent, in other words, it amounts to 3.6 tonnes for each person on this planet. Exploding only 1% of these stockpiles is enough to cause a "nuclear winter".

Undernourishment and Starvation

The number of people in need of food exceeds 850 million people, which means one in every 7 people does not receive the required amount of calories in their food. Over 5 million children die every year from starvation.

Poverty

The World Bank estimates the total number of poor people living on less than 2 dollars a day to be 2.5–3 billion people worldwide. That includes 1–1.2 billion people who live in extreme poverty (on less than 1 dollar a day). In other words, 40%–48% of the world's population are poor, while 16%–19% are extremely poor.

Resource and Energy Crisis and
Hydrocarbon Energy Sector

Oil reserves will last us 47 years, gas 57, iron ore 54, and copper 38 years. Copper traded on London Metal Exchange and the other four main non-ferrous metals will run out ever sooner: nickel reserves will be exhausted in 34 years, tin in 18, zinc in 16, and lead in 15 years.

Pandemics and Epidemics

The world's infection mortality rate has reached 17 million people per year. Tuberculosis is the second most deadly infectious disease, malaria is the fourth, AIDS is the fifth, and hepatitis B is the sixth. There are over 200 most common diseases, while rare infections appear on a regular basis. Over the last 35 years, 35 new diseases have been registered that have epidemiological significance, out of which 68% are viruses, and 29% bacterial. Today, over 42 million people are HIV-positive in 210 countries of the world. Lung tuberculosis affects 20 million people a year while 2 – 3 million people die from this disease.

As a separate issue, many sociologists, political scientists, practising politicians and public figures, especially those who espouse opposition to globalism, problematise the relations between the global world, individual nations, and regional organisations. This is caused by the differences in development between the active and coerced participants of the globalisation processes.

It is remarkable, however, that the global problems themselves, whatever they touch, only stimulate a further process of globalisation. They do not require quantitative expansion as much as qualitative change, its own evolution and transition to something higher in terms of organisation, goals, and essentially, human integration. This is quite logical, because the global character of these problems (the environmental crisis, mentioned earlier, or the current state of the environment and the inertia of biosphere processes) incommensurately exceeds the solution potential at the disposal of individual states and even some international associations. The fact of the matter is that these countries or associations do not possess all of the resources or the rights to use them!

However, instead of decisive integration, the global world keeps or even allows the acceleration of disintegrative and destructive processes. Humanity must be united; it is largely globalised, but has not yet become truly united in mutual help and solidarity on a global scale. This is what should be the real target of criticism of the global world, and of the review of its structural-organisational foundations and functional practices.

What is it that must be obvious and decisive in the essence and understanding of the global world today, at least at the level of quite justified expectations? Of course, the integrated state of humanity, not known before and, evidently, the historically happy state of people–their community and unity deriving from a common source–their own nature! Nature, in the sense of human nature, common to everyone, i.e., the unity of the species, a unique biosocial phenomenon, a product of protein life evolution and a historical development of society as a special form of population. Moreover, nature in the sense of an ecosystem of a large home that is common to everyone, whose laws modern people understand much better than their ancestors did even 50 or 100 years ago, and which is manifested in a successful synthesis of natural and technical sciences as well as the whole nature transformation activity.

This human integration is quite natural, and is derived from the very heart of the global world; it appears to have to create appropriate features, conditions and structural forms of a harmonious world design over the whole political and environmental spectrum. However, what do we see in reality? The direct opposite of what we ought to expect logically! The current global world is not only disharmonious, asymmetric, and unbalanced, but is also rightly considered to be undergoing a crisis. Moreover, instead of human integration (both in terms of its biological and social nature), its key definition is that of a crisis, a global systemic crisis caused by *global problems*, a crisis that has almost become a perpetual form of existence for humanity. For the last decades, due to their crisis nature, the global world and globalisation with its concepts, practices and culture have incurred harsh criticism from various camps, at times quite convincing.

Criticism of the global world has targeted both positive and negative globalisation aspects, practices, and consequences. It is worth reminding that the positive, productive, and progressive aspects normally include: the cosmopolitanisation and review of the concept of citizenship; increased mobility of movement and communications; gradual opening of borders and the possibility for global problem solving and threat minimisation. The negative globalisation aspects are primarily considered to be the following: infringement of national sovereignty; prevalence of economic management motives over political motives; deficit of openness and freedom of speech, as well as unclear responsibility mechanisms in the operation of supra-governmental and supra-national institutions; life standardisation and unification, blurring identity and individuality of nations and the loss of ethno-national and cultural uniqueness; unequal development of different participants of globalisation processes.

Cosmopolitanisation or the *global citizenship* is criticised for the break with the original, native, local citizenship implying a person's ethno-national and cultural identity, and deriving from it loyalty to his or her country's political regime. Perceiving himself a global citizen, a man of the world, an individual can behave with discrimination, demandingly, and even with prejudice to the conditions and quality of life in his country, its traditions and customs, laws and moral rules, political practices, arts, beliefs, consumption standards, and way of life. Such non-conformism may not always receive welcome from the authorities, loyal community activists, opinion leaders, and especially nationalistic and ultra-right ideologists.

The increasing mobility of people results in: experience acquired by members of closed societies, and authoritarian and totalitarian regimes while travelling abroad; interaction with people from other countries; and exposure to other cultures, consumption standards, and way of life. This threatens the conservative governments of those countries, because, again, such experience can undermine the political, social, and electoral loyalty of people whose rights and freedoms have been limited, and whose quality of life is not high.

Gradual *opening of borders* presents various risks and threats to archaic and uncompetitive social institutions, economic entities, as well as economic and organisational-legal systems. As a rule, it affects underdeveloped local producers of products and services, and sometimes, administrative and judicial bodies as well.

Prevalence of economic management motives over political motives may sometimes infuse rationality and utilitarianism into the foreign and domestic policy of some governments. This tends to have a positive impact on economic processes and people's lives, as well as the country's international image, but it may irritate reactionary leaders, radical opposition, religious fundamentalists, and their followers.

Lack of transparency of global institutions: nationally-minded elites in some countries have strong and deeply ingrained suspicions that the infrastructural elements of the global world such as the UN, IMF, WTO, IAEA or UNESCO, are guided in their activity by the interests of the most globalised countries, primarily the USA. They are often accused of violating the principles of global democracy, and of lacking real, effective responsibility mechanisms.

According to adherents to local national cultures, *standardisation and unification* of life inevitably leads to depersonalisation, and the loss of the ethno-national, religious and spiritual identity, and historical individuality of people; and, by doing that, it violates their inalienable right to have their own culture and authentic cultural code.

Asymmetry in the development of different participants in the globalisation process: developed countries continue to prosper, while the so-called developing countries are getting poorer and more impoverished. The gap in wealth between them is getting wider. The regionalisation of economies as a concrete objectification of market globalisation encourages economic, technological, and social polarisation. Outsiders emerge alongside leaders that become donors of cheap labour, territory and resources; and they find themselves dependent on international investment, foreign help and "humanitarian injections" of alien cultures.

Indeed, the global world is not perfect; it is full of faults and risks, including global ones, which jeopardize its existence and the existence of the planet itself. People have not yet united and even at the global level, have not understood the necessity to unite despite current contradictions. However, it is this need that must be ultimately recognised as the most important and urgent one, and accepted categorically by humanity. It will happen first at the level of transnational elites and opinion leaders, and then at the level of comprehensive mobilisation supra-political ideology.

Nevertheless, not all criticism of globalisation and the global world can be considered flawless in terms of social practices, scientific truth, and moral rightness, which are understood even in the most general sense. For instance, some opponents' fears that globalisation and the world market would destroy national sovereignty of some countries have proved wrong. At least, they have not proved right at this stage. On the contrary, even the tiniest of states, at least diplomatically recognised ones, are full subjects of international law and masters of their domestic policy. By the way, this is often characterised by idiosyncratic, exotic, and even quite barbaric "peculiarities" of some countries' social, cultural, and political life. Many of them violate human rights and damage the environment, while global institutions are not always capable of rectifying this. Therefore, from an objective point of view, these institutions should be criticised for their inefficiency rather than for their repressiveness.

Talking about economic transformations caused by capital re-distribution, labour migration, and business standardisation, we can say that they have become a blessing or at least a historic chance. We mean here those regions that, for some internal reasons, have not developed their own modern, sustainable, and competitive economic infrastructure. People in these countries survive today because they have had the opportunity to take some place—a cluster fragment or a network cell—in the modern geo-economy. So here, too, we can justifiably talk about a humanistic role of globalisation in the life of some nations and their economic systems.

Another harmful myth about globalisation is that it threatens nations' cultural, ethnic, and religious authenticity. There is a clear substitution of notions, and a misunderstanding of the evolutionary nature of the historical process. The first argument worth mentioning here, as an objection, is that: global business is interested in different cultural, religious, and ethnic subjects as sources of supply and demand and to be active players of the commercial processes simultaneously in several markets ranging from the public opinion industry, to the tourism industry. The second argument is that: disappearance and extinction of some traditional forms of socio-cultural and historic self-organisation are natural processes, and they take place as such forms become archaic and outdated, while globalisation does not always play the leading catalytic role. The third: in response to globalisation, many beliefs, myths, traditions, archetypes, and other components of historical-cultural and ethnic authenticity characterising many countries of the world, are restored as if receiving a new life. Having been disposed of, they suddenly rise in value including as a selling item in the direct sense of the word.

What can be the genuine object of criticism and resistance in the architecture and system of the global world from the point of view of basic logic, sense of justice, and common sense? It can hardly be an extended longevity, achievements in medicine and the entertainment industry, e-commerce or network communications, the level of technology, or an expanded human understanding of the universe! There are, of course, those critics who put forth fanciful and pretentious claims, adherents of traditional values, "the soil", religious dogmatism, exotic beliefs and spiritual systems, isolationist cults, and totalitarian sects. However, we are not talking about these people here, because they do not have considerable public support, they are not in, as are anti-globalists. What then? First, social and economic, and partly political and cultural injustice, has emerged as the agenda when economic agents, with different levels of development, started to play on the same market field.

The gap between the level of life in developed and developing countries in the context of globalisation is growing. It is encouraged by the factor that is often referred to in literature as the "race down". Powerful transnational corporations prepare to relocate their production facilities (including hazardous) to countries providing the most beneficial conditions such as cheap labour and less stringent environmental legislation. These facts often violate the rights of citizens of these industrial "workshops" and testing sites, and seriously harm the ecology of these countries.

The natural basis of both theoretical and practical resistance to globalisation is the rejection of the West-centric pivot of the global world, and its orientation towards Anglo-Saxon, Protestant values, and the liberal market model of social relations. Despite the fact that historically, it has demonstrated its effectiveness, giving birth to dominant economies, leaders in scientific-technical, economic and political competition, representatives of non-European cultures reject the mono-centric and unipolar world as the only acceptable template of social design.

The problem here is that they want not only to keep their national-historical, spiritual and political uniqueness, traditional identity and the "memory of ancestors", but that they also reject categorically the discriminatory Golden Billion Theory. Finally, at the level of mythological-ethnic self-identity, some nations still believe in their "choiceness". Even more nations adhere to their archaic spirituality of a closed nature as the only guarantee of survival, fearing and resisting external influences, whichever products of civilisation they might try to encompass. The actual way of life of these people is built on the simplest reactive algorithm: "ours – good / not ours – evil". However, history has taught us that even such collective archaic subjects tend to abandon with time the ideological bastions of their isolation, and emerge into the light of progress.

As we see, the basis of opposition to globalism and situational non-alignment to the global world is ideologically strong, scientifically objective, and morally viable. Therefore, to forestall the disintegration tendencies, save the global world, and take the global world to a new phase of development, it is necessary to solve cardinally the problem of injustice in the distribution of natural and production wealth, and the resources and incomes from their use. This problem-solving mechanism will be revealed in this book. By the way, a system of fair distribution and symmetrical development of local economies as part of the global economy can become the basis of creating organisational-financial, supra-political foundations for resolving problems of the global world. A way out can be found from the crisis the world faces today, and the threat to the life of the human species can be removed, as well as the danger of an environmental catastrophe on planet Earth.

It makes absolutely no sense to try to solve problems caused by globalisation, which have become problems of the global world, based on the established *pro* and *contra* arguments of the Golden Billion Theory supporters and anti-globalists. We should have a qualitatively different scientific-practical platform encompassing conditions not only for constructive criticism but also for practical harmonisation of world design. However, it can be possible only if real integration of humanity takes place on the basis of a common plan of self-preservation, under the leadership of the most progressive and humanistically minded international elite, and administered by a system of world development management created by it.

Otherwise, no such activity or criticism of globalisation from the standpoint of private interests or individual problems will ever be constructive, nor will it ever alleviate sharp contradictions of the global world, or resolve essential problems that have reached the level of the planet's survival. Tackling problems from any nationally oriented bridgehead whether it is Russia, Catalonia, or Liberia, will never yield any long-term strategic results either for these countries themselves or for the world community, and is doomed to failure. Such protest movements just cannot have any positive, humanist future.

The current global world is increasingly plunging into the crisis, but this does not mean that globalisation is a "mistaken" scenario of human development. The current global world is not the end of civilisation, but its pinnacle. A further prospect of the development of the world and humanity can be seen, provided planetary resource management is systematised and centralised from this superposition.

It is impossible to resolve global problems, remove contradictions, and minimize risks to global world design when only one or several countries are involved, even if these countries have the largest populations and strongest economies. These are global, international issues, at least because they have international legal status and require colossal funding. The need to achieve universal justice in the world forces us to take account of the interests of all participants of the process. Even the remotest participants in geographical terms from the epicentre of any problem qualify, because it is caused by a global problem. We cannot allow either any exceptions or minorities whose interests would be unaccounted for or ignored.

Productive criticism of globalisation aimed at improving the health of the global world, and putting it into the mode of harmonizing the world structure, can be thought through and conducted in a systematic manner only based on *much more global* positions than global ones! We are talking here about defining and providing arguments for a *planetary position* that includes a planetary agent and its resources, interests, needs and demands.

CHAPTER 2

Unification of Humanity: Utopia or an Alternative

No alternative to human integration. Real basis for global humanity and possibilities of unification. Global platforms: universal human values and human rights; international social and political institutions; global business; the Internet and global communications; and the unity of the technosphere. Obstacles, risks, and certainties on the route to global unification of people and their life-support systems. Possibility and admissibility conditions for unification.

Today, as we have already said in the previous chapter, unification of humanity is the key and singly most important global goal of humanity as both a biosocial species, and as a planetary and cosmic phenomenon that is in danger of self-destruction. The process of self-destruction has a long history: people have long meticulously killed each other, and have developed and practiced both primitive and sophisticated ways of harm, violence, murder, and suicide. These include: invasive and religious wars, genocides and ethnic cleansing, slavery, political repressions, infectious diseases, and destructive cults and sects activities. In the age of globalisation, the following factors, whose scale and destructive potential had not been seen before the advent of modernity, represent the most probable pessimistic instruments for destroying humanity, our civilisation, and nature itself: weapons of mass destruction; technogenic impact on the ecosystem as a result of irrational nature management; epidemics and pandemics; general depletion of resources necessary for life and its reproduction; and overpopulation.

Dreams about a united humanity and a united world, which are built on the basis of a common understanding of goodness and moral duty, have been embodied in myths, spiritual systems, religious teachings, philosophic theories, and arts. Science has been much more cautious and modest in these issues not to be accused of utopianism. Nevertheless, even some scientific disciplines and traditions have developed various projects resembling global integration modelling and justification, as well as the transformation of people to correct their nature and improve their life. To be true, the public fate of such attempts has not treated them well: they have been dubbed pseudo- or semi-scientific, "non-reflective" or radical, extremely ideologised and, again, utopian! Among such projects are Marxism, Russian Cosmism and Mondialism, to name just a few.

Mondialism, as a term derived from the French word *monde* meaning *world,* has at least three meanings today:

1) the concept of planetary human community able to exist on a common national-political basis;
2) social movement of "citizens of the world", which emerged after WW2, whose aim is to unite people around the ideas of pacifism, cultural freedom, historical responsibility, and social equality;
3) goal-oriented practice of creating a new world order with an appropriate ideology and political system, whose centre is said to be located in the USA.

Some people believe that mondialism ideas can be found in both moderate European socialism ("the Fabian Society") and communism, and also in the liberal-capitalist ideology of big transnational business.

The essence of mondialism as an ideology, and as a political and cultural philosophy can be represented in the following points:

- peoples and nations of the Earth must be united as one human community;
- separate regions of the world must be united on a federal basis;
- the united world must be governed by a World Government accumulating national sovereign mandates;
- the political-legal system of global governance shall be built on the principles of Western bourgeois democracy.

In terms of political practices, there are the "right-wing" mondialism, favouring Atlanticism globalisation, and the "left-wing" mondialism, allowing the equality of the Eurasian sector with the Western sector.

Criticism of mondialism from different perspectives ranging from conservative to the left is based on the following:

- suspicion that it represents a secret plan to create a World Government spreading its power all over the world;
- a statement of superiority of Euro-Atlantic liberal democracy and cultural model based on Western values;
- a belief about the need to remove racial, religious, ethnic, national, and cultural restrictions;
- preference of supra-national over national legislation, and supra-national governance bodies over traditional power structures;
- similarity to *globalisation* ideas and practices;
- similarity to *pan-Americanism* ideas;
- serving the interests of Western political establishment;
- activity of such closed political financial organisations as, for example, Cecil Rhodes' Round Table Group, Garry Davis' World Government of World Citizens, Henry Usborne's Crusade for World Government, Carnegie Endowment for International Peace, J.P. Morgan sponsored Council on Foreign Relations, the Bilderberg group and the Trilateral Commission.

In any case, theories are of interest saying that the current global political institutions such as, for instance, the UN or UNESCO, are the fruits of 19th century mondialism.

Until recently, *utopia* was either an artistic genre or a voluntary social design ending up with some negative consequences. Today, what resembles utopia, namely human unity and a harmonious and systemically-managed world based on such unity, has no alternative if we are to survive as a species and save the Earth as a planet. The necessity for world integration does not derive from some abstract moral-ethical considerations and ephemeral utopian dreams or secret plans of an anonymous world government. It derives from a critical state of the global world and is dictated by the survival instinct, which we can comprehend at the level of *common sense*.

Common sense is a very important conceptual science-based category of the current worldview. Rooted in the seventeenth century philosophy of René Descartes, pioneer of new European rationalism, the notion of common or good sense (le bon sens) has come to be synonymous with reason (la raison) or, more exactly, an ability of rational reasoning. Rene Descartes wrote in his "A Discourse on Method" (1637), that good sense or reason is the power of judging aright and of distinguishing truth from error.

In the eighteenth century, the category of common sense starts resembling a natural science method represented by Newton's physics. In the English philosophical tradition, the notion of common sense is close to Latin *sensus communis*: the *reasonable* and *common* are interpreted almost identically. This means that the ability to judge reasonably is understood as a faculty of people, the human kind, and society.

Today, when we talk about *common sense,* we mean the ability of a person to reason based on rational logic, empirical data, and cultural-theoretical constants accepted in a dominant civilisation paradigm. The cultural subtext of common sense is no less important, it implies a person's ability to recognise mistakes, prejudices, mystifications, and resist their influence without accepting uncritically their unsupported statements. Common sense points at belonging to a general aggregation of evolutionary and civilisation experience. Due to its historical maturity and volume, this experience contributes wholeness to a worldview that it has constructed. This worldview will also include the experience itself at the level of its fundamental possibility and basic presumptions of existing. Therefore, it is not only a root layer of a worldview and a mechanism of sustainable worldview reproduction, but also a form of socially acceptable and encouraged thinking and behaviour.

In the current context of global problems and world crisis, human common sense must receive objectivation at the level of *global goodwill* capable of becoming an ideology and movement to form appropriate social institutions. In turn, the launching and fully-fledged functioning of these institutions will lead to solving global problems and harmonise world design. This will ensure necessary conditions for the implementation of an alternative civilisation, historical, and socio-anthropological scenario, taking people to the new horizons of evolutionary development, and making them *planetary* beings and even higher—*cosmic* beings.

To achieve this highly important civilisation-historical program of moving from salvation—from self-destruction to global problem solving, to sociogenic and environmental risk minimization, to world order harmonisation, to the transfer to qualitatively higher social and evolutionary development—humanity needs to unite, become integral, and cast itself as the single living species unified both by common problems and common needs, solutions, and prospects.

Humanity will not be able to complete this programme in any condition other than an integrated one (at the level of institutions, elites, communities, assets, and technologies). The time of disparate, sporadic, and differentiated progressist missions has gone! The global character of the world has made it more vulnerable than in any other period in human history. In this situation, no nation, wherever its geographical location, can be exempt from the negative processes of our times; nor can it stay out of the process of resolving these issues to let humanity survive as a species and nature survive with its ecosystem and habitat.

It is comforting to see that several social-historical phenomena have already emerged as established, full-fledged, generally recognised institutions, which can be viewed as *platforms of natural integration of humanity;* and which, by the way, can be boldly attributed to globalisation! Conditionally, they can be divided into political-legal, economic, infrastructural-technological, and cultural. In any case, they are all products of modern civilisation, and results of the best achievements of previous civilisations. Each of these sustainable phenomena and processes, institutes and practices, which have already become in essence global integration platforms, deserves a brief overview.

1) *Universal Human Values and Human Rights*

The image of a united humanity has become a fragment of the civilised nations' *cultural code* and found a legitimate correlation to the universal human values category. It is hard to agree with the idea that cultural concepts and norms have in their root an ethnic and national-historical nature and therefore can be very different. Another thing is that near the end of history, even contrary cultural agents will have to recognise universal human values as signalling lights indicating moral-ethical boundaries of human activity.

Universal human values are a quintessence of moral-ethical axioms, a result of the historical development of society and a product of civilisation as a maximally possible form of social organisation. Universal human values are universally applicable and undetermined by any individual, narrow ethical systems, moral codes, spiritual doctrines, or religious beliefs. On the contrary, universal human values are embodied in some form in specific cultural traditions, forms and types of value consciousness. It is by this criterion that we can judge the humaneness and social maturity of these mental phenomena. They were only recently recognised at such a highly abstract level, perhaps, only in the twentieth century.

Universal human values are built on the priority basis of personal needs and interests, and reveal human nature, his desire to co-exist with other people, and the transcendental world (the world of higher beings). By reflecting universal and essential qualities of human existence, universal human values are free from national, political, cultural, and religious limitations and focuses.

Universal human values include life, happiness, freedom, comfort, health, safety, love, family, friendship, faith, learning, truth, status, and professionalism.

Today, despite numerous attempts by radicals and conservatives to negate universal human values, they play a hugely important role as a buffer zone and a "peace-making" resource at the time of cultural contact.

As we see, universal human values include inalienable natural needs, rights and weal of a person as a living, rational, and spiritual being, living in the natural and human world. The concept of universal human values has crystallised from a diverse mass of human historical experience, despite its paradoxical discreteness and, at times, often mutually exclusive layers of meaning.

In social practice, universal human values are objectificated in the institute of *human rights* and partly of international legal norms.

The *human rights* category includes a whole range of cultural-historical, social, and legal concepts. Overall, they concern an inalienable human faculty, the basis of a person's role in society and an indispensable condition of his self-identification and development. Human rights are a concentrated expression of universal human values embodied in an individual.

By reflecting objective democratic principles, human rights serve as a means of protecting a person from the infringement of the state and other social entities. Given to people at birth, they form their sovereignty, delineating the sphere of their freedom, self-expression, and other aspects of their individual being. At the same time, they contain the concepts of personal freedom and independence limited by the interests of other people. The goal of such limitations may be only common harmonious co-existence of individuals.

Human rights are recognised to be given by birth and inalienable for each and every one irrespective of the person's sex, age, race, ethnicity, nationality, and religion. They are necessary to guarantee and protect the person's life, dignity and liberty, equal status, and to safeguard against coercion and violence. Human rights are conditionally divided into personal, civil, political, socio-economic, cultural, collective, and environmental.

Human rights are part of the Universal Declaration of Human Rights. However, despite this document's colossal historical importance and humanitarian value, its norms are only recommendations; therefore, they are interpreted differently in different national legal systems.

So *universal human values* and *human rights* are the first of the most obvious and accepted integration platforms for humanity. It makes no sense to deny this fact, at least due to the scientifically proven psychosomatic human identity at the level of a biological species.

2) *Global Social Institutions*
Global social institutions not only exist, but also enjoy the world's rightful respect.

Today, *global social institutions* include international organisations that, in turn, divide into international intergovernmental (interstate) and international non-governmental (public) institutions.

International organisations are international associations created on the basis of legal agreements, and the principles of voluntary, sovereign, and equal membership. International organisations enact recommendations. Currently, there are over 4,000 international organisations.

They are created, and work to represent and protect their members' interests and achieve political, economic, civil, social, ecological, and cultural goals in accordance with their statutes. The main feature of international organisations is the range of issues they deal with, and that they have a membership of a minimum of two countries.

International organisations are classified according to different criteria:

- membership (universal or regional)
- mandate (intergovernmental or supra-governmental)
- functions (law-making, consultative, mediation, operational and information)
- way of joining (open or closed)
- jurisdiction (general jurisdiction, e.g., UN and other general integration associations; special jurisdiction, e.g., political, economic, currency, credit and financial, trade, communication, cultural, health, military, customs, and environmental organisations).

At the general level, common markets, free trade zones, transborder agreements and partnerships, international banks, regular forums and transnational corporations, are also considered to be global institutions.

Unfortunately, we have to state that despite its considerable international authority, global institutions are not as influential as they should be. They take an active part in developing, passing, and supervising very important and large-scale solutions concerning entire nations and countries, and the world community, but they are very far from completing their mission in its full scope and meaning. Highly bureaucratised and bound by complex procedure, and with internal and external limitations and conditions, global institutions are cumbersome, money consuming and inefficient; this is further aggravated by a number of their own ineffective practices, including financial and economic ones. However, a separate chapter in this monograph is dedicated to the criticism of international organisations and improvement proposals. At this point, it is sufficient to state that the irrefutable fact of global institution existence, activity, and recognition is yet another proof of the objectivity of human integration platforms, which have so far justified and supported globalisation and are quite capable of becoming the foundation of *planetary unification*.

3) *Global Business*

Global business grew out of the age of great geographic discoveries, periods of scientific-technical progress, and industrial revolutions. By the 19th century, a global business prototype had emerged in the form of expanding and institutionalising intercontinental trade, and it became the world's leading economic project; while in the 21st century, it is a no-alternative reality whose key figures are transnational corporations, international trade, and financial-industrial institutions.

Today, *global business* operates with the structure of two types of international corporations: transnational corporations, and multinational corporations. They can be conditionally differentiated by the ownership principle of their parent companies; company branches of both of these types are located in different countries. The majority of modern international corporations are transnational corporations and therefore, their parent company belongs to the capital interests of one country. Essentially, transnational companies are national monopolies with foreign assets, i.e., they own companies having subsidiaries and offices in two or more countries. Thus, their production and trading operations are conducted across borders.

The international status of international corporations is reflected in the indicator of the percentage of sales outside the country of residence. Forty per cent of the asset value of the 100 largest international companies (including financial institutions) is based in the territory of other states. According to UN methodology, an international corporation can also be identified by its asset structure.

Most transnational companies are located in the USA, EU and Japan. Transnational companies control up to 40% of industrial production in the world, and half of the international trade. Around 80 million people work for them, which is practically one in every ten people, employed worldwide including in agriculture.

Transnational companies are characterised by:

- regional (intercontinental) division of labour: formation and sustaining the system of international production spread across different countries
- centralised management and control in owner countries
- relative independence in local operational decision-making
- high standardisation of business processes
- development, transfer, and use of cutting-edge technology within closed corporate structure
- use of complex infrastructure including banking services
- high intensity of internal corporate trade between offices based in different countries
- global staff structure and international manager mobility.

Most transnational corporations' investments are placed in the industrialised world: approximately three quarters of all direct investment abroad is divided between developed countries. Nevertheless, transnational corporation participation is also growing in developing economies.

The nature of global business is that it practically fails to recognise borders and sovereignties. With the current state of global transportation, information, and communication networks, capital flows to countries that have favourable business climate and the biggest profit potential. Nevertheless, global capital mobility and business processes face resistance from the instability of the planet's macroeconomic and macro-social processes. This already concerns politics. Yet, it should be admitted that global business, the global economy, trade, production forces dynamics, and production and consumption standardisation, are now the most objective part of the human integration basis.

4) *The Internet: Global Communications and the Virtual World*

The Internet is the global information and communication network. It has, perhaps, the unspoken status of being the most useful modern product; at any rate, both globalisation supporters and opponents make equal use of it. Some people believe that the World Wide Web is an ideal planetary world model or, perhaps, in some ways, its invariant. The virtual space is said to be the image of an expanding galaxy. In any case, the significance of the global web cannot be overestimated: as a driver of an information revolution, it transforms the very principles of social organisation, the structure and structural-functional mechanisms of the life of society.

Information revolution is defined as a transformation process of social relations under the influence of considerable changes in information exchange and processing. Society and human life acquire new qualities because of such transformations. History has examples of a number of information revolutions. Currently, humanity is undergoing a fifth information revolution whose nature is in integrating communication and telecommunication means, software, information databanks and knowledge as well as any symbolically expressible content in the world's single information space. It implies creating transnational global information and telecommunication networks and storages, and ways of their interaction capable of influencing both masses of people and every individual. The Internet is an example, result, symbol and active agent of the current information revolution, which causes a vast increase in the rate and scope of processed information, dissemination and amalgamation of knowledge, as well as of human communication and activity, including the production of products, services and added value as well as profit making.

The fifth information revolution has ultimately made *human consciousness*, both social and individual, a possible and promising object of labour. With new opportunities, it has brought new risks including effective mechanisms of manipulating people and modelling their motivation and behaviour.

In the economic sense, the current information revolution has transformed information into a liquid product and a valuable resource. In the historical sense, it has triggered a social formation process of creating a new type of society, an *information society*. The paradox of it is that information and communication technologies greatly outpace in speed the development results and potential of the social system, transportation and, in some sense, most users' intellectual abilities.

Among the most formidable consequences of the current information revolution, we can identify the following:

- division of labour transformation at all levels ranging from a sector of the national economy to an international level

- the strengthening of a network-type division of labour between economic agents irrespective of their location and object of labour
- emergence of new co-operation forms
- a new innovation cycle
- increased prestige of labour using informatics, programming, computer engineering and other related skills
- better access to information, and information and communication mobility
- lower status of the state and institutional and cultural practices
- science transformation in the direction of science globalisation in terms of object, agent and method
- emergence of new sciences revealing the world of infinitely small quantities (microelectronics, bioinformatics, genomics etc.)
- priority status of intellectual-spiritual technologies over material-practical ones
- emergence of information weapons and transformation of the concepts of national-state and corporate security
- priority status of non-material products: the intellectual product and intellectual property as the most expensive type of wealth in post-industrial economy
- widening gap between rich and poor countries in terms of development and quality of life levels.

The virtual world as a digital metaphor (and an objectification, if you will) of the noosphere has brought real world changes that we can boldly consider irreversible for our civilisation. The cancelling of these effects would only mean that people would degrade from the current civilisation level to the state of barbarism and savagery, abandoning their intellectual-humanist positions backed by progress, free choice, and the political will of several previous generations. Indeed, the Internet has made this world more compact and open, and people more mobile and universal. The main thing is that it has greatly increased the volume and accessibility of global competences, knowledge, and needs expanding the field of value, cognitive, and aesthetic elements of the current worldview. At the level of experience constants, communicated knowledge and skills, the Internet has made different cultural languages closer to each other: a *common cultural code* is crystallising in the virtual reality of the global human universe.

Nowadays, the Internet has become one of the most popular communication, learning, and work tools — over one third of the world's population uses it. This fact alone demonstrates that we must see it as a real and quite effective integration platform. Further, we will talk specifically about its application in the implementation of the design and plan of post-global human integration.

5) *Unity of the Technosphere*

Despite the fact that industrial and post-industrial society types co-exist in the modern world, we can, albeit conditionally, talk about the unity of the *technosphere* as a material basis of modern civilisation. At least, we can talk about a family of the following interconnected global technological systems (infrastructures) organised by single scientific-methodological and management principles:

communication, energy, transport and logistics, as well as space systems.

The global technosphere is a manufactured environment of human existence, socialisation, production activity, and consumption. Its global scaling has become possible due to energy sources and means of communication. The global technosphere currently includes all functional varieties of object-material, material-energy, electromagnetic, transportation-logistic, and information-communication infrastructure. We can say that the global technosphere serves not only as collective scientific intelligence and production activity, but also contains enormous possibilities of development in the form of historically self-unfolding ideological-theoretical potential of human thought. The global technosphere is a combination of science, machines, and technology; it transforms the biosphere and affects the quality of life and social relations.

We can already say now that the technosphere is generating its new, hybrid post-industrial technogenic forms, when its individual subsystems are becoming more complex, increasingly autonomous and ubiquitous, such as *virtual reality*.

According to Elena Dergacheva, the author of the paper *Specific Features of the Global Technospherisation of the Bioshpere in Modern Times*, "global technospherisation is taking place in the form of uniting production complexes of different countries used at different stages of the technological cycle in order to implement the same economic objectives, production technology improvement, exchange, and consumption of products produced with the maximum economic efficiency. At this stage, links of a single world mechanism of technogenic processes reproduction and dissemination, ranging from new equipment and technology implementation, to technogenic changes of the biological matter of the biosphere, including human body changes. This techno-urbanistic frame laced with information-technospherical networks presents the core of global technogenesis of the modern world community."

Correctly coordinated and effectively managed, the globally technosphere is capable of becoming a new evolutionary force, and compensate for the damage human civilisation has inflicted on nature during the years of its fast development.

It is much more difficult to attribute world economies to the same technological paradigm: to do that, we must admit, they are too different and do not even match each other. Still, the prospect of technological paradigm renewal, when the Sixth Techno-economic Paradigm will succeed the fifth one, is an objective possibility for economic practices irrespective of their development level. Practically everyone considers it a *global challenge.* As such, the transition to a new technological paradigm, as any other global challenge, this one must be viewed as a full-scale integration platform.

Technological paradigm, as an economic term, has to do with scientific-technical progress theory and points to the level of economic system and production force development. The technological paradigm concept is said to have originated from Nikolai Kondratiev's economic cycle theory.

Technological paradigm is understood in two ways: either as 1) a combination of technologies characteristic of a specific production development level, or 2) a system of interconnected system of different production processes having a single technical level and developing synchronically. Nevertheless, the concept of techno-economic paradigm characterises an economy in terms of its production activity, and its object, agent and method.

The notion of techno-economic paradigm is applied in economic history referring to the time of the first industrial, and the early stages of industrial capitalist economy, i.e., approximately from the last quarter of the eighteenth century, onwards. The core of each techno-economic paradigm is reflected in several core components: first, it is a dominant energy type; second, it is a combination of industries where it is used; third, technologies and innovations per se; fourth, the most progressive and technologically equipped industry temporarily becoming a driver of economic development; fifth, ways of production activity organisation and management, as well as capital dynamic (correspondingly, ownership forms).

It is no less important that historically, no national economy has yet met the criteria of any single techno-economic paradigm: different industries and production-economic complexes with such an economy would include development with different rates, some are more mobile, others are more conservative, which is caused by a number of factors, the key one of which is still the energy sector. The more industries and infrastructures of a particular production system meet the most forward techno-economic paradigm, the more developed it should rightly be considered.

Four techno-economic paradigms have already changed, now we are living through the fifth one; the Sixth Techno-economic Paradigm is looming on the horizon: it is forecast to arrive by 2035 – 2040, but some of its signs and tendencies are already revealing themselves today. By 2020 – 2025, a new way of scientific-technical revolution and a new cycle of scientific-technical progress are expected as a result of interdisciplinary synthesis.

The Sixth Techno-economic Paradigm will be characterised by breakthroughs in nanotechnologies, biotechnologies, genetic engineering, quantum and membrane technologies, microelectronics, informatics, robotechnics, micromechanics, and photonics. Its basis can be thermonuclear energy and, according to some expectations, a systemic use of alternative–natural– sources of energy. Some believe that the advent of the Sixth Techno-economic Paradigm will make it possible to develop and widely use new social system management forms and methods. Production and consumption individualisation, energy and material efficiency, tailor-engineered materials and organisms, as well as longer life expectancy are said to be new paradigm civilisation achievements.

The new techno-economic paradigm arrival of problematisation concerns social, economic, and cultural changes, and the preparedness of modern humanity and its live-sustaining subsystems. Predicted risks derive from production force development asymmetry, investment climate, infrastructure sectors, and elements. It has to do not only with having technically "under-equipped" or with "underdeveloped" individual production system components: it has to do with the fundamental contradictions and problems of the capitalist formation as such. Moreover, the system architecture and functionality of the global world have demonstrated that classical capitalist contradictions have been augmented by new contradictions, hidden conflicts and crisis trends of the common economic space. The most significant of them deserve detailed overview.

There is a contradiction between dynamically developing science-consuming material production technologies and archaic re-production capital systems. Another contradiction is between rational possibilities of new economic approaches and irrational big capital storms (world financial crisis, narrow-minded and selfish exploitation of fuel and energy technologies, etc.).

One more problem is the extreme unevenness of markets (product supply markets, consumption markets, and labour markets). This is the cause of many global problems: environmental contamination, starvation, and epidemics.

The growth of small and weak economies depends on large and strong ones. The emergence of managed markets within post-industrial economies, which clash with the original freedom of entrepreneurship, causes the reduction of capitalism's driving force and development potential.

Tension grows between the separatist ambitions of local elites and the integration aspirations of national economies. Production growth periods, which relieve social tension, are replaced by crises sometimes leading to conflicts between different social groups, including anti-government, and anti-globalist protests.

Inter-ethnic tension and nationalist resistance to globalisation encourage terrorism, which has become a dangerous mass anti-social phenomenon with the background of the availability of weapons of mass destruction, and extremism. This is practically the most noticeable class struggle manifestation.

Large transnational corporations play an increasingly important macro-economic and geopolitical role; this concerns especially resource monopolies whose capitalisation exceeds some national budgets.

Media and commercial art, which generate new and ever more powerful psychotropic and pathogenic effects, are playing an increasingly important role by negatively affecting people's mental health on a massive scale.

A conflict is growing between the post-modernist cultural shift, social organisation, and communication systems on the one hand and traditionalist revanchism on the other. While the former has found its expression in globalisation processes and trends, the latter, in religious fundamentalism, new mystical teachings, nationalism, and the restoration of archaic social organisation models.

Thus, it would be fair to conclude that at the beginning of the 21st century, the global need for the supra-national and supra-political integration of humanity is inevitable both as being *forced* in the face of global threats and risks, and as *natural-historical* and *evolutionary* because humanity is ready and able to become one as a planetary phenomenon. The necessity for global human integration is so evident that it can now be considered as a criterion of the social, civilisation and humanistic maturity of man, the elite society, and a social institution. Human global integration, globalisation, and global problems concern society as a whole, and each of its members in particular.

It is not ephemeral or utopian: as we see, it is timely from the evolutionary and historical points of view; it is prepared by all objective prerequisites; and therefore, it is quite real and *vitally necessary*. However, surprisingly, it is not a *fait accompli* or even a process that has a goal-oriented direction or managed development. Why is it so? What prevents us from launching this process, managing it centrally and systemically, and resolving humanity's global problems on the way? What prevents us from recognising the possibility, necessity, and timeliness of global human integration?

Even on a superficial level, we can see a number of reasons and factors for human disintegration in the world. They can be classified as political, ideological, religious, cultural, social, and economic ones; but even this classification or other classifications will be largely conditional. The main thing is that all the obstacles on the way to global human integration are generated and dominate at the mental level, the level of mass and group consciousness. It means that they are all subjective, even if the subjects are large social entities!

So, *what is in the way of global human unification?* We can mention the following factors:

- Absence of a systemic science-based unification model, which includes: structure, goal setting, principles, limitations, conditions, strategy, and implementation mechanisms
- Incongruence of levels of economic and social development of countries and peoples, and political conflicts between them
- Stockpiles of weapons of mass destruction causing the countries possessing them to

have an illusion of strategic superiority, and to encourage military-political confrontation
- A new stage of the Cold War
- Inefficiency of global political institutions
- Differences in resource bases of national economies
- Hydro-carbon fuel-based energy sector as the economic basis leading to irrational use of natural resources
- Contradictions between national and universal (supra-national) interests in the world
- Mutually excluding and conflicting pictures of the world and ideologies
- Inertia of mass consciousness, narrow-mindedness, and archaic cultural-ethnic mode of thinking.

Characteristically, not a single disintegration reason or disunity factor has a global (not to mention organic or planetary in its essence) character unlike integration reasons and factors: they are all quite particular and situation-dependent; so they can be corrected and transformed!

It is of fundamental importance, however, that no global human integration conception has yet been formulated that would be understandable and acceptable to everyone by being: systemic, compromise-based, convincing, attractive, clear, and allowed no alternative. It is also clear that the problem here is not only in the message itself, but in the target audience that the message should be communicated to, and by which it should be accepted at the level of their interests or, at any rate, it would not reduce again these interests. Various projects, paradigms and integration plans, be it monotheistic, communist, or fascist, and mondialist, environmentalist, or technocratic, have suffered from an array of drawbacks, which have made them incapable of becoming a real global human integration philosophy. These drawbacks are listed below:

- Understanding of global human good, or happiness, was not universal, because it was often detached from its objective basis—natural biosocial needs
- Other values, which were proclaimed in private integral projects, were characterised by narrowness and specificity. This prevented them from claiming the role of global human values; besides, they tended to contradict each other even when combined in the same worldview
- Integration goals were neither clear nor obvious; they were too particular, artificial and variable
- The actual integration object was too controversial in some theories: the concept of humanity allowed discrimination of some social, cultural, and national-ethnic groups
- Historical, civilisation, political, and other specificity of countries and nations as well as traditions of their social practices and way of life, value and worldview were disregarded
- Fundamental environmental conditions, including the ecosystem, weather and climate zones, biospheric processes, etc., were not taken into account
- The integration message target audience was often unclear or not concrete at all: even if the integration object was treated as "the whole

of humanity", the driver, active agent, driving force, vanguard or leader, were not identified or remained abstract. There was often little justification to vest in him such a historically important mission
- No undisputable arguments were presented for the necessity of global human integration: hardly any arguments could have sufficient convincing power for everyone except those that have to do with global problems, increased risks of human self-destruction, and the death of all life on the planet, or threats of a thermonuclear war, or ecological catastrophe.

Having analysed the mistakes and drawbacks of previous integration projects and models, we can conclude that a systemic change and paradigm review should be made of global human integration to make it logically impeccable, historically organic, conceptually consistent, ideologically compromise-based, economically justified, organisationally realistic, and therefore the *only one possible*. At least, as an initial model, deserving decisive intellectual and financial investment in order to complete, popularise among international and national elites, and subsequently implement it in practice. Such paradigmal formatting would be based on the conditions of the new integration project's global relevance. This way it will give a clear answer on what kind of global human unification is possible and acceptable to avoid the hard path of globalisation and multiplying its problems.

Such unification of humanity is only possible from a historical-cultural point of view of the unique way of life of different nations, natural and climatic conditions of various regional ecosystems, and acceptable from the point of view of international law, and personal rights and freedoms that:

- is based on natural and social needs of a person and humanity
- is carried out consistently, by stages, in accordance with an approved unification plan and model
- does not contradict the cultural-historical and social-political identity of nations
- does not violate the principles of rational use of natural resources and social-economic justice
- is profitable for national economies
- is supported by a scientific economic study, with planning, management, and control based on it
- is founded on adequate public support and an efficient institutional system
- does not use a mechanism of coercion and suppression
- is implemented in a legitimate and open manner
- is based on global mobilisation ideology.

The real integration of humanity is not only institutionalised and underwritten organisationally and financially, but thought through as a system, at least at the level of transnational elites and all those who take global economic and political decisions. It is an alternative to the current crisis for the global world and its destructive consequences, which will not wait long to materialise if left without comprehensive solutions.

Since the process of global human integration, as with any other large-scale social process, must have reliable financial-economic foundations and effective organisational mechanisms, we must address them now in more detail. In this regard, it makes a lot of sense to examine the Concept of Sustainable Development, which is interesting both as an integration model and as a macroeconomic paradigm; it must be thoroughly analysed and reviewed to crystallise the ideological and methodological basis of the *Planetary Project*.

CHAPTER 3

Criticism of the Concept of Sustainable Development

The Concept of Sustainable Development: definitions, pre-cursors, brief historical overview. Ideological basis. Key points, fundamental principles and main avenues of development. Implementation problems. Lines and arguments of criticism. Possibility of transformation.

As we said at the end of the previous chapter, contrary to the highly contradictory global human integration models of different periods and belonging to different intellectual traditions, it would be encouraging to look at the Concept of Sustainable Development. This is because it embodies an attempt at finding economic solutions to global problems based on some integration processes. At least, that was the first serious theoretical attempt to provide a systemic basis for world integration in the face of common historical challenges. Another thing is that the practical implementation of the sustainable development strategy has run into a number of difficulties; the analysis of this has served as the starting point of the Planetary Project covered in this book, and to which we are gradually leading the reader.

The *Concept of Sustainable Development* derives from a scientific and social-ideological study of the systemic civilisation crisis and the world's problems. The progressive part of the world's scholarly community and political elites had recognised their existence by the end of the twentieth century. They looked at the coming 21st century as an era of uncertainty and escalating global catastrophic processes. Some people believe that the term was first used in the UN Program for Global Change to identify humanity's development trajectories, which was adopted by the UN International Commission headed by former Norwegian Prime-Minister Gro Harlem Brundtland. It is believed to have been used for the first time in the 1987 report "Our Common Future". The phrase *sustainable development* was used to denote the key idea reflecting the meaning and values of the global anti-crisis movement.

The institutionalisation of the sustainable development category took place at the United Nations Conference on Environment and Development (UNCED) in Rio de Janeiro in 1992. It was there that the Concept of Sustainable Development was made the foundation of anti-crisis environmental modelling.

The notion of sustainable development was first tied to the sphere of the relationship between man, society, and nature. Sustainable development implies: normative-legal and other mechanisms of restraining human economic intervention in nature; other side effects of globalisation based on scientific assessment and forecasts; and some other principles approved by global international institutions. The goal of sustainable development as a modern civilisation economic policy concept and strategy is to move humanity to the state of *global dynamic balance* and *organic growth*.

The classical, model definition of the *Concept of Sustainable Development* is contained in the book *Our Common Future*, published, as we have already said, in 1987: "Sustainable development is development that meets the needs of the present without compromising the ability of future generations to meet their own needs. In its broadest sense, the strategy for sustainable development aims to promote harmony among human beings and between humanity and nature. The Concept of Sustainable Development as an anti-crisis civilisation paradigm had formed by the 1980s, and it became world famous in the early 1990s. In the early 21st century it became part of the economic, sociological and political agenda as a global trend, and a fully-fledged domestic policy direction in a number of developed and developing countries (over a hundred states developed their own sustainable development strategies), as well as the international policy of global institutions. However, many trace its origins to the scholarly thought and social practice of much earlier times. With a certain degree of conditionality, but meeting historical justice and scientific exactness requirements, we can see the sources and precursors of the modern Concept of Sustainable Development in a number of research works (from Huques Lagrange, to Thomas Robert Malthus, to Hunter Lovins) and social-political practices (the Club of Rome and the UN as well as international environmental and human rights forums).

When looking at the history of the *Concept of Sustainable Development* and the resulting national sustainable development *strategies*, analysing the ideological and practical basis and precursors, we can single out several key milestones and defining names.

The English cleric, demographer, and economist, Thomas Robert Malthus, who is considered to be the earliest prophet of a "natural apocalypse", should be the first one on this list. In his infamous "An Essay on the Principle of Population", he put forth a thesis about the inevitability of poverty, destitution, and starvation on a massive scale as natural processes resulting from the limited resources and population growth. He talked about the unevenness of human reproduction rates and the rates of supplying humanity with means of subsistence, the law of soil degradation, and the necessity to restrain population growth and birthrate control. Despite the fact that Malthus' theory was reactionary and later successfully critiqued by Marx, it was very influential at the time. In any case, such controversial theories can often be useful: doomsday scenarios have always been, and will be necessary to draw the global scholarly community's attention to the possible negative consequences of the centuries-old mode of production that still exists today.

Cognitive optimism characteristic of the 19th century natural and "positive" sciences as well as resulting engineering advances and industrial growth were succeeded by the horrors of the imperialistic and world wars, disillusionment in progress and the criticism of technogenic civilisation. The idea of the interdependence of people and nature through consumed resources received a new revival at the beginning of the second half of the twentieth century leading to the problematisation of the state of the environment. An issue was raised about the dangers of anthropogenic influence on the ecosystem as a result of economic activity and the need to protect nature on a systemic basis. Rachel Louise Carson, an American biologist, wrote in her book *Silent Spring* (1962) about the destructive effects of pesticides on living organisms, and was the key milestone in this regard. We cannot say that nobody had thought or written about it before: scientists had constantly raised environmental and related issues, but they had done it in basic research removed from practical application. Rachel Carson's work, however, became a sort of starting point for the process of public focus on the problems of a *natural processes evenness crisis*. It is important that the book appeared when humanity was ready to accept new realities requiring decisive action. The wide discussion that the book generated gave impetus to an environmental movement in the USA, whose aim was to prevent harm to the ecosystem and living organisms, including humans.

At the world level, the *Club of Rome* was the first to discuss threats to human existence and nature. The international non-governmental organisation was founded by the Italian industrialist and public activist Aurelio Peccei and OECD Director-General Alexander King in 1968. Scientists, politicians, social activists, as well as representatives of the world's financial, political, and cultural elites joined the organisation. The club's activity focuses on examining global problems, risks, threats, catastrophic factors, processes and their dynamics, as well as ways to solve and prevent them. Results of such studies have regularly come out since 1972. The

Club of Rome experts have proposed a number of original ideas and methods of predicting the future of the biosphere, society, economy, technology, and public consciousness. Their ideas about global economic restructuring, economic division of labour between different regions of the world within a single production system, organic growth, and the necessity to transform public consciousness in the direction of harmonizing the relationship between people and nature went a long way to the creation of the Concept of Sustainable Development. It is of fundamental importance that the results achieved by the Club of Rome regarding systemic global problem analysis, and the formulated objectives to be addressed, soon reached an international level due to the worldwide authority of the club.

The United Nations has made possible the transition from theory to practice in the fields of environmental protection, natural resource use, and solving poor countries' problems. In this regard, the most fundamental starting points included the UN Stockholm Conference of 1972, and the above-mentioned 1987 World Commission on Environment and Development report "Our Common Future" of the UN International Commission, and the United Nations Conference on Environment and Development (UNCED), held in Rio de Janeiro in 1992. These and later international elite forums organised by the global institution of the UN have developed civilisation development principles and appropriate action programmes, including national *sustainable development strategies* in more than a hundred countries. The purpose, of course, was not to stop or reduce economic growth, but to present new requirements for it, such as the qualitative assessment criteria of its effectiveness: environmental neutrality and clear social orientation. Thus, in essence, a shift has taken place in the understanding of scientific-technical progress and civilisation progress: humanistic changes have been introduced into their core characteristics.

It is important that sustainable development ideology be based on the correct principles of scholarly tradition and social-political reflexion of the early modern period and modern times. The ideas that gave birth to the Concept of Sustainable Development, and have been interpreted by it, are as follows:

- Population growth causes increased natural resource consumption. Human needs are limited by the resource available for their subsistence; whether we want it or not, this relation is objective. Meanwhile, Earth's resources are not unlimited, they are exhaustible; increased wasteful use of natural resources on a regular basis leads to their depletion, and does not allow them to renew.
- In the twentieth century, industrial growth accelerated unprecedentedly in comparison with previous historical periods. This became possible due to the technological realisation of the many 19th and twentieth century scientific discoveries, and the conditional levelling of leading economies and market globalisation. The main effects included economic growth, huge demographic shifts, and dramatic environmental changes some of which are irreversible: the Earth found itself on the brink of exhaustion, because humanity consumes more resources than the planet can produce.

- Many renewable natural resources have ceased to be renewable due to anthropogenic effects: air, fresh water, and fertile soil, many types of flora and fauna, as well as entire ecosystems.
- Industrial pollution constantly increases: solid wastes, greenhouse gases, and the accumulation of hazardous synthetic substances in animals and humans that cause pathological conditions or stimulate pathogenic mutations.
- To date, three large environmentally destabilised zones covering about 20 million square kilometres of land have grown in Europe, Asia and America, while fewer than 10% of natural ecosystems can still be considered intact. Some of the countries located in these zones are developing economically at a rapid pace, and are constantly increasing their polluting emissions.
- Unrestrained economic growth, as we now understand, does not resolve global problems; on the contrary, it aggravates them causing mass impoverishment and starvation, wealth disparity between poor and rich countries, rising unemployment and crime levels, as well as the spread of new and cured diseases.
- Economic interest, national wealth and economic growth cannot be the only goals of the international agenda, but must be combined with equally important global issues such as ecological security, public health and quality of life.
- Environmental issues, natural resource use, and social-economic development problems should be treated as global, valuable in and

of themselves, and vitally important. At the same time, they cannot be treated separately from each other or locally within the limits of individual countries.
- Ongoing deterioration of ecosystems, the foundation of people's well-being, is directly linked to perpetuating disproportions both between countries and within individual states, aggravated by impoverishment, starvation, public health decline, and illiteracy.
- Catastrophic tendencies in modern civilisation development are caused not only by incorrect interaction between humanity and the biosphere, but also by an unfavourable interaction climate within the global community.
- Human dependence on nature has not been overcome; on the contrary, it has acquired a qualitatively new, *global* character: people clashed with nature in the twentieth century when human abilities matched nature at the level of civilisation abilities. Social crisis is developing in parallel to the environmental one; by reaching the international level, the latter is to a great degree stimulating the former.
- At the end of the twentieth century, it became clear that unrestrained economic growth could lead humanity and the Earth's ecosystem to the final catastrophe and perish by the middle of the century. Integration of all economic practices into a single system, its transition to simple reproduction, massive improvement of the health of the environment, and population growth control could be a way out of this situation.

- A comprehensive approach alone to environmental and development problems treated with due attention will contribute to satisfying basic needs, improving humanity's standard of living, protecting and using ecosystems more rationally, as well as ensuring a safer and prosperous future. No individual country can do it alone: it can be achieved only by joint effort based on global partnership.
- There is a fundamental possibility to solve global problems, because modern humanity has reached the level of civilisation development that allows it to maintain production growth in practically any industry of the progressing economy without additional resources and energy. This means that humanity can live twice as well while using twice as little resources (Ernst Ulrich von Weizsecker, Amory Bloch Lovins, L. Hunter Lovins, 1997).
- Systemic, centralised, and coordinated measures to save the Earth and its life including humanity as a whole, and individual nations in particular, must be united as part of a single concept alternative to unlimited economic growth, and one-sided global economic development, which favours the richest countries and are implemented by such international organisations as the UN.

It is impressive that the Concept of Sustainable Development looks the most presentable compared to all previous variations on the global integration theme. At least, it has a solid scientific basis (based, by the way, on advances in both social and natural sciences), logical and compromise-based content, humanistic principles, a clear goal and reasonable objectives. It is worth saying, therefore, a few words about the content of the Concept of Sustainable Development. Overall, it has many very useful points for global human integration modelling and global problem solving.

Sustainable Development Concept Key Ideas

- The twentieth-century dominant economic growth model must be seriously adjusted by introducing environmental and social orientations, requirements, and limitations.
- The sustainable development category makes sense only in relation to the entire humanity and nature: the task of sustainable development strategy formulation and implementation is posited both at the level of modern civilisation as a whole, and an individual state in particular. Sustainable development must not only include the economic and environmental perspectives, but a social one as well, because people tend to focus primarily on resolving pressing social problems.
- Environmental protection must constitute an integral part of human society's life, and it cannot be treated in isolation from it. A comprehensive approach alone will ensure sustainable development as a worldwide strategy (it is futile to implement it at a lower level).
- Human poverty and the environment are not compatible. The poorer the population, the more harm there is to the environment.

- While environmental orientation is a priority for sustainable development, its main objective is to care for people, to achieve a high level of quality of life, and to ensure conditions for a healthy and productive life. Even more so, that with this approach the state of the environment is not disregarded, because a direct connection is established between the people's level of life and the quality of the environment.
- It is important to note that sustainable development is not only defined as one that rationalises economic growth, but also as one that distributes fairly its outcome, reviving the environment rather than destroying it, as well as enlarging people's potential rather than reducing it.
- Human survival implies not only maintaining the life balance of the current human population, but also ensuring natural resource use conditions for future generations.
- Saving and protecting nature implies keeping and improving the health of the biosphere as a natural basis of life on the planet and ensuring its sustainable reproduction and further evolution.
- The active vector of the sustainable development strategy is aimed at creating such a biospheric system that could be capable of resolving globalisation contradictions. Primarily, it has to do with the evolutionary-historical contradiction between resource limitations and needs growth (nature and society), developed and developing countries (economic growth levels), rational economic development

requirements, and national interests (global and local).
- Achieving a *strategic balance* between human activity and consumption, and maintaining biosphere regenerative capacity, can be considered to be the most important sustainable development criterion on a world scale.
- Transition to sustainable development and following its course implies the environmentalising of all production and consumption modes, as well as other drastic transformations of human activity, attitude, and consciousness that have to proceed in a goal-oriented and systematic manner.
- Managing the transition to sustainable development implies decisive actions in uncertainty and risk conditions, because neither the slowing down of social-economic dynamics, nor stopping social-economic growth would resolve global problems or remove the threat of an environmental disaster.
- The sustainable development strategy can be implemented only if a new civilisation model is introduced, which would require selection, re-orientation, and transformation of several social processes. For example, it includes increasing the social status of education and science. These institutions play the leading role in sustainable development strategy implementation, because scientists are meant to form global public consciousness and define noospheric priorities.
- The comprehensive nature of sustainable development means that goals and objectives should be set as part of major human activity

spheres such as economy, environment, the social sphere, state governance, science, upbringing and education, security and defence, as well as international relations.
- Sustainable development is defined as a transitionary stage from the current crisis state of modern civilisation to a future harmonised one. It is planned to resolve global problems and alleviate global risks by using such measures as: needs optimisation; production structure, distribution, and consumption transformation; as well as human consciousness evolution towards a rational-humanistic value system. It is expected that these measures will ensure a new worldview formation oriented at survival and improvement of the health of people and nature.
- The concluding stage of sustainable development is the noosphere as the most desired and best state of humanity, when the environmentally acceptable impact of society on nature has been achieved as a result of human needs rationalisation.

So what are the radical differences between the Concept of Sustainable Development and the economic growth industrial paradigm? The answer to this question is crucial to understand the concept, because it defines itself, first, as an alternative to unlimited economic growth. We believe that the most important difference and novelty is in the demand of modern civilisation with its production basis to replace its expansive natural resource use with the need to accommodate the biosphere, observe its laws, and take into account its prohibitions and limitations.

The market economy is based on the prevalence of profit-making and increasing material wealth on a competitive basis without taking it out of the capacity of the biosphere and its local ecosystems; however, the sustainable development economy will aim at creating harmony with the environment. To do this, it must be based on qualitatively new principles, largely deriving from the *environmental imperative*, i.e., the highest requirement of human behaviour and activity to meet the interests of nature, the biosphere, and universal human values.

The fundamental principles of sustainable development were outlined in the Declaration and other documents of the United Nations Conference on Environment and Development (Rio de Janeiro, 1992), the 19th Special Session of UN General Assembly (New York, 1997), and adapted in several national sustainable development strategies in later years. Their principles can be assessed using the following categories.

1) *The anthropocentric principle:* care of man, protection of his rights for a healthy and productive life in harmony with nature and society in an environment that is favourable for him. This principle defines world power co-operation in rooting out poverty and standard of living, and human need satisfaction disparities, as the necessary sustainable development condition.

2) *The comprehensive principle:* the sustainable development model encompasses the interests of saving nature, social justice and care for the future.

3) *The saving principle*: human survival depends on the rate of transition to new economic activity methods and forms: resource saving, energy saving and health saving, which could be based on science-based technologies and implemented by the motivation of decision-makers.
4) *The principle of the rational use of natural resources* requires harm-free management of renewable natural resources, efficient use of non-renewable ones, and their optimal consumption; finding alternative sources; timely waste disposal and safe burial.
5) *The principle of prevention of going beyond the limits* of ecosystem economic capacity concerns, in particular, limiting the use of economically unaffected parts of the planet's landmass and the World Ocean.
6) *The security principle* requires carrying out safe economic activity and minimising its social and environmental risks.
7) *The prevention principle* includes precautionary and preventive action in the event of serious and irreversible environmental danger, prevention of man-made disasters and emergency situations, carrying out health and safety measures, and preventing other global problems (the economic efficiency principle is consciously decentred in this case).
8) *The sovereignty principle* is one of the most content-extensive sustainable development principles. It encompasses three activity, process, and relationship types. First, it establishes the right of states to define their national natural resource management

policy, including the exploration of the state's resources. They are required by the international community to ensure the environmental safety of their activity vis-à-vis other countries. Second, it protects international trade against hidden restrictions and discrimination based on arbitrary environmental protection measures. Third, it forbids conscious "importing" of hazardous activity from one country to another.

9) *The justice principle* establishes equal development rights for current and future generations, and between all countries of the world without exception.

10) *The synergy principle* requires all countries to interact in the transition to sustainable development, and appropriate strategy implementation, in their economic, political-legal, and social systems. It also implies the global unification of effort in learning about the world, global problems, and their solutions. In particular, it talks about scientific-technical information, research findings and technology exchange, including innovations. This co-operation must acquire a global partnership character.

11) *The adaptivity principle* relates to environmental legislation regarding environmental standards, regulation principles, and environmental policy priorities, which must meet individual countries' conditions, where they are adopted, including economic conditions.

12) *The selective priority principle* emphasises the significance of developing, especially the least

developed and environmentally vulnerable countries' current conditions and needs.
13) *The responsibility principle:* all countries of the world must carry responsibility for maintaining the Earth's environmentally stable zones, its ecosystems and resource reproduction, as well as its plants and animals. The liability for harming the environment in any way must be ensured both at the national legislation level, and at the level of international law, with world powers co-operating in developing such legislation.
14) *The environmental harm internalisation principle* talks about the necessity to find a possibility to redistribute economic means to cover harmful environmental effects based on the premise that the polluter must cover such effects.
15) *The optimisation principle* requires the discontinuation of unsustainable production and consumption models as well as encouraging an appropriate demographic policy.
16) *The openness principle* guarantees public availability of environmental information at the national level for every individual, and at the international level for countries' official representatives, mandated to take environmental security and emergency situation decisions. Information rights must be endorsed by appropriate legislation.
17) *The pacifism principle* is based on the premise that wars and military conflicts have a destructive effect on sustainable development: peace is the most important and necessary condition for environmental protection, and

introducing a new, noospheric civilisation model.

18) *The ecological principle*: environmental and nature-saving orientation and saving life on Earth must become a dominant feature of economic and educational policy, modernising economic practices, social relations and public consciousness, and the core of environmentally conscious economic development.

19) *The gradualism principle*: transition to sustainable development must have evolutionary character avoiding sudden leaps, coercion, or any actions that could result in conflict or resistance at a regional or international level. The terms and rates of production-technical, economic-political, organisational-administrative, or other social transformations, must be goal-orientedly co-ordinated relative to the time of the predicted global environmental catastrophe. The goal is to put off for at least several decades the environmental calamity, to be able to complete the comprehensive environmentalisation of economic and social practices, as well as public consciousness. National transition strategies to sustainable development must be based on appropriate regional, infrastructural, and social specifics. The more developed and resource-rich economies could act as leaders and senior partners in the environmentalisation and general improvement of less developed countries economically and socially. At the same time, it does not imply one-sided "donorship", but rather full-scale co-operation, so that all participants

comply with international legal norms and provide genuine contributions to the process.

20) *The voluntary principle:* different states and nations interact on a global partnership and goodwill basis, which is also the source of international sustainable development law.

The above principles are reflected in the concretisation of sustainable development directions, collectively worked out at the end of last century.

The main sustainable development directions were proposed at the World Summit in Copenhagen on 6-12 March 1995:

- Wide civil society participation in developing and carrying out solutions, determining society functioning and well-being.
- Large-scale sustainable economic growth and sustainable development models, and demographic aspect integration into economic and development strategies, which accelerated sustainable development rates and rooting out poverty, and will contribute to achieving demographic goals and improving people's quality of life.
- Just and non-discriminating distribution of benefits conditioned by the growth among social groups and countries, and expanding access to productive resources for destitute people.
- Interaction of market forces, encouraging effectiveness, and social development.

- Government policy directed at overcoming factors leading to social antagonism and the respect for pluralism and diversity.
- A favourable and stable political and legal structure that contributes to mutual improvement of the connection between democracy, development, all human rights, and the main freedoms.
- Political and social processes characterised by preventing isolation and complying with pluralism and diversity, including religious and cultural diversity.
- Strengthening the role of the family in the interests of social development, as well as the community and civil society roles, in accordance with the principles, goals, and responsibilities proclaimed in the Declaration of the World Summit and at the International Conference on Population and Development.
- Increased access to knowledge, technology, education, healthcare and information.
- Strengthened solidarity, partnership, and co-operation at all levels; as well as government policy that gives people the opportunity to lead healthy and productive lives.
- Protecting and saving the environment in the context of human-oriented sustainable development.

Thus, it is obvious that the Concept of Sustainable Development can be considered quite revolutionary for science and public consciousness. It was the first to systematise a whole range of ideas originated between the eighteenth and 20th centuries, which have to do with the destiny of humanity influenced by the relationship "people–society–nature". It has suggested an alternative economic growth model in the form of noosphere-oriented transitional type civilisation.

In light of global human integration, the following is most important for global problem solving. The Concept of Sustainable Development has set the correct objective to maintain the biosphere, ensure biotic regulation, stabilize and improve the health of the environment and society. It is worth noting that the 12th principle of the Rio de Janeiro Declaration on Environment and Development postulates the necessity for the Earth's countries to unite their efforts in creating a comfortable and open economic system that could lead to economic growth and sustainable development in all countries.

Life has shown, however, that the attempts to implement the Concept of Sustainable Development have not been sufficiently radically successful to make it a pivotal moment in resolving global problems and taking the modern world out of the current civilisation crisis. On the contrary, they have run into problems that have proved to be partially or entirely unsolvable, at least using the Concept and strategies of sustainable development.

The following are the most noticeable and common problems of sustainable development strategy implementation.

The demographic problem is, perhaps, one of the most important and delicate. First, no clear, and more importantly, legally and ethically acceptable world mechanism has yet been developed to decrease the population growth rate. Second, even from the financial point of view, the problem is hard to solve due to the paradox of reverse proportionate dependence between the standard of living and birthrate in various countries.

The problem of overcoming poverty, and the disparity of the standard of living in developed and developing countries are being resolved very slowly. Efforts made in this regard have little effectiveness due to: inflation; high population growth in Third World countries; incorrect schemes and methods of calculating the poverty line; a minimum standard of living; and the international poverty level, etc. The most important factor is that the very practice of so-called government and international help to the poor is superficial and futile, because it changes nothing in the actual genetic foundations of the problem, and its reproduction mechanisms.

A suggestion to transform the world based on the programme of *uniting natural resources* was voiced at the Davos World Economic Forum in 2007. This route was shown as the only way to save the biosphere, including humanity, but it has not yet been deemed acceptable by many countries of the world. In countries whose economy is largely based on natural resource production and export (Russia, Iran, Algeria, Turkmenistan, Venezuela, Indonesia, etc.), natural resources remain the primary or only national income source, and often act as the instrument of putting pressure both on individual importing countries, and the entire world community (e.g., through the energy market). To them, resource internationalisation could mean sovereignty minimisation or loss.

Meanwhile, *environmental conditions* continue to deteriorate. The UN alone has spent several trillion US dollars on environmental programmes for just over twenty years of sustainable development strategy implementation. Despite some local improvement, the world's environmental situation has considerably worsened, with new risks and threats emerging. This is easy to explain by the fact that only developed countries have passed and observe strict environmental legislation; they also fund adequately their environmental programmes. Moreover, they help the poorest countries, which often cause dismay and indignation amongst their elites who feel that justice is violated. No doubt, developed countries accept their responsibility in the context of international sustainable development efforts. They take into account the emphasis of their societies on the global environment, and on the technologies and financial resources they possess. Nevertheless, as we have seen before, the resources spent in Third World countries change practically nothing in their economic structure. This is not because they are inadequate; but because they are not invested in creating a civilised production and consumption market, instead of plugging the holes that re-emerge practically immediately.

Thus, the contradictions, identified in the course of sustainable development concept implementation, demonstrate its internal logical paradox. *The incompatibility of national interests to global human interests* takes one of the central places among them. It is demonstrating itself prominently already. At the current consolidation and human integration stage for global problem solving, it would be naïve to suppose that any country would entirely abandon its own interests for the sake of global human interests when it involves global project practical implementation. However, all countries realise that the global community has a common future, and in the event of the predicted collapse, the whole of humanity will be affected. In this case, there is no sense to enumerate and dwell upon existing contradictions. It is enough to mention just one of them.

The Kyoto Protocol situation is an example of such a deep-rooted mismatch of national and global human interests.

The 1995 United Nations International Conference held in Madrid officially recognised, as an established fact, the global warming that took place in the second half of the twentieth century. This resulted in the signing of *The Kyoto Protocol* in 1997 by most countries of the world. It established the necessity to strictly control industrial atmospheric emissions, and to actively develop alternative energy technologies that would not affect or minimally affect the environment.

The Kyoto Protocol situation demonstrates the fact that despite the high rhetoric, no country wants to forfeit its national interests. Many countries have not ratified the Kyoto Protocol yet, while the USA and Australia have left it altogether stating that the agreement violates their national interests.

Many are not satisfied with the approach to determining countries' contributions to pollution used as the basis for the Kyoto agreements. For instance, the USA position was quite categorical: they left the Protocol. This is understandable: first, Kyoto environmental policy would lead to a radical increase in energy prices; and second, it is unjust in principle to developed countries, because it excludes 80% of the world's nations from complying with the Protocol recommendations, including China and India, which are leading production gas polluters. Introducing emission limits would reduce their economic growth, and therefore, impede their poverty programmes.

Thus, it is clear that the Kyoto Protocol, just as any multilateral international agreement, infringes the different interests of its participants. Even if we look at just one example of the contradiction that arose during the development of Kyoto Protocol endorsement mechanisms, we can see that the primacy of national interests over world community interests is currently evident. Every country, with a varying degree of intensity, solves development problems at the national level.

Therefore, almost twenty years have passed since modern global institutions officially set upon the course towards sustainable development, and no single economic, environmental or social policy model has been elaborated. Global problems have only accumulated. Acknowledging the Concept of Sustainable Development, we must repeat that the failures and difficulties of its endorsement cannot only be explained by practical barriers, but are rooted in its ideology. This concerns the very theoretical-methodological foundations of the Concept of Sustainable Development.

Becoming popular worldwide and finding its reflection in several important international documents, decisions, and practices, the Concept of Sustainable Development, we note with pleasure, has not been turned into a dogma; on the contrary, it has been criticised from different angles.

The traditional objective criticism of the Concept of Sustainable Development coupled with our own observations can be summarised in the following aspects:

1) *The incorrectness of the term "sustainable development" and its internal logical contradiction*

    In his book *Humanity: To be or not to be?* the Full Member of the Russian Academy of Sciences, Nikita N. Moiseev states that "the concept of development is the opposite of the concepts of sustainability and stability. Sustainable development is simply impossible: if there is development, there is no stability!"

2) *The narrowness of the term and the provocative tendency to confine global problems to the environmental context*

    Many scholars, politicians, social activists, and industrialists believe that environmental protection issues cover the entire sustainable development strategy.

    For instance, in their book *Main Civilisation Challenge: A Russian View of the Problem* (2005), Viktor Danilov-Danilian, Kirill S. Losev, and Igor E. Reif, describe sustainable development in terms of the theory of biotic regulation of the environment. They see the real goal of sustainable development not only in reducing the anthropogenic pressure to the level meeting the biosphere economic capacity, but also in releasing some areas to allow biota to perform its planetary stabilising mission.

    This approach may be a step forward compared to the situation when there was no adopted national programme at all, but it does not comply with global community recommendations. However, there cannot be ranking preferences in identifying global problems that contradict the systematic character of scientific thinking. These problems can be resolved in isolation from each other, but in the situation of the absence of possibilities, this should be done in a comprehensive manner. Even an unconscious desire to address one problem as the condition of resolving another one is not harmless.

3) *The absence of a single concept of sustainable development, with multiple concept definitions causing considerable implementation difficulties*

Anatoly Kostin states in his book *Ecopolitology and Globalism* (2005) that multiple concepts of sustainable development derive from the multiple treatments of "development", conditioned by different ideas of the relationship between political, economic, environmental, and social development, as well as global prospects as a whole." He identifies five conceptual positions in the treatment of sustainable development. These are the protective position, environmental modernisation position, structural ecologisation position, radical traditionalism position, and noospheric reconstruction position.

4) *The selectivity of the Concept of Sustainable Development, its original elitism and imperialist character*

There is an opinion that the implementation of the concept of sustainable development can only bring benefits to a certain part of humanity rather than to all people. Thus, in his book *Globalism: Theory, Methodology and Practice*, Ernest Kochetov, who is the Head of the Centre for Strategic Geoeconomic Research at the Higher School of Economics, writes that "post-industrial ideologists are trying to prolong the life of the post-industrial machine in its highest, technogenic phase, and one of such attempts is the concept of "sustainable development", i.e., the process of resource absorption must acquire a "sustainable" character for further functioning of global reproduction links where the world income is formed and distributed between a tiny group of "developed countries", without any participation of "third" parties with their natural, human, intellectual, and financial resources."

5) *The controversial character of several methods used by the Concept of Sustainable Development*

The extrapolar modelling used as part of the Concept of Sustainable Development is not a final verdict: we must understand that the predictions made based on it will materialise unless humanity, all other things being equal, changes its resource consumption policy. If the necessary corrections are introduced, the predicted collapse can be avoided. The fact of the matter is that there is no such thing for technical progress as the law of declining production factor effectiveness. The law is only valid with an unchanging technical level of production, but it ceases to work once that level grows. Obviously, human intelligence underwrites technical progress. However, the problem looks extremely different if the scientific-technical progress potential is not limited by anything. To be exact, there are limitations, but they have to do with the social sphere, i.e., the social form of production forces.

Indeed, there is much more than just resources to an approaching global catastrophe. Besides resources, we must take account of the internal dynamic within the global community, which is the same social factor. By dominating the process, it unfolds not only from its objective side, for example, economically motivated, but from its subjective side as well, in the elements of social consciousness (values) and even of mass unconsciousness (archetypes).

6) *The diversity in understanding the goals of sustainable development, naturally arising from the different worldviews of the participants implementing a new civilisation model, and countries and people representing cultural, social and political diversity.*

Without doubt, The Concept of Sustainable Development goals are aimed at creating a just and balanced world design. Nevertheless, we must not forget that different countries, scholars, and politicians interpret "justice" and "balance" differently. The very question of humanity's and individual nations' *readiness* for global integration, which will require a major transformation of their political and economic systems, is quite controversial. It has a historical character and concerns the actual basis of civilisational and evolutionary maturity of the modern Homo sapiens;

it encompasses cultural issues, man's moral-ethical self-identification, reasonableness, and responsibility. In addition, of course, it has a direct relationship to the socio-cultural status, influence and authority of science, rational worldview and prognostics. Obviously, it bears a clear connection to the Concept of Sustainable Development. In this regard, it is hard not to agree with Arkady Ursul and Alexander Romanovich who said in their book *Security and Sustainable Development* that "we have to bear in mind that transition to sustainable development is only possible as a result of creating a conceptual-theoretical model of the future, which is more rational than the current one-dimensional economic model. From the outset, this approach to the future has noospheric orientation; therefore, the very beginning of moving along the sustainable development path separates the chaotic period of human history from the noospheric one when it is rationally created."

An open question remains whether history used to have a chaotic character and what opportunities people have to influence their own history. Official science has not yet given any single or clear answer to this question, and the chaotic statement is a default but unproven version of the dominant historical discourse. How can we talk about humanity's readiness for noospheric orientation in modelling its future, or any global integration projects at all, when the world community is so divided, and the economic development asymmetry between various countries is so drastic?

7) In light of the above, we must note *that the main target of criticism* of the Concept of Sustainable Development (unless this criticism is provided for the sake of criticism, rather than as the basis of further development and evolution of the initial concept) must include the absence of *systemic implementation mechanisms* organisationally and financially underwritten. The subsequent chapters of this monograph will be dedicated to the discussion of these issues.

Thus, in any case, both the critics and followers of the Concept of Sustainable Development are united in believing that transition to sustainable development requires dramatic transformation of the current civilisation, the core of which is the environmentalisation of all major human activities. However, the world is stuck again not being able to stop looking at the environment as the source of resources, otherwise the current economic system based on hydrocarbon energy would negate itself! The afore-mentioned and any other possible problems with the practical implementation of the sustainable development strategy are rooted in the fact that the modern economy does not "satisfy" the biosphere, while the "biocompatible" economy does not satisfy modern civilisation. It is only possible to resolve this contradiction through technical means if there are changes to modern man's worldview, civilisation identity foundation, and value system, and a radical technological leap. What is meant here is a noospheric re-orientation of public consciousness: it must be possible technologically, and acceptable socially, to transition from hydrocarbon energy industry and economy to those based on alternative sources of energy.

This step could usher in a new era in human development, a step to a new kind of civilisation. A lot of work is needed to accomplish this task and colossal financial resources. However, the concept of sustainable development says nothing about the sources of funding, nor does it talk about the mechanisms of its implementation. This is exactly where the root is of the theory's current lameness and untenability; and why it is time that we stopped deliberating and expounding slogans, and turned to real actions because we do not have much time left to save the world.

CHAPTER 4

Planetary Project: Premises, Basis, and Definitions

Planetary Project premises and essence: re-globalisation and planetary modelling. Fundamental hypotheses. Key ideas of Planetary Project philosophy. General principles. Introductory information about planetary property, rent and infrastructure. Planetary Project target groups. Planetary Project timelines as a product of scientific and business practice development.

Despite its theoretical solidity, international authority, and partial success, the Concept of Sustainable Development has run into fundamental implementation issues and divergent opinion regarding its interpretation and implementation. This is the reason why it has not yet made any significant progress in global problem solving, including the saving of the biosphere and harmonising the social-economic structure of society. Internal contradictions are revealed both in its ideological-methodological frame, and in the global institution practices that have taken up the role of enforcing sustainable development in economic, financial, administrative, and other subsystems of modern society. The Concept of Sustainable Development's global mission has not been fulfilled, which implied laying out the foundations of *a new type of civilisation* that would adapt people and their life to the environment through the worldwide application of the appropriate strategy.

Nevertheless, the task of global human integration is not cancelled; rather, it is becoming increasingly urgent in light of modern environmental and geopolitical threats and risks. Global problems, none of which has been resolved or considerably reduced in its dynamic, have accumulated a critical mass. There is not much time left before the Earth's life-subsistence resources are irreversibly exhausted. Radical and efficient solutions based on a systemic scientific-practical anti-crisis economic model are necessary. The environmentalisation of all activity spheres, environment protection and social transformations must be realistic, manageable and supplied with resources both in the methodological and material sense.

It is also clear that the Concept of Sustainable Development cannot be carried out when so many of its true points, correct principles, and promising proposals, require evolution, re-working and review, based on constructive criticism and modelling focus shift. For instance: the categories of "progress" and "development" require conceptual review; while the terms "sustainable development indicators" and "the quality of life" need a systemic detailed overview; and there has to be a total re-evaluation of the notions of "biocentrism" and "humanism". Finally, *the environmental imperative* and *biocompatible ethics* should be filled with concrete and accessible meaning. The main thing, however, is to develop an organisational basis, and resource mechanisms of global human integration and global problem solving to avoid the situation when they remain as admirable wishes and delusionary future projects never to be implemented.

This work must start where a gap is found in the Concept of Sustainable Development, and where the Sustainable Development Strategy has lost its way. Still, correct ideas have allowed the adequate formulation of *what* should be done and *when*; while *how*, *who* and *with what resources* remain the weak link in the argumentation of sustainable development followers. To address these issues, we propose our own comprehensive ideology and methodology referred to as the *Planetary Project*. This book discusses its timeliness and underlying ideas, as well as implementation spheres and prospects.

The very idea of the Planetary Project as a new and realistic model of solving global problems, as a concept of global human unification, and a civilisation paradigm, was born in 2006. Initially, it emerged as criticism of the Concept of Sustainable Development: as discourse of correcting and augmenting some of its points; developing ways for its implementation; creating the resource base and institutions for enforcing the strategy of sustainable development; and clarifying its goals and objectives. It gradually became clear that we, the authors and developers of the *Planetary Project*, reached the horizon of *re-globalisation,* which implied modelling society and its processes that are essentially an alternative to the "golden billion" format. The optics of *planetary modelling* has become possible due to a new angle and a certain focus shift.

It is impossible to solve global problems, and remove or alleviate global contradictions, most of which lie in the economic dimension or at least are rooted in it. Therefore, we saw real possibilities of radical solutions in revising the notions of *planetary resources*, *planetary property*, *planetary rent*, and the *re*-distribution of income from it.

Indeed, what has become the barrier for international attempts to implement sustainable development strategy? Generally speaking, any obstacles can be confined to the three most significant aspects:

1) conflict of interest in the process of discussion and resolving global problems (along the following juxtapositions "global–national", "international", and "national–regional–local")
2) absence of scientific-technical projects and proposals to solve global problems
3) ideological and value contradictions between global players and the absence of a single platform for the understanding and evaluation of global problems, as well as the necessity to resolve them.

It is clear that to develop and implement an effective policy to remove these obstacles (ensuring balance of interests in the first case, carrying out necessary research and obtaining optimal technologies in the second, and raising awareness of the above in the third), we must have, first of all, adequate financial means. The Planetary Project contains its own theory of financial sources and mechanisms.

Talking about the essence of the Planetary Project, it is sufficient to point to the fact that it proposes the following *basic hypotheses*, to be substantiated through practical activity:

- *resolving global problems* of the contemporary world is difficult and costly, but possible, provided these are in place: an adequate resource base, material means, clear planning, correct organisational scheme, and a realistic financial mechanism;
- *levelling off the disunity factors* of peoples and countries of the world to the level when they do not present obstacles to the process of global human integration, is possible with the gradual removal of inequality of wealth distribution between agents of planetary development;
- planetary unification is possible when *a compromise-based model of civilisation is created,* in which conditions are acceptable for different people, states, and cultures;
- *developing necessary scientific-technical solutions* sufficient for a painless transition to the Sixth Techno-economic paradigm, and achieving a qualitatively higher level of collective scientific intelligence organisation, and also designing a comprehensive and all-encompassing approach to global challenges, threats and risks are possible providing planning is done correctly, while research, experimental, and

design work are carried out in compliance with environmental and noospheric priorities as well as with an adequate level of funding;
- coherent *modelling of instruments* of solving global problems and global human integration is possible, and is carried out justifiably as part of the *Planetary Project*;
- we can completely rely on *support* for the Planetary Project from the progressively minded international and national elites if we present to them a well-argued justification for the degree of their interest, participation, and responsibility.

Whether the hypotheses are proved, confirmed, and serve as the development basis for additional and associated directions, can only be shown by the practical implementation of the Planetary Project.

The Planetary Project philosophy is constructed along the following lines:
- identifying the most important global problems;
- recognising their fundamental resolvability;
- proclaiming the planetary scale of the activity, and the necessity for global human unification;
- formulating basic hypotheses;
- formulating key principles of planetary integration;
- recognising the possibility of creating a single human civilisation able to develop in harmony with nature;
- determining means and mechanisms of global problem solving and planetary integration;

- forecasting and programming prospects of planetary civilisation according to the new evolutionary scenario.

Consequently, a brief overview of the purpose, content and direction of the Planetary Project would follow the logic of this scheme; and put concrete meaning into its provisions and their interrelation in this and following chapters. Thus, the purpose of the Planetary Project is to solve global problems threatening the present and future of humanity.

We believe that the following problems are the most important, and urgent today:

- poverty, unemployment, social inequality and social injustice;
- starvation, undernourishment, deficit of fresh water and food as well as its poor quality;
- threat of a nuclear war and the proliferation of weapons of mass destruction;
- climate change;
- environmental crisis and environmental degradation;
- rising deficit and non-renewable depletion of natural resources;
- spread of existing and new mass diseases (including infectious and virus);
- terrorism and local wars;
- international mafia structures, etc.

The ideology of the Planetary Project is based on the premise that global problems of today's world are essentially solvable only if the following conditions are met: unified understanding and assessment of problems, and the need for their solution achieving the balance of interests of all parties; a reliable organisational-financial scheme; and the integral co-operation of united agents. The main thing is that global problems can only be solved on a *planetary scale*: there is no real possibility of solving them in any other way.

Pre-empting the question of why we use the term "planetary" instead of the conventional "global", we will explain it as follows. We purposefully use the notion of **planetarity** in both the name of the project, and in the terminology about its vectors, content, goals and specific objectives. There are two reasons for doing this: firstly, its scale indicating the cosmos character of the Earth, the biosphere, humanity and man; and secondly, to get away from the odious notion of *globalism*. Unfortunately, *globalism* causes negative associations in many people, because it has been discredited by the opponents of globalisation and the "golden billion" ideology. "Planetarity" does not just have a purely mathematical meaning of the maximum imaginable calculable amount of the Earth's objects, including organic and non-organic matter as well as primitive and highly organised life. It is also representative for the understanding of evolution as a cosmogonic process in which *integral people* can play an active part. **Planetarity** *is a form of existence in which any division between people is removed and loses its meaning and significance.*

Within the Planetary Project framework, resolving global problems and global human integration as the key condition for human survival, and the emergence of planetary humanity as a new agent of history and evolution, can only be possible based on some fundamental principles deriving from the analysis of the UN, the world's integration practices, and historical experience.

The Planetary Project general principles are as follows:

- survival and health improvement of the biosphere, surviving world ecosystems, resource saving, and use of alternative resource substitutes, are of priority importance for the existence and development of the world community;
- equality and equal rights for all races, nations, cultures, religions, states, and other forms of social organisation are postulated as part of the human integration process;
- forming a planetary institutional infrastructure, which will be a system of supra-national *planetary governance* organisations, is necessary for solving global problems of civilisation integration and world design harmonisation;
- for this, it also makes sense to develop public diplomacy and civil control over official international organisations;
- national, regional, continental, and international elites become active participants, drivers, and agents of planetary development, which contribute to the development, financing, and practical implementation of social, economic, and political planetary programs of harmonious development of a unified human civilisation;
- a new format of global civilisation development must be worked out along the lines of re-globalisation, which would contrast with the

globalisation serving the interests of the "Golden Billion;"
- the authors and designers of Planetary Project ideas and its supporters profess scientific optimism in regard to current reality, belief in people and nature, their integral organic unity and kinship, as well as the victory of mutual harmony.

The above general principles will be the basis for special principles, axioms and algorithms of the Project's individual sections.

Today, it may sound idealistic to talk about the possibility of harmonising the relationship between people and nature and social development *harmony* in noospheric unity format, when the world is wrought with a multitude of fundamental contradictions. Pessimistic experts predict escalation and even collapse in regard to some global problems, which can result in the death of humanity, the biosphere, and the Earth itself. The authors of the Planetary Project consider themselves scientific optimists: we believe in the reason and spiritual power of people, in their ability to make sense of their needs and regulate them. It would not be surprising if in the ancient past, barely remembered now, our ancestors already found themselves on the brink of self-destruction, but were able to save themselves by uniting in the face of danger. Today, there is hardly any other scenario for people than an integration one. In this case, however, as perhaps in any other mega-project to be implemented in market conditions based on the *similarity* and *conflict of interest*, everything depends on the "price tag." In other words, it has to do with the costs involved and the financial mechanism of the entire work cycle ranging from designing and approval to implementation and quality control.

The achieved level of science and economic activity has given us the possibility to identify the *source of material basis* for global anti-crisis activity practically in all needed aspects. We have realised that the institution of *planetary property* could become the basis of the planetary supra-national institutional infrastructure, and of planetary programmes. *Planetary property* is the most important natural resource that has no national borders and belongs to the whole of humanity. It is a huge long-term source of income and a factor of economic unification of the planet's entire population. It includes:

- space resources (solar energy and the planet's gravitation);
- world ocean resources and its potential;
- air resources and its potential;
- humanity's intellectual potential (basic research, natural sciences and humanities, as well as human capital), etc.

According to the Planetary Project ideology, we had to make sense of the *planetary rent* and develop practical mechanism for its appropriation to use the planetary property potential to its fullest. This work has been done, and its results are presented in the subsequent chapters of this book.

As an example, we can examine the Earth's atmospheric resources. Air circulates around the world as wind and hurricanes. Unlike the air space for air travel, which is regulated over national territories, it is impossible to identify national boundaries of the atmosphere. Every person or company uses the atmosphere, consuming oxygen, and polluting it by hazardous emissions.

The 1997 Kyoto Protocol mentioned above can be considered the first attempt to introduce an internationally accepted mechanism of using the Earth's atmosphere. According to the agreement, emissions quotas are allocated to each country. Countries must pay fines if quotas are exceeded, while unused quotas can be sold to other countries or economic entities using natural recourses in their production. Despite the controversy over the criteria used in determining quotas, measuring real emissions in their dynamic, and defining the cost of environmental damage, etc., this mechanism is one of the ways to appropriate and concentrate the *planetary environmental rent*.

Creating a *planetary institutional infrastructure* is necessary for the management of the formulation of global human interests, and for its co-ordination, systematization, and protection; as well as for a whole set of actions involved in the design, planning, and implementation of the world integration movement that preserves historical cultural diversity. Their prototypes (*global institutions*) have been in existence for several decades. They include the United Nations, its committees and commissions, the Organisation for Economic Co-operation and Development (OECD), the International Monetary Fund (IMF), the World Bank, the World Trade Organization (WTO), and others. Their authority and achievements in politics, economics, the environment, and peace making are internationally accepted. Nevertheless, they need to be constructively criticised, and some methods of their work need to be objectively modernised and revised.

According to many politicians and scientists, the existing global institutions are not effective enough. Suffice it to mention the UN modernisation attempts made at its 60th Session in 2005. The weakness and organisational laxity of supra-national institutions are rooted in the prevalence of block (group) interests, and the dangerous disparity between the levels of economic development and the standard of living in different regions of the world.

The Planetary Project idea derives from the necessity to unite existing global institutions into a single infrastructural system, beneficial to all nations and acceptable to them. This is both necessary and possible. All the necessary conditions and instruments exist for that: global information networks, the Internet, the virtual communication space, a 50-year experience of many global institutions' efficient work and their publicity capital, as well as professional diplomats, economists, political scientists, and ecologists. We must only add to it the planetary goodwill, the interest of *planetary development agents* (motivated elites), a clear and compromise-based integration-institutional programme, and the initiator of the process. The Planetary Project takes upon itself the latter role.

From the point of view of the Planetary Project, the compromise-based planetary institutional infrastructure can tentatively look like this:

1. *Spiritual-ideological* institutions (the World Academy of Sciences, the World Information and Education Space, the World Dialogue of Churches, etc.);

2. *Political* institutions (a modernised United Nations, the World Parliament, Continental Parliaments, planetary political parties and social movements);
3. *Economic* institutions (Planetary Property Institute, the United Planetary Development Budget, and a system of planetary and continental development programmes);
4. Supra-national *governing* institutions (the Planetary Council, the Security Council, Regional Councils for Economic and Social Development, and a modernised UN);
5. *Administrative institutions by sector* (a modernised WHO, a modernised IAEA, the United Space Institute, etc.);
6. *Environmental expertise* institutions (they carry out a comprehensive oversight and review function, and have casting vote rights in all nature management and development decisions).

When modelling planetary institutional infrastructure, we must understand that any serious integration processes in today's world are restrained by concrete contradictions between national and global human interests, both of an objective and subjective nature. The hyper importance of national over international interests impedes many global decisions, and will present the same threat to planetary decision making. This must be expected and taken into account. Therefore, the task of identifying Planetary Project *target groups* acquires special significance. These target groups must be able to understand the Project's main message, goals, values, and programme of action, and become its supporters and influential world agents. We believe that at first, these groups will include *elites*: accepted leading minorities, decision makers, owners of strategic assets (ranging from means of production to valuable knowledge), power-vested individuals, and those people who interpret the interests of the groups led by them.

World history shows us that entire nations or entire humanity (this notion still appears problematic to us) have never really driven progress or incited radical changes and transformations (whether they be political, scientific, economic, religious or cultural). Even if we talk about some kind of *passionary ethnos*, the drivers of its development were its chiefs, leaders or members of its elites. Populations have always been guided by their own, or even alien, exogenous elites. The masses are blind, inert, and unguided without leaders who own initiative and *vision*.

Minorities rather than majorities, have always possessed creativity, commanded kick-starting mechanisms, and had power, authority, and governance capacity. This is how roles are distributed in society, and it is quite natural: it is easier for a majority to obey, based on overt or covert agreements and delegate decision making rights, because this majority tends to minimise its responsibility for others, and save the psychological costs involved in process launch and management. Moreover, when they are born, people are differently endowed with potential, creativity, courage, penchant for risk taking and experimentation, and responsibility. This is a fact, it is normal, and it is not a tragedy. Thus, it is also justified that the distribution of power, privileges and resources is not even in society, and tend to concentrate in the hands of a minority that is more functionally decisive and effective.

We do not want to condone here social injustice manifested in uneven or asymmetrical distribution of material or spiritual goods; but we talk about social competition as a special, complex form of *natural selection*. This task belongs to the future if we are to talk about the humanistic overcoming of this law involving the noospheric-spiritual evolution of people and humanity, which would result in the increased number of leaders, or a dramatic transformation of everyone to an autonomous and self-governing person. However, there is still an open question about how desirable or humane such a task may be.

Why do we hope to get the elites interested in the Planetary Project and encourage their active participation in it? The fact of the matter is that real members of the political, business, or scientific elites have a special type of personality. Having achieved success in their profession, they move on looking for new ways to apply their energy, talent, and creativity. Their entrepreneurial proactiveness turns into self-sacrifice. Besides the professional and income-earning activity, they always strive for self-realisation in the social sphere.

The Planetary Project is ready to offer the elites:

- a qualitatively new type of activity that is differentiated from others by its scale, originality, and paramount historical and civilisation importance;
- a long-term investment project involving all kinds of investment as well as unlimited entrepreneurial possibilities;

- a genuinely messianic role in world history; and a real possibility of personal contribution to an ambitious goal of saving the biosphere, harmonising society, creating the basis of a new civilisation, and ensuring the future for all humanity.

Particularly, national elites and political leaders have to develop and implement the mechanism of delegating parts of their power to supra-national bodies. UN and European Commission experience could become the starting point for the development of such a mechanism, and engraining it in international conventions.

Any social institution, especially functioning on a planetary scale, can work effectively only if it is adequately funded. For example, the activity of the UN, its committees and commissions demonstrate the necessity to attract additional funding sources, including those that would not require the approval of national governments. The economic mechanism of funding planetary institutions is thoroughly worked through in the Planetary Project, and this will be given due attention in this book.

Scientific research and findings are also a very important constituent part of the Planetary Project for its design and implementation. Thus, we expect to develop, for example, a contradiction-free *needs assessment technique* in relation to the most important resources, which are necessary to solve pressing planetary issues.

According to some assessments, food aid alone worth 1.5 US dollars a day per person, amounts to 200 to 250 billion US dollars annually, to maintain subsistence of poor people in countries unable to cope with the poverty problem. It is estimated that there are between 400 and 500 million poor people worldwide. Large amounts of investment are spent to boost Third World countries' economic activity. War on international terrorism also needs additional spending. Finally, global funding is required to restore the global environmental balance on different continents worldwide. Another thing is that, even with its volume, this spending is not as effective as it could be. Therefore, the issue of the effectiveness of current spending on global problem solving is a separate research and design topic altogether, which is open for suggestions and review.

To develop and implement Planetary Project ideas, we plan to create an organisation capable of achieving research and public awareness objectives. The main goal of its activity must consist in harmonising the social, economic, political, cultural, and spiritual life of the Earth's population as a whole, and in individual regions, subregions, countries, and territories, by implementing comprehensive interdisciplinary and socially significant economic, political, social, cultural, and environmental practically oriented projects. These programmes and projects are intended to converge in the single Planetary Project qualitatively improving people's lives in their social and natural environments.

To achieve the main goal, it would be desirable to engage in the following activities:

- basic, field and applied research, that is comprehensive and interdisciplinary in nature

(the comprehensive and interdisciplinary character of research manifest themselves in the fact that they include specialists from such scientific fields as economics, sociology, political science, cultural studies, philosophy, history, law, social, and political psychology, environmental science, etc.);
- facilitating the implementation of practical projects and programmes based on comprehensive and interdisciplinary research;
- participating in the expert assessment of programmes and projects developed by various research organisations that are connected to the Planetary Project's main goal;
- forecasting social, economic, political, cultural, and environmental development;
- organising and supporting virtual and real communities made up of scientists, politicians, civil society activists from different countries who would be interested to develop and implement Planetary Project ideas and innovations (such communities can be considered as an important research quality control source);
- organising and conducting virtual and real scientific and academic conferences, seminars, symposiums, forums to disseminate, discuss and promote research results and other measures;
- organising the development and support of information databases, electronic libraries, portals, and websites in their field including providing planetary-scale access to such resources through modern telecommunications and information networks;

- encouraging the wide dissemination of its own work results through its own publishing activity and by publishing papers in journals and the media;
- participating in regional and international projects and programmes connected with the Planetary Project's main goal;
- conducting other activity contributing to the Planetary Project's main goal.

At a mature stage of its life cycle, the Planetary Project concept and strategy implies transforming it into a distributed network organisation with elements of virtual, intellectual, and educating activity. These objectives will require some in-depth explaining.

As we all know, network structure is an association of independent individuals, social groups or organisations which are involved in co-ordinated actions on a long-term basis to achieve agreed goals. This association has a common image and common infrastructure. The main functional ideology of the network is competitive co-operation.

If we look at the structure of a network organisation, we can identify three groups of elements: a network centre, a system of servicing organisations, and network membership.

The network centre's functions include:

- reconciling members' interests;
- representing them vis-à-vis outside organisations;
- lobbying members' interests;

- co-ordination and support of the network's image;
- conducting appropriate information and propaganda policies;
- ensuring interaction between network members: the Centre is the information and communication core of the network;
- creating the network's single information space, infrastructure and organisational mechanisms;
- ensuring the possibility for members to interact with each other directly bypassing the Centre;
- organising the work of servicing companies or distributing some service functions between network members.

Network members can have different status. The following statuses can be established: "full member", "associated member", "first, second, etc. level member".

According to the Planetary Projects authors, the network centre will be represented by the scientific research organisation (institution) "The Planetary Project". It will unite all charter-related research participants. In its nature, it can be a dispersed (distributed) organisation, because research groups are expected to be located in different countries and cities.

By definition, a virtual organisation is an association of functional partners managing the design, production, and sale of products and services using modern information technologies, and a contract system with independent working groups and entities. One of the main characteristics of a virtual organisation is that it sets up connections, and carries out managerial activity based on integrated and local information systems and telecommunications. Of course, one can say that the main product of the scientific organisation "The Planetary Project" is information as a virtual and ideal product. Consequently, using modern information and telecommunications technologies is a natural way to enhance information exchange and improve the quality of the organisation's products and services.

Any scientific organisation can be called an intellectual one. From a theoretical point of view, an intellectual organisation is defined as a "free society" of many interacting centres. Its main characteristics are plurality and discussion providing the opportunity for completing points over a wide array of comparable issues. As far as the rights of such an organisation's members are concerned, they would include freedom of speech, and the right to communicate freely with other members irrespective of their rank and structural unit boundaries. The main qualitative sign of an intellectual organisation is that it replaces administrative control and coordination with the direct responsibility and self-control of performers, working in interdependent groups that are made up of equal status members. This equality in status makes it possible for the members to use their intellectual potential most effectively. Any modern organisation strives to increase the effectiveness of using human potential.

Combining the advantages of network, distributed, virtual, intellectual, and educational organisations is the main organisational strategy of the Planetary Project.

From a network point of view, we, as the authors and creators of the Planetary Project, see it as a prototype of planetary institutional infrastructure that will achieve its objectives by way of *global network co-operation*.

In conclusion, the Planetary Project concept can be defined as follows. It is:

- the result of the criticism, review and reconstruction of the Concept of Sustainable Development taking into account modern facts and trends;
- a non-commercial scientific research project with a view to transform itself into an international institution of re-globalisation, modernisation and planetary human integration;
- a response to current challenges representing a model of global problem solving, threat alleviation, and risk minimisation;
- a real alternative to the modern world of risks and threats as well as a unipolar westernised world, because the Planetary Project ideology allows local cultural diversity in the planetary civilisation context;
- an instrument of supra-political unification of humanity for the sake of global problem solving using planetary and noospheric resources as well as the optimal schemes and effective mechanisms of their use.

Even in its today's form, the Planetary Project is first of all a scientific-humanistic movement that offers a new world economy paradigm, a global human integration model, and practically a new historical and evolutionary scenario based on the actualised interpretation of such terms as "development", "progress", and "civilisation", to which the environmental and planetary humanistic imperative requirements are applied.

We believe that the Planetary Project ideas and proposals are extremely timely, because:

- the Project fits current conditions and addresses the Sixth Techno-economic Paradigm challenges due to its cosmic scale and the globality of its comprehensive objectives;
- the Project's comprehensive proposals promise favourable impact on the Earth's biosphere;
- it is a project that can unite the entire humanity, despite its political disunity, on the basis of genuine humanism, higher justice and the single goal to save and develop the human species;
- the Project's ideology and proposals meet the similar needs of local and transnational elites of harmonizing world processes to achieve market stability.

Therefore, we believe that the practical implementation of the *Planetary Project* could contribute to the qualitative improvement of the lives of current and future generations, when everyone can have a long, healthy, active, and happy life in harmony with nature in the ecologically friendly environment.

CHAPTER 5

Planetary Project Design: Goals, Specific Objectives, and Methodology

Planetary Project general goal and main directions. Planetary Project philosophic-ideological, research, economic and political-administrative objectives. Basis of interdisciplinary planetary research methodology. Central planetary problem. Methods of scientifically grounded facilitation of world development harmonisation.

The previous chapter discussed the goal of a scientific organisation as part of the Planetary Project. The scientific organisation's goal, however, is much narrower than that of the entire *scientific-humanistic movement,* which the Planetary Project is meant to initiate. The Planetary Project goal, in its grand form, is relatively large-scale. It consists in: resolving global problems of modern civilisation and minimising global world contradictions; achieving harmony in society and its relationship with the environment; saving and improving the health of the biosphere based on the re-distribution of incomes from planetary resource use and the intellectual assets of economic systems and communities. In this sense, the Planetary Project simply had to emerge; it is something that humanity eventually had to arrive at.

It is important to understand that, fundamentally, we do not separate environmental and social-economic issues, because we believe that only successful economic transformation both in terms of production technologies and in terms of the distribution system can fundamentally change nature management policy, and relieve the ecosystems of excessive pressure. The key force, which is capable of kick-starting the movement processes towards the designated goal and achieving it, is the *collective scientific intelligence* and the *planetary goodwill* of our contemporaries' world over the manifestation of the *noospheric potential* of current generations. We believe that in order to achieve this goal, we must use the resources of natural and intellectual assets held in planetary ownership. This movement should meet the interests of the biosphere objectivised in the *environmental imperative,* the Planetary Project's basic principles, and the images of harmony known to us from the time of Pythagoras. Therefore, the vector from *sustainable development to managed harmony* will be most relevant to characterise the Planetary Project goal.

By the way, the rehabilitation of the concept of *harmony* as a scientific category, and its inclusion in the planetary discourse, will be one of the central meaningful and value focuses of the Planetary Project philosophy.

Indeed, the concept of harmony figures most prominently in aesthetics. However, this category also has a full-fledged general scientific meaning. It is harmony that characterises movement and development in the objective world. Some Greek philosophers, including Pythagoras, and the Pythagoreans, Heraclitus, Empedocles, Plato, and Aristotle, talked about the harmony of the cosmos. We would like to quote here the Soviet philosophers Alexey F. Losev and Vyacheslav P. Shestakov, who said that "harmony belongs to the categories that characterise general structural principles ("measurability" and wholeness of a thing) ... and characterise the *content* of a structural whole, which presupposes both the existence of the whole and its divisibility, qualitative dissimilarity and opposition of the elements composing it at the background of uniting wholeness. Therefore, the category of harmony is closely connected with the notion of unity of the opposites." Thus, as a philosophical and scientific category, harmony means many things. It is the commensurability, proportionality, and orderliness of the parts of the whole in movement and development. It is the unity of developing diversity. It is the agreement of form and substance of a developing object. It is the reflection of the unity of the opposites and of the natural development of holistic reality, etc.

We used to talk a lot about the necessity for a person to develop his personality in a harmonious way. Nowadays, we talk as much about the necessity to harmonise relations between different nations and ethnic groups as well as the relationship between people and nature. A concept of harmonious production is a natural follow-up of the concept of flexible, saving-oriented production, etc. In this sense, we can say that the Planetary Project Concept of Managed Harmony is a natural revision of sustainable development ideas from the point of view of social scientists and economists.

The general goal of the Planetary Project is to save the world that found itself on the brink of destruction at the beginning of the twenty-first century. It implies a long-term prospect of modelling an environmentally oriented noospheric civilisation based on biocompatible economy and biocentric ethics, as well as of generating an *integrated WE-humanity*. This general strategic goal and vision of the future find their organic fruition in the Planetary Project specific objectives, which can be divided into philosophical-ideological, scientific research, economic, and political-administrative.

The Planetary Project philosophical-ideological objectives include:

- developing a theoretical-methodological basis of re-globalisation (including global human integration);
- formulating an environmental imperative;
- revising the categories of progress and development;
- modelling the categorical-conceptual and structural-functional bases of a noospheric civilisation as a harmonious world design;
- developing a system of biocompatible ethics and the basis of different kinds of spiritual activity;
- creating a new mobilisation ideology based on the values that can unite humanity;
- other associated objectives.

The task of creating a special language is at the core of any theory. This language must be capable of communicating key terms and constants as well as defining the object, subject matter, and method of analysis. The key task of any theoretical language is not only to verbalise fully the researcher's ideas about the object, subject matter, and method of theorising, but also to show their non-contradictory relationship and abstractification in the context of a single discourse. The theory principles and axioms must act as internal reference points for the coordination of theory concepts. These principles and concepts must be able to act as the theory's apodictic basis or elementary (further non-analytical) truths. However, they need identification themselves. Any theoretical language is representative if it has reference to other semiotic systems and semiotic spaces. In other words, a theory can only be judged as a complete description and interpretation of its subject matter, if it can be translated into other languages. The potential of theory terms and their methodological symbolism capacity determine the strength of the fundamental joints of the world described in the theory. As far as the planetary context is concerned, we inevitably face the necessity to construct a synthetic metascience language capable of communicating concentrated knowledge from the fields of natural science, philosophy, technical, and social sciences to find the shortest way possible from their suggestive representation to practical implementation.

The Planetary Project *research objectives* include:

- taking stock and assessment of the current status of global problems;

- review and systematisation of sustainable development indicators;
- development and justification of interdisciplinary planetary research methodology;
- creation of a unified system of studying and designing planetary processes;
- creation of a common planetary theory through a synthesis of noosphere theory, bio-centric ecology and sustainable development theory;
- development of scientifically warranted facilitation of world development harmonisation;
- modelling and justification of optimising and rationalising the use of natural resources;
- development of strategy and technologies of resource substitution, search for and implementation of sources, carriers and technologies of the alternative energy sector;
- other associated objectives.

When setting *research objectives* within the Planetary Project framework, we must understand the fundamental importance of the fact that we are aiming at creating qualitatively new scientific thinking. It is not guided by the classical orientation at finding truth cleansed of any external value, but is based on the humanistic-noospheric needs of *integral man*, which are guided by his main goal of saving the biosphere and resolving the global issues of the modern crisis-ridden civilisation. On the one hand, such an anti-crisis mobilisation purpose endows scientific research with innovation-practical character, and on the other, strengthens it with a *bioethical* basis. In this regard, even the most fantastic scientific-technical solutions and technological innovations are not viewed as intrinsically valuable achievements, but rather as rescue operation tools. Progress will have to revise several of its intermediate results and rectify the consequences of an excessive anthropogenic impact on nature. It is not surprising then that a number of research objectives will be dedicated to resource saving, and resource substitution solutions. Resource saving and resource substitution gained popularity at the end of the last century. The reason was not even because natural resource limits were "counted", and the energy and resource crisis was predicted. The interest in such innovations was also motivated by the desire to minimize expenses and production costs characteristic of any economic activity. Both past and present research of economic resource management systems argues that the development and implementation of resource saving and resource substitution-based development strategies lead to the long-term sustainable functioning of a company. Moreover, in the post-industrial economy, the resource efficiency and resource substitution criteria are growing in importance. Design, implementation, and self-development solutions based on alternative resource and energy supply sources for production, which derive from breakthrough innovation technologies, have become an established fact under the name of the *creative economy*. It is left to us to give the trend a large-scale and mass character.

The Planetary Project *economic objectives* include both theoretical and practical ones, including:

- creation of a quality of life assessment system;
- development and justification of the concept of intellectual resources;

- development of a planetary rent calculation method;
- development of the concept of an integrated planetary economic-distribution system;
- development of an economic mechanism for financing planetary institutions;
- creating conditions for new growth points and economic development zones;
- other associated objectives.

Interestingly, even the Vatican proclaimed a large-scale task of global economic integration as early as 2011 in the wake of the global financial-economic crisis of 2008-2010, and the expectation of a new crisis. Calling for a radical reform of the world currency and financial system, the Pontifical Council for Justice and Peace spoke about the necessity to decentralise financial institution governance, capital flow management, the co-ordination and regulation of banks, currency exchange systems, as well as stabilisation and insurance funds. That integration initiative was driven by anti-crisis interests related to a particular local situation. Today's motivation is even more radical based on the need to save the planet.

The nature and purpose of the Planetary Project *political-administrative objectives* are quite similar to the ones above. They include:

- developing a comprehensive system of international targeted programs, organisations and funds;
- creating a political concept of supra-national governance of the world integration process;

- developing an international concept of disarmament and stockpile reduction of weapons of mass destruction;
- developing a planetary governance institution infrastructure model;
- developing a program of modernising existing planetary infrastructure institutions and creating new ones;
- other associated objectives.

It is paradoxical, but the world is increasingly experiencing the *lack of global management*. It has to do not only with the high geopolitical and political-ideological risk of tension between antagonistic systems, but also with the difficulty for partner countries to reach consensus over major world issues under the aegis of global supra-national institutions, such as the UN, the EU or NATO. The inefficiency of international organisations, as they exist now, is becoming increasingly obvious: they are cumbersome, bureaucratised, limiting themselves by archaic norms and complex approval procedures, disunited internally, and often concerned with narrow interests. The task of re-organising them is gaining ever-growing prominence due to the growth of culture-genic mutations (including *archaisation*), political aggression viruses, and the probability of *resource wars*.

A number of very authoritative scholars and public figures believe that management globalisation (including integration process management in all spheres of social life) can be a great benefit for us today. What is important is to tune in, direct, and make use of the synergy of global governance and management, as well as to ensure a certain dispersion of authority, influence and power through global institutions. At the same time, planetary governance tasks must be based on such basic principles as historical experience and national identity of current states, the balance between different political cultures and social formations uniformly understood planetary interests and goals.

Solutions to some of these problems will be described in this monograph; other problems are so large that they require comprehensive studies to be published elsewhere as part of the Planetary Project research. All of the above objectives have one thing in common: their methodological basis. This is because both their formulation and implementation have not been arbitrary or governed by chance, but rather have resulted from a natural development of current crisis analysis and rationalisation, as well as a systemic sense making of global problems and the scientific project of noospheric re-globalisation. Thus, it would be quite relevant now to describe the *methodological basis* of interdisciplinary planetary research.

The problem of method, which is essential and receptive for science as a form of social consciousness, is one of the most characteristic ways to abstract attitude to reality and a mode of human life in this world. This problem reflects the eternal desire of our *ratio* to possess a flawless "organon" – an instrument of the productive search for and finding the truth. Indeed, method is meant to ensure continuous consistency of the process of learning and a scientific rigidity of its results. Including theoretical and practical devices, rules, ways, norms and principles, method is a sort of reflection of the entire science, akin to the way a drop of water can give the impression of the biochemical composition of the body of water from which it came. At the same time, method is always a reflection and objectification of consciousness that makes sense and transforms reality. Therefore, it is correct that you can judge the level of knowledge and the system of activity based on this knowledge at a particular period of history by the method.

As regards the Planetary Project, its *methodology* is important in both its senses: both as a combination of learning activity procedures; and as teaching about theoretical instruments and their application as a system in various relevant contexts and environments. It is clear that the actual question about methodology in relation to the planetary research subject matter, scale and objectives, firstly, is doomed to be interdisciplinary; and, secondly, is fundamentally open to dialectical changes, development, and evolution.

At the same time, it is obvious that the self-defining methodology of planetary research cannot ignore the nature of today's science that is currently characterised by such features as post-modern eclecticism, openness, non-linearity, admissibility of subjectivity at the level of formatting goals, compromise between rigidness and conventionality, etc. Current scientific thinking can be defined as hybrid, and this is not strange since it has to keep balance when civilisation values are devalued, progress is discredited, and classical rationality has given way to mythogenic archaism. It views method as a subsystem of the entire science combined from different, but historically compatible elements of philosophy, basic and applied research, classical and non-classical sciences that place importance not on the origin of these elements, but rather on their combinatory applicability to concrete problems. It is important in this regard that planetary research has, at the very start, immunity to dogmatism and multi-modelling and pluralist orientations. A so-called poly-paradigm approach typical, for example, of modern sociology, is very promising in this respect. From a methodological perspective, its essential purpose is to go beyond one isolated paradigm (in the role of a combination of its methods) in terms of certain research, interpretation, or practical procedures. On the contrary, the poly-paradigm approach allows the use of any appropriate method to describe, analyse, predict, assess, or solve a concrete interdisciplinary (in our case, planetary) problem that could fit, and be effective in solving, a specific problem or achieving a specific objective. Optimal combinations of tools, which are different in origin and functionality, give a comprehensive and flexible methodology that can be applied to a more complex level of goals than any individual paradigm.

The universal general scientific *systemic approach* has revealed a number of drawbacks when applied to the subject matter and issues to be studied, e.g., social issues. Therefore, efforts have been made to correct and develop it to form the methodology of interdisciplinary planetary research. The results of this adaptation of the systemic approach to interdisciplinary *planetary research* were reflected in the formulation of some critical arguments against sustainable development and in some ideas of the concept of managed harmony.

Many complicated and extremely complex processes, principles and the problems of their functioning, require interdisciplinary research through the setting up comprehensive research teams. Such super-complex entities include planetary objects, processes, and issues. A methodological problem arises in interdisciplinary research that implies a choice of a methodological approach (or approaches) capable of becoming the basis for integrated new knowledge, which could be shared by the whole research team and communicated to the outside world. This problem is aggravated by the fact that the notion of "methodological approach" in traditional epistemology is quite vague and often very controversial. For some researchers, it is a way of looking at a problem; for others, it is a way of goal achievement; still others interpret it as a starting position that guides the development of research; finally, there are those who see it as a certain scheme for attaining new knowledge.

Science has now developed a number of approaches claiming to be interdisciplinary. Each of them has its own framework, requirements, and rules. They include, for example, systemic, synergy-based, comparative, reproductive, dialectical-materialistic, statistical, evolutionary, and other approaches. To develop a planetary interdisciplinary research basis, a comparative analysis of traditional research approaches has been conducted with a view to assessing their adaptability to planetary research, which concerns complex planetary problems.

Planetary principles, processes and problems have always been studied using a systemic approach that includes: *systemology* as a supercomplex diverse system; *systems engineering* as practical guidelines on how to design complex systems or regulate its work; and *system analysis* as research methodology.

The core of Planetary Project research is to ensure harmonious world development in interaction with the environmental and social-economic subsystems.

This paradigm of managed harmonious development has no alternative, if we are to resolve global issues and save the biosphere. Science, human intellect and the collective ratio can provide the fundamental possibility of setting current civilisation on the path of harmonious development.

The notion of *the collective ratio,* and the phenomenon it designates, has fundamental importance for the purpose, ideology, and implementation of the Planetary Project. From our point of view, it is not a beautiful metaphor or hypothesis, but a reality of the level that, perhaps, we are not yet able to interpret within the framework of the dominant worldview. However, for this reason this reality is less real.

In an approximated and non-strict sense, the image of the collective reason brings out allusions to a whole range of concepts from Neo-Platonism to Marxism, and from mysticism to intuitionism. Philosophic and social science literature tends to equate the collective reason with *public consciousness,* which is understood from the perspective of historical materialism, with *common sense* treated from a positivist perspective or with *collective experience* represented in various civilisation theories. If we imagined a maximally varied, but semantically homogeneous "collective portrait" of the collective reason, it would be based on the following premises:

- collective reason could not have emerged together with individual reason due to the biosocial natural of man;
- it is a natural phenomenon, a product of the mutual evolution of individuals and society which takes

shape in parallel to increased need for information exchange and collective decision-making;
- the genetic source of collective reason is joint human activity as a process generating and multiplying *information*;
- collective reason development outpaces individual reason development in the majority of cases; it served as the source, platform and, in some sense, genetic mechanism even at the outset;
- some people believe that collective reason is constantly growing in significance for the subsistence of some communities and most people;
- many believe it to be a source of scientific, technical, economic, and spiritual achievements of humanity;
- many believe that the human ability to use functionally objects and devices, which people do not understand, proves that collective reason exists;
- division of labour and network co-operation have become possible due to collective reason, the former being the key conditions of the latter;
- today, collective reason manifests itself in mass co-operation, network co-operation, and *open source intelligence* – alternative sources of information, platforms of group creativity and public voice.

The factuality of collective reason can be put under question, because it exists within no narrower boundaries and with no less degree of objectivity than such similar derivatives of collective activities as, say, *language*. Indeed, if following the German philosopher Martin Heidegger and the Russian philosopher Vladimir Bibikhin, we consider language as a *carrier of meaning* - not only the "mirror" but also the "creator" of a person's world - then the ontological meaning of collective reason as the *creator of language* becomes apparent. We can say the same thing about mathematics, the universal language of describing reality as both clearly accessible and conditionally accessible to man. These relationships remind us of the similarity of collective reason with a *thinking ability* as the specific identity of humans as a species.

By the way, thinking gave rise in the 1980s to the concept of *collective intelligence* or *group intelligence* in the context of collective decision-making research. The core of the concept is that group intellect is more effective in producing new knowledge and impetus than individual consciousness due to *synergy*.

If we consider collective reason as the quality of the whole of humanity and information civilisation, it surpasses its own previous levels. Moreover, according to some estimates, it surpasses all the levels put together. It happens due to the system of interaction between elements represented in the following sequence: "information – knowledge – software and hardware – individual intelligence – group intelligence – education system – institutional information-communication systems – mass media and mass communication media – public consciousness". Modern collective reason, therefore, can be characterised through the notion of *symbiotic intelligence*. Undoubtedly, the Internet, one of the integration platforms of humanity, and the virtual world it has created are its largest agent and conduit. Symbiotic intelligence also manifests itself in developed countries, at any rate, in such forms as:

- social consensus and social capital;
- political and civil initiatives;
- social media;
- information-communication technologies and artificial intelligence;
- crowdsourcing projects, etc.

The Planetary Project philosophy treats collective reason in line with the rational-ethical tradition of the early modern period and modern times, including Emmanuel Kant's *transcendental subject construct*, Vladimir Vernadsky's *noosphere concept* and Nikita Moiseev's *concept of global human intelligence* on the *supra-individual basis* of *intelligence and ethics*. The synthesis of these universal notions with biocentric needs gives us an understanding of a single *planetary consciousness*. A special chapter of the book is dedicated to the above issues.

The idea of harmonizing world development must include not only the reconciliation of ethnic and national values, i.e., social reference points, with industrial development as an economic process, but also saving the environmental balance as social responsibility to future generations. Harmonising planetary processes as a comprehensive and supercomplex task requires the use of scientific findings in various fields; therefore, we must involve planetary research scholars and specialists who have achieved interesting and promising results. The figure below depicts the set of sciences to be included into targeted planetary research and transformation programmes.

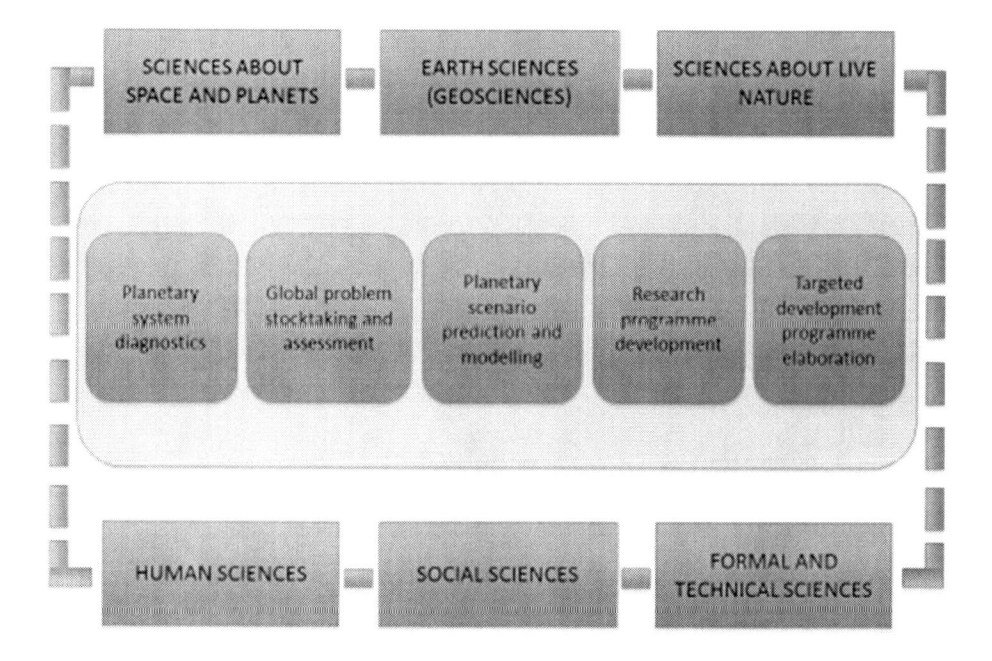

Fig. 1. Planetary Process Research and Design System

At the same time, in order to form a comprehensive research team with interdisciplinary goals and ensure its productive work, we must do the following:

- develop a targeted research programme;
- develop a common paradigm vision and a relevant language;
- develop an approval procedure.

As far as such planetary theoretic perspectives as globalism, alternativism, prognostics and futurology, they are all characterised by a *pre-paradigm* state described by the American historian and philosopher of science, Thomas Samuel Kuhn.

In his famous work *The Structure of Scientific Revolutions*, published in 1962, Thomas Samuel Kuhn reviewed the essential development of scientific knowledge. He stated that each field of science has two periods: a pre-paradigm period, and a mature science period. Transition to mature science is characterised by the fact that one paradigm receives a dominant position. It is more competitive and is capable of explaining available facts and resolve outstanding problems that science deems within its scope.

A pre-paradigm period of scientific knowledge development is typified by:

- immaturity of the scientific field that represents itself by the lack of a single, widely recognised point of view on major issues the field covers;
- co-existence of multiple conflicting schools with varied views regarding the object of study in the field;
- a possibility to do research without specific and necessary paradigms;
- a feeling that we must build knowledge anew starting from its very basis;
- relative freedom of choice in terms of research methods to justify new knowledge.

It is worth noting that the pre-paradigm level of interdisciplinary approaches to planetary problem research, and to the resolution of planetary objectives, opens the possibility both to develop new theories and to develop traditional theoretical constructs based on various methodological approaches. Thus, the choice of a methodological approach and theoretical basis for practical implementation of harmonious world development through comprehensive planetary programmes should be based on the enhancement of the practical usefulness of global design theorising.

The following ideas reveal the criteria for the practicality and usefulness of the Planetary Project theory:

- Practically useful theory is born out of real life and directed towards it.
- The product, which is a result of practically useful theory objectification, has external application, i.e., it is consumed outside the sphere of science or, in other words, in practical life. This consumption is not a mere contact of the scholarly community with existing reality as part of an empirical study, when scientists only act as observers of various aspects of this reality. Practically useful product consumption is directly connected to the value position of the scholar activist, scholar reformer, scholar politician, scholar administrator, etc. and, thus, has a social impact and social consequences.
- A practically useful theory is a theory on whose basis one can perform in the existing conditions scientifically warranted transformations of reality, putting the possibility to practise or refrain from such transformations, keeping the status quo. Moreover, a practically useful theory is capable of transforming its content into an application method by itself, because this facility is implicitly built in it.

- The practically useful theory "language" can be "translated" into the "language" of real life, despite their fundamental differences. A practically useful theory can guide its consumer to specific applications of its findings.
- A practically useful theory forms in its user the ability to apply it. In this case, the process of mastering the theory goes through three stages: grasping the theory; forming skills how to use it; and developing adapting and articulation skills.
- The product that is created, when a practically useful theory is applied is the result of its content adaptation to a specific time and space in the process of applied research, and it has a normative and instructive character for an outside user. The external consumption of such a product forms and reproduces correspondence between the outside reality and its reflection in the user's mind. This creates opportunity, and determines social ability to perform effective action.
- The usefulness of a practically useful theory goes in two directions, as the theory product is useful both for an outside consumer and for the user who applies it.

The above characteristics determine a special methodological approach to the development of a practically useful theory that is different from those used in the development of descriptive and explanatory theories. These differences are in the choice of concepts, theory design, and the relationships between claims and supporting arguments theoretically representing the objective character of external reality.

Any theory simplifies reality, but a practically useful theory also explains its basis and movement, and guides practical actions as the product of its application. This makes us assess methodological approaches claiming to be interdisciplinary in terms of the possibility to build based on such approaches a practically useful theory capable of facilitating global problem solving and world development harmonisation. This work is expected to continue above all within the framework of the Planetary Project philosophical-methodological and research directions.

Meanwhile, general schemata of the development and practical implementation of the comprehensive Planetary Project can be proposed as a scientifically warranted world development harmonisation technique.

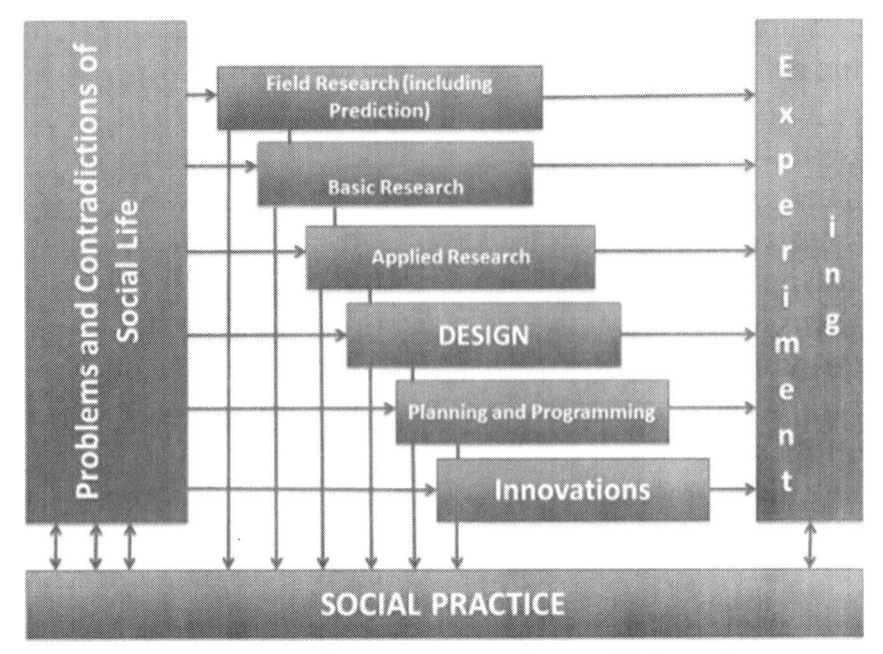

Fig. 2. Scientifically warranted world development harmonisation technique

This book primarily focuses on the theory and methodology of the Planetary Project economic and partly philosophical-ideological directions.

CHAPTER 6

Planetary Resource Base

New classification of planetary resources. Space energy and resources. Atmosphere. Land and World Ocean. Inland water bodies. Biosphere. Human resources. Humanity's intellectual capacity and the global intellectual potential. National intellectual culture. Asymmetry of scientific and technological development of different countries and its factors. Intelligence spiritualization.

One of the most radical novelties of the Planetary Project is a *new resource base classification* of modern civilisation that is perceived as a combination of *planetary resources* with which humanity enters into two kinds of relationship: as an agent, and as an element. Scientific analysis will allow us to systematise them and reveal their economic potential. It is important to us as well that the united resource base is a natural and objectively historical platform of global human integration.

Economic theory has traditionally understood the term resources production factors: land, labour, and capital used by economic players in varying degrees. Since the agrarian economy dominated until the twentieth century, land was considered the main resource. Industrial society pushed means of production, industrial equipment, and capital to the forefront of economic development. Post-industrial society made the services sector the dominant economic resource pool, which includes such key components as knowledge, information and human intellectual abilities. This simple division of resources into the three groups of 1) *land*, 2) *labour*, and 3) *capital* is adequate for microeconomic purposes, and explaining a businessperson's choice of economic sector. Macroeconomics, however, needs something more sophisticated than this simplified approach, if it is to describe a national economy, let alone characterise a global economy. A more detailed and systematised notion of the planet's resources is needed.

Based on the model of the Earth as a planetary phenomenon, a general classification of planetary resources can be suggested that can be developed in detail and expanded in the future. Three parts are identified in it: *cosmic energy and resources; atmosphere, land and the world ocean, inland water bodies, and the biosphere; and human resources.* We should say a few words about each of them.

Cosmic energy and resources: Earth exists and moves in the cosmos, humanity explores cosmic space, and organises interaction with cosmic processes. The main cosmic resource, which life itself depends on, is *solar energy*. The power and strength of solar light determines Earth's temperature, seasonal changes, and plant life reproduction, as well as day and night life rhythms. The degree to which solar energy and its reserves in organic fuels (oil, gas, coal, shale, and wood) are harnessed determines the bases of the energy sector.

Outer space is being explored, including electromagnetic and gravitation fields, as well as the space being used by satellites or to be used by spaceships for inter-planet journeys in the future. A total of 1,000 satellites are circling the Earth at the moment, which requires internationally recognised rules governing the use of space. The role of the Earth's *ozone layer* needs to be taken into account, because this layer can be considered as a buffer zone protecting the planet from solar radiation. *Cosmic communication* means that fields and frequencies have also gone beyond their military uses and become accessible to civilian organisations and individuals.

Atmosphere is the second main source of human, animal, and plant life subsistence. All living organisms need oxygen to live. It takes several minutes for suffocation and subsequent death to occur once access to air is cut off. People, equipment, industrial, and energy facilities consume oxygen. Although plants reproduce oxygen, environmentalists are still concerned with the misbalance of oxygen consumption and hazardous emissions levels.

Atmosphere is a resource for air transportation, radio and telecommunications. The density of air routes and air corridors is increasing. Air companies and passengers are interested in cutting down air travel costs per kilometre. Radio frequencies distribution is important for organising radio and television broadcasting, as well as mobile communication.

Our planet is covered with **land** and the **World Ocean**. The Earth and its crust are being exploited; they provide us with a wealth of natural resources and raw materials for various industries, including the food industry. The Earth or its fertile layers, to be exact, are used in agriculture as cropland, grazing ground, and roads. Cities and towns as well as recreation and entertainment areas are located on land. Extracting industries use the Earth's crust to give us fuel, energy sources and ore.

The World Ocean and inland water bodies are also being explored. Fish, sea animals, seaweed, mineral resources on the sea shelf, water, and oxygen, are used for production and consumption. Sea transport and pipelines have actively been utilised for passenger and cargo transportation since the Age of Discovery. Tidal energy, river, and storm water hydro energy, and bioenergy, are also widely used in economic activity.

The biosphere is a source and supplier of important resources such as food. Food production and consumption are vital human needs. Plant and animal life products have long been used by humanity, but we are still facing huge problems of starvation and food shortages. Microbiology is making it possible to put to good use bacteria, viruses and other microorganisms, e.g., as protection against pathogenic viruses such as "bird flu".

With the development of anthropo-sociogenesis and culture genesis, a new form of existence, referred to by Vladimir I. Vernadsky as the "noosphere" or the sphere of reason, has emerged. In post-industrial society, **human resources** are business-driving forces, and determine its character and effectiveness especially in such neo-economic sectors as science, innovations, education, telecommunications, culture, and arts. It is the quality and intensiveness of human resource use that give the neo-economy its advantages and effectiveness.

Human resources are the most important part of the world intellectual potential. To understand this concept, we must focus on the relationship between the categories of "potential", "resources", and "capital" from the perspective of economic theory. *Potential* is the combination of all available means, possibilities, and energy of an object or system. *Resources* are the means that are ready to be used, as well as factors and conditions ensuring the production of products, results, or effects. The notion of *capital* encompasses resources or means whose use brings income or additional benefits. In this sense, human resources represent the part of human potential actualised and available for use, sale or conversion.

Today, human potential is growing and being enriched by the processes unknown to pre-modern age civilisation: the relationship "man – machinery and technology" has acquired a reverse influence effect. In the information society, people and humanity can transform themselves qualitatively based on labour humanisation and increased creative self-realisation possibilities.

Human capital is considered one of the forms of expressing human potential, and human potential realisation in social-economic relations. This phenomenon has high social value, because it manifests itself successfully at the institutional level, e.g., in the market context.

One main quality of human groups and communities characterises phenomena of any generalization or realization level: from the micro-level of family and company workers, to the macro-level of an ethnic group or an entire nation, to the mega-level of humanity. This quality is *synergy*, being a co-operative interaction effect, when the power and outcomes of the collective activity of a set quantitatively and qualitatively exceed those of individual subsets. Today, the learning, methodological, and administrative problem of human resources, is that this category is used almost exclusively in the micro or macro scope and context (an organisation, region, economic sector, production-economic complex, and national economy), while the mega level of humanity remains untouched. We believe that it is time that we started studying human resources, their management, and improvement possibilities on the scale of an integrated planetary agent. We see an obvious desirability and applicability in the results of such research.

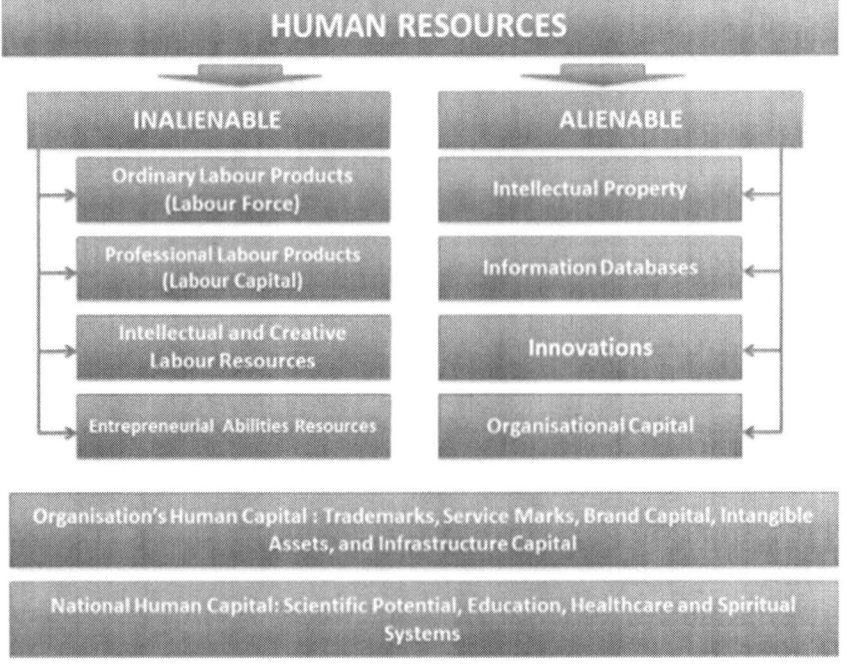

HUMAN RESOURCES	
INALIENABLE	**ALIENABLE**
Ordinary Labour Products (Labour Force)	Intellectual Property
Professional Labour Products (Labour Capital)	Information Databases
Intellectual and Creative Labour Resources	Innovations
Entrepreneurial Abilities Resources	Organisational Capital

Organisation's Human Capital: Trademarks, Service Marks, Brand Capital, Intangible Assets, and Infrastructure Capital

National Human Capital: Scientific Potential, Education, Healthcare and Spiritual Systems

Fig. 3. Human resource classification

The first group of human resources is embodied in the *individual human capital* of every economically active person. Knowledge, abilities, experience, culture, motivation, and physical and creative forces are inalienable parts of human personality, and constitute his individual potential. Human qualities employed in business and bringing profit become the basis of individual human capital.

Alienable knowledge, information, intellectual products and licenses, constitute a special group of the institutionally established personal intellectual property and authors' rights. Every economic entity, e.g., an organisation or company, also owns intangible assets and brand capital. National human capital embodies competitive positions and advantages of any country.

The resources of a potential world economy are diverse but *intellectual resources* are the most significant. They ensure the material and spiritual development of society, and determine the role of nations in the world economic system. At the end of the twentieth century, intellectual potential changed its role from an auxiliary factor of production to a force of production in and of itself, whose function is the working out and systematisation of knowledge about the environment and its practical use.

Humanity's intellectual capacity is a world intellectual potential that on the one hand represents scientific advancement and directions of the world's science, and on the other, members of the world scientific community. The use of these very resources can ensure considerable growth of labour productivity, and qualitative changes in its structure, content and quality, as well as contribute to the growth of people's level of well-being and raise the standard of living of the planet's population.

The notion of the *intellectual potential* is closely connected with the concepts of the *creative society* and the *creative economy*. It is also actively investigated within the framework of the *knowledge society* paradigm and is used in economics, philosophy of science, sociology, and social system management.

The thesis stating that intelligence plays the leading role in the development of society and post-industrial civilisation has now received wide recognition. There exists a whole range of intelligence concepts: it is treated from logical-philosophical, evolutionary-anthropological, social-historical, and psychological-behavioural perspectives. It is important that every theory of intelligence characterises it as:

- An ability to take in, understand, retain and process information, as well as use it in appropriate contexts and situations;
- Operate abstract notions, values, ideas, concepts, and other theoretical constructs, as well as apply them in practice;
- Systemic, reflexive and rational thinking skills, as well as self-learning and personal development abilities;
- Problem-solving skills and an ability to address external challenges based on one's own knowledge and intellectual properties, while adapting to changing circumstances.

As we all know, there are three types of intelligence: *general* (universal human intelligence whose development level depends on age, socialisation mechanisms, occupation, and way of life); *special* (oriented towards individual knowledge fields and activity types, and connected to the so-called talents and gifts, which are individualist in nature); and *professional* (connected to a person's occupation, his main job, special knowledge, and competences). General intelligence is considered to be the basis for the formation and development of special and professional intelligences.

From the point of view of economics and social life, it is important that both individual and collective intelligence could realise its potential in socially valuable applications. Indeed, dynamics in all types of activity and contemporary social reproduction modes depend on intellectual potential. This includes carrying out an innovation cycle that has the following stages: "basic research – applied research – experimental and design work – production – implementation – dissemination – mass use".

Intellectual potential is the source of intellectual resources and intellectual capital. The logic of their relationship remains the one we have already established between the notions of human potential, resources, and capital. Current definitions of intellectual potential include the following aspects:

- Historically accumulated civilisation experience of people, nations and cultures (primarily, this includes ways of learning about and making sense of reality, spiritual and rational bases of different worldviews as well as productive practices traditions and techniques);

- Systems and models of knowledge organisation, languages of science and cultures, progress paradigms and concepts;
- A set of information and communication instruments and strategies of the whole social system and its individual subsystems, knowledge channels and carriers, as well as the ways of disseminating, exchanging, and assessing knowledge;
- Comprehensive self-identification and self-assessment of society in terms of its cognitive and creative capacities, motivation, and long-term goal setting;
- Innovative frame of reference, strategic goals, prediction, and planning.

Intellectual potential of any level of community manifests itself in all spheres of life; this is just its nature. Intellectual potential replenishment and development is stimulated by education and science. Humanistically oriented values and open cultures create the best conditions for these things to happen.

In terms of structure, intellectual potential consists of the following subsystems:

- Human potential as a set of features and qualities community members have that can transform into socially useful activity results (assessed in terms of the quality of life, social and cultural policy, labour market, and people's intellectual level);
- Information potential (characterised and evaluated by such indicators as the systemic approach to organising and disseminating knowledge, information openness and accessibility, and

the level of development and use of information systems and technologies);
- Institutional potential (roughly, it is created by all social institutions contributing to the qualitative development of society, including education and science infrastructure, research and development funding, legislation, civil society institutions, competitiveness, and practical usefulness);
- Organisational process potential (methods and technologies ensuring the organisation and functioning of the main society life-subsistence subsystems: economy, politics, social governance, and culture);
- Innovation potential (trends and benchmarks of scientific-technical development, basic and applied research direction, invention and scientific-technical creativity, the level of high-tech sectors, market trends, and protection of intellectual property rights).

Each subsystem has its own assessment criteria, performance indicators, dynamic scales, and change indexes. At the same time, the world's actual intellectual potential is hard to assess in terms of quantity, including cost estimates. On the one hand, it is closely connected to such quality-quantity objective factors as the countries' level and development vector, their social structure and economic nature, the state of science and civil society, available legislation and legal relations, socialisation mechanisms and communication tools, as well as the type of society itself. On the other hand, the real level of science, education, science-consuming production, high technologies, communication systems, etc. is so different in different countries that even a hypothetical picture of the world's intellectual potential would inevitably be asymmetrical and contradictory, at least at the current moment.

In terms of intellectual resource development and use, different countries approach this differently, and this difference is based on their historical and social-economic development and depends on cultural-ethnic, socio-political, and economic factors. These differences lie in the scientific activity organisation, the structure and volume of scientific potential, and research priorities and their special features. The number of these differences equals the number of countries engaged in global intellectual and research activity. Every country is unique in this respect. Nevertheless, we can still put similar national intellectual cultures into the same technological groups.

The notion of *intellectual culture* is said to have emerged at the junction point of psychology of personality and psychology of learning; and in literature, it is applied usually to human personality. We consider it to be applicable to any community, including a people or nation, because such a collective social-historical agent is organised in the form of a nation state whose intellectual potential and intellectual traditions are institutionalised.

The notion of culture is universally applicable to any phenomenality having to do with man, and produced by people and society. Therefore, among other things, it also includes individual and collective intelligence, intellectual activity with its organisation and operation mechanisms. Equally, the intellectual culture characterises both a private and collective agent of socially articulated activity.

In this sense, intellectual culture will characterise the group of nations and peoples using the following criteria:

- Education level, the state of educational system, teaching methods and technologies, education prestige, and economic conditions in the education services market;
- Scientific and creative labour traditions aimed at learning and reality transformation goals;
- Inclusion of a specific agent (nation) in the entire civilisation experience and progressive world development processes;
- Making sense and assessment of universal human values, their real position in the social (mass) consciousness of a particular nation, and this nation's self-identification and critical thinking levels;
- The ratio of intellectual labour, including science, art, various creative economy industries and forms, and primitive, unskilled labour in the structure of the national economy;
- Productiveness and effectiveness of the intellectual (science-consuming) sector in the national economy and its contribution to the country's GDP.

Interestingly, in terms of its meaning, the concept of a nation's intellectual culture, irrespective of its methodological status, is intuitively close to concepts such as a nation's *way of thinking* and *national mentality*. It is clear that these are not synonyms, but the way of thinking of a collective agent, and its mentality, value consciousness, and self-identity, can act as both general culture projections and lie in the culture's deep basic archetypal and stereotypical layers. In other words, national intellectual culture includes, on the one hand, tools, ways and methods of thinking, learning and creative attitude to the world; and on the other hand, it defines and assesses intelligence, rationality and a systemic worldview as a social force and manifestation of its own historical activity.

Intellectual culture is not a nation's experience, but rather the way it organises and adapts to changing conditions, meets internal and external challenges, and learns from this experience. Equally, we can say that the culture of society is a direct manifestation of its collective intelligence and attitude to science-consuming activity, and its social-ideological value that has both a moral and a relatively material, including financial, dimension.

Intellectual culture has a direct relation to self-development, self-organisation, self-study, and innovative abilities. Moreover, some people believe that the task of intellectual culture is to create new, more progressive forms of thinking, learning, and activity. In the social world, there is the same interrelation between the intellectual culture of society and the pro-active approach to life of its members. This is because intelligence itself, as a set of human thinking abilities, unlike its individual components (e.g., analytical reasoning or aesthetic judgment abilities), is characterised by a pro-active, reality-transforming look at things.

Intellectual culture of a nation is an ideological and instrumental collective thinking and self-identification fund extending beyond the academic community that is organically open to the inside and outside world. This fund realises itself in speech, everyday consciousness, communications, and social institutions. The key feature of intellectual culture is its dynamism, adaptability to external influences and internal changes, complexity, and a systemic character. At the same time, it is worth pointing out its dependence on society values: however free thinking its nature might be, its products are implemented depending on economic opportunities, social service order, ideology, and moral filters.

To identify an intellectual culture type, we must have a special methodology and performance indicators of intellectual resources. The nature of intellectual resource parameters does not allow us to easily change them methodologically. Intellectual capacity indicators include resource characteristics, scientific findings and innovation results, as well as their internal and external relations.

The totality of humanity's intellectual capacity assessment indicators can be systematised in the following way:

Table. 1. Humanity's intellectual capacity assessment indicators

№	Qualitative certainty	Quantitative certainty
1	Research staff	Number, structure, and sufficiency of research staff
2	Material-technical base of intellectual activity	Adequacy of material-technical base
3	Basic and applied research	Sufficiency and direction of basic and applied research

4	Social-economic orientation of intellectual activity	Progressiveness of social-economic organisation
5	Research and development funding	Adequacy of financial and economic support
6	Licensing fund	Degree of involvement in the world's scientific-technical progress
7	Intellectual activity outcomes	Effectiveness of research, findings and innovation activity
8	Value component of vocational training	Education orientation towards innovation activity

The above indicator groups in their totality ensure comprehensive assessment of the composition and dynamic of intellectual resources in their organic unity.

Today, the world's research potential is concentrated in those countries that are engaged in implementing global innovation projects capable of solving pressing social, economic, and environmental problems facing humanity. The research community is changing its structure due to changing social development priorities. If we re-distribute the demand for scientists and specialists across regions and countries, it will prove to be limited and differentiated not only in terms of qualification, but also across various disciplines. Specialists in the fields that set the main trends in humanity's intellectual capacity are in most demand. These fields include physics, mathematics, informatics, microelectronics, cybernetics, biology, chemistry, medicine, and space research.

Research-based knowledge became the chief economic resource as early as the beginning of the twenty-first century. Basic, cultural, applied and innovation knowledge, spread in society through a network of research institutes, educational institutions, mass media, and mass communication media. Therefore, their development level and effectiveness determine not only how equipped society is from a scientific-technical point of view, but also how developed its intellectual culture is. Knowledge must not only be accrued and kept, but it must also be reproduced, disseminated, adapted, developed, and implemented in practical life. For these processes to be successful, the state must pursue adequate financial-economic policies in the scientific and educational spheres, innovation and science-consuming technologies, human resource management, and the investment climate.

The modern global world is characterised by an asymmetric development of scientific, educational, and information and communication resources. The reasons for these fundamental differences are rooted in economic-political factors (funding priorities in national-state development programmes, government and private investment in science and education), and socio-cultural factors (intellectual traditions and culture, social service order, and ideology). Research and development staffing and institutional structuring, as well as the industrial demand for its findings are also very important.

In terms of scientific-technical development level, world economies are judged according to the following indicators:

- Research and Development expenditure share in a country's GDP;
- High-tech sector share in the national economy;
- Science-consuming sector share in manufactured exports;
- National economy share in the world's science-consuming products and high-technologies market;
- Technological balance (license and patent trade balance);
- Number of research and technical workers in Research and Development (share of total population or of national labour force);
- Number of international prizes for outstanding scientific achievements;
- Citation index (number and frequency of instances that a nation's research is cited in scholarly journals in the world).

Research and Development effectiveness is also evaluated based on private sector involvement in scientific-educational activity. In this regard, we must not forget about international co-operation that manifests itself in the international co-financing of research projects and programmes, scientific outsourcing, international scientific-technical alliances, global higher education standardisation, as well as creating and promoting global information resources.

Intellectual and research results are usually judged using an economic effect criterion that is often hard to evaluate. This assessment can be based on society's expectations characterised by increasing demand for scientific and technological achievements. Society is becoming increasingly involved in choosing research priorities and research funding decision-making. Today, the possible social effect of research results is so huge that neither companies nor society as a whole can use them to their full potential.

Currently, the situation remains with the uneven development and practical implementation of research findings, design, and high technologies. This is despite the globalisation of Research and Development, both in terms of international co-operation of scientists from different countries and scientific schools, and in terms of international funding. On the surface, we can see Research and Development funding figures, intellectual property trading (especially, in technologies) and patent cross-licensing data.

Various research results show that the countries that lead in innovation development (e.g., the USA, China, Japan, Sweden, and Finland) have high values in such categories such as: Research and Development spending; government spending on education; the number of scientists and patent applications; and high-tech investment. Research and Development funding have many sources in developed countries. They include the state, local self-government bodies, the private sector, and company-owned funds. Apart from direct investment, indirect investment instruments and possibilities are used, including tax benefits, government-subsidised loans, and depreciation write-offs.

Funding is often provided through creating and developing innovation institutions: venture capital funds and technoparks that are autonomous from government. Small private innovation companies play an active market role with government support.

Developed countries' governments and economic elites aim at keeping the science-consuming share of the GDP between 3% and 4%. Over the last ten years, most of them have increased government spending on Research and Development by 1% or 2%. Private sector investment has also increased in the field. Foreign investment into science and high technologies, including the venture business, has also grown. At the same time, private sector and non-governmental organisation funding for Research and Development is estimated at 60% to 75% in these countries. Public-private partnership mechanisms have also shown their effectiveness.

South-East Asian countries including South Korea, Hong Kong, Taiwan, and Singapore are catching up with the USA, China, and EU countries, the leaders of science-consuming economy.

A country's intellectual resource level determines the country's competitiveness and its place in the scientific and intellectual system of the world. National competitiveness is a key indicator of a society's development level. Many analytical centres in various countries study this. The two Swiss institutions—the World Economic Forum and the International Institute of Management Development—are the most influential among them. Two indicators determine competitive rating: the Growth Competitiveness Index and the Business Competitiveness Index, which reflect macro- and microeconomic conditions in a country.

Microeconomic conditions, state institutions, and technological development level underlie the competitiveness indexes calculations. The Business Competitiveness Index (BCI) is based on the level of production processes, company strategies, and the *index of* the *quality of* the *business environment.* Some indicators, which influence rating results, are based on statistics (macroeconomic indicators, university enrolment ratio, etc.), while the rest are based on top-management polls.

The Competitiveness Index is understood as a general, relative indicator of economic system development characterising the system's middle-term stable growth potential. More concrete notions of *Business Competitiveness Index* (BCI) and *Global Competitiveness Index* (GCI) are sometimes used. The latter operates the following assessment criteria:

- Basic factors (macroeconomics, government and civil society institutions, infrastructure, social policy, healthcare, and secondary education);
- Effectiveness enhancing factors (secondary vocational and higher education, market mechanisms, and the technical and technological level);
- Innovation factors (Research and Development, innovations, and business development level).

The factors that stimulate national economic competitiveness growth also include: intellectual property rights protection; developed legislation and a strong judicial system; the high level and prestige of education; labour force qualifications; wide access to new knowledge and technologies; and the quality of information and communication processes.

According to the methodology used by Columbia University Professor Xavier Sala-i-Martin to create the Global Competitiveness Index in 2004, GCI has 113 variables that fully reflect the competitiveness level of different countries characterised by different economic development levels. It is important to bear in mind that no individual variable in isolation can have a substantial impact on a country's competitiveness: all variables are interconnected and work in unity. This resulted in the conclusion that the countries that become the world's competitive leaders are those whose government and business elites are able to pursue a united systemic socio-economic policy aimed at maintaining the balance between all competitiveness components.

At the same time, economic competitiveness factors work differently in different countries, because they depend on a number of conditions and the existing level of development. These factors themselves are subject to historical changes both in form and in substance.

According to World Economic Forum estimates, Switzerland, Finland, Sweden, Denmark, Singapore, Germany, the USA, Japan, the UK, Norway, and the UAE, have been the most competitive economies for the last ten years. WEF researchers and experts emphasise the fact that highly competitive countries tend to ensure a high standard of living for their citizens.

In the age of informatisation and high technologies, if we are to close the gap between various nations, we must develop a socially promising world policy aimed at developing and sustaining humanity's intellectual capacity.

Thus, from the Planetary Project point of view, intellectual resources will become the leading force of world economic transformation in the nearest future, because they must become the key factor of the main production mode in the Sixth Techno-economic paradigm scenario. For intellectual resources to take the leading role in the planetary resource system, and to be able to start carrying out their saving mission of resource substitution (especially in relation to non-renewable resources), they must be put on the single track of global human integration. The purpose of this integration is to save the biosphere, and create a new agent of planetary development—a humanity of the future, WE-humanity. The Planetary Project is meant to initiate this large-scale, humanistic in its essence, movement to reassess, popularise, promote, and develop the intellectual resource on a planetary scale.

Spiritualisation of the intellect is extremely important for the future fate of individual persons and an emerging integral humanity. This spiritualisation means bridging the gap between rational thinking and extra-rational emotions constituting the content of spiritual experience reflected in religions and mystic doctrines. Scientific consciousness made breakthroughs in the field in the twentieth century when it returned to searching for foundations and possibilities to synthesise rational-analytical and mystical-intuitive views of the world to understand it in its entirety. In this context, we understand the mystical experience as an individual, formally unstructured experience obtained, through means different from the discursive cognition in the classical sense. The intuitive type of perception gives coherent images and pictures of objects, relationships, processes, and the world as a whole. Sometimes, intuition leads to great discoveries capable of transforming science and social life.

Why is it important? Early civilisations believed that *there was nothing outside us that we did not already have inside us.* The meaning of this statement is not to point out the wisdom and greatness of man, but to emphasise the organic and total connection of people with the united cosmos, including phenomena and forces that people cannot yet see, understand, or appreciate at a given moment of history. It follows that the conflict of people (whether a concrete individual or a collective entity, a group of any scope) with the outside world, including nature, another person or people, and society, is rooted not only in external objective circumstances, but also in the internal conflict of "original man". Figuratively, this situation is often described as the *rift between soul and reason.* Rationally, it can be represented as a problem of unaddressed tension between various cognitive abilities, values, and principles of several orders, as well as instantaneous motivation versus systemic, long-term motivation. If we try to understand the self-preservation instinct comprehensively, we will see that the self-preservation motivation must not only apply to the current but also to future generations as well; it must encompass nature and other living things as part of the common natural habitat. In this sense, the concept of cognitive and behavioural responsibility can be interpreted not just as a personal history, but also as one that would ensure a full range of vital possibilities, and conditions for organic life, to continue on this planet.

A systemically spiritualised and self-aware intelligence can see and cognate the universal interconnectedness of phenomena in nature, the world, and the cosmos. This intelligence can therefore understand its place in it, and carry its own responsibility for it. By becoming holistic as a result of overcoming conflicts and contradictions between channels and ways of knowing and evaluating reality, it not only becomes an instrument of solving current and future problems, but also – in some sense – becomes a source of life meanings forming mental and behavioural motivation.

Today, spiritualisation of the intellect has a fundamental importance for transforming the intellect into a planetary and cosmogonic force. This type of intellect combines an ability to act for the sake of this day's achievements, and benefits and serves elementary needs, with the role of a spiritual compass whose ethical orientation would allow us to steer in the direction of the interests and values of all life on Earth, including the generations who will come after us.

CHAPTER 7

Planetary Property and World Income

Planetary property as the economic basis of future civilisation. The problem of calculating aggregate world income.

When speaking about global human unification with the purpose of saving the planet, we primarily count upon the economic platform of integration and, specifically, the economic unification of people. This means transforming them into owners of planetary resources; since the character, purpose, and efficiency of any resource use is determined, first of all, by the type of ownership and only after that by the industrial technology and production, or business organisation. It must be said that the development, and the first years of implementation of the sustainability strategy, had as a natural result the recognition, legislative consolidation, and institutional implementation of planetary ***property***. We consider this result to be a promising concept for further development and investigation, because planetary property in universal resources is going to become the economic basis for future civilisation. It will provide the vital resources and the revenue necessary to finance the work on the solution of global problems.

Currently, most of the natural resources are formally included into national state property systems. The relevant institutions existing in different countries, national legislation and economic traditions regulate them. At the same time, many problems require coordination of national and planetary interests, activities, programmes, and projects.

The issue of working out the mechanisms for planetary property implementation is especially acute in connection with the current situation in the field of natural resource use. Economic theory typically divides natural resources into appropriable and inappropriable. This classification leads us directly to property relations, as a concise definition describes them as relations of appropriation in a particular social form.

Paul A. Samuelson and William D. Nordhaus, in their *Economics* suggest the following approach to the form of natural resource use: "Economists make two major distinctions in analysing natural resources. The most important is whether the resource is appropriable or inappropriable. A commodity is called appropriable when firms or consumers can capture its full economic value. Appropriable natural resources include land . . . mineral resources like oil and gas . . . and trees . . . On the other hand, a resource is inappropriable when some of the costs and benefits associated with its use do not accrue to its owner. In other words, inappropriable resources are ones involving externalities." Examples of inappropriable resources would be the air quality and the climate, which are connected with externalities caused by such activities as burning fossil fuels.

It is specifically in the range of problems associated with this distinction that we need to look for a solution to the following fundamental contradiction: the incompatibility between the attitudes of the general public, interested in preserving the environment, and the position of business entities, which, objectively following their commercial interest, cause damage to the environment. Here, the issue of "no one's property" comes to the fore. Quite understandably, the attitude to a resource that is somebody's property will differ from the attitude to a resource that does not have a definite owner or manager. The situation is both understandable and paradoxical at the same time. From a standpoint of formal logic, if a certain object is involved in the production process, this creates relations of appropriation and, consequently, property relations as well. The owner is always there, but it is sometimes hard to identify the relevant relationship, or rather, it is not always possible to identify the owner correctly. Even if the property right is clearly defined the mechanisms for exercising this right sometimes remain unclear.

Here, the question arises why are natural resources divided into appropriable and inappropriable. From the general public's point of view, unless we address this from the limited economic standpoint, they are all equally vital for human existence. What is of more importance to us: land or air? A question like that will sound strange to an ordinary person; but it would not sound strange at all to a manufacturer, whose main goal is the attainment of profit. And again, this will not be just any manufacturer, but an active business entity existing within the economic system of reference.

The sector of transnational property has emerged, and is rapidly developing today, due to the strengthened economic integration process; a good example would be the International Space Station (ISS). Travelling in orbit around the Earth, the ISS clearly illustrates the advantages and opportunities of international co-operation when solving the most complex problems of science and economy. Space has become the arena of interstate projects and programmes, even though relapses into formal alienation of space objects do occur from time to time, for example, the practice of selling sites on the Moon and Mars to private buyers.

Transnational property is increasingly used to solve planetary environmental problems: in the studies of the World Ocean and the Earth's climate; in geophysics of the Earth's crust; in the search for possible explanations of such natural disasters as earthquakes, volcanic eruptions, floods, hurricanes, and others. The opportunities provided by interstate property can be used to solve social problems of human development, employment, and poverty alleviation, which the UN and regional interstate associations direct their efforts at.

The logic behind the development of international forms of property leads to the understanding of the urgent need to create and expand its ultimate form; which is: **public planetary property** in the objects of common use in space, the Earth's atmosphere, the World Ocean, and the international fundamental research. This concept requires further investigation and development. Planetary public property, however, can definitely serve as an objective basis for implementation mechanisms of the harmonious development strategy for humanity as a whole, and for countries and regions. According to the Planetary Project concept: in order to serve the purpose of global human integration, the Planetary Governance System (the infrastructure of planetary institutions) has to take control not only of the consistently insufficient resources collected from the member states, but also its own economic base necessary for addressing planetary problems.

There are several reasons behind the high potential of planetary public property. First, at the global level, planetary property serves as a framework within which strategic issues of the survival and development of human civilisation are addressed. This results in serious and often irreversible changes in the productive forces and economic relations, which are life changing for the people, the continents, and humanity as a whole. The role of international organisations and institutions is increased by changes in the economic structure of society, and by the emergence of new international and planetary lifestyles with an ever-increasing degree of self-sufficiency and autonomy. The most important things that need to be changed, however, are the functions of international economic centres and the methods that can be used to exercise the necessary influence on countries and communities. In view of anti-civilisational, disintegrative forms of economic behaviour, it is especially important to create a system of laws that protect the interests of humanity as a whole. First, the laws should be restraining and regulatory economic, environmental, and social legislation, built on a rational basis.

Planetary ownership of natural resources clearly demonstrates the social form of appropriation directed at conditions of human vital activity. A good and typical example of this is appropriation of benefits provided by the Earth's atmosphere. Each of the more than 7 billion people comprising the world's population every minute naturally breathes in and consumes oxygen from the air, thus actively maintaining their body's metabolism. The need for oxygen is essential and absolute. The oxygen balance is restored in a natural way as well. If the right to use atmospheric air is natural and universal, then there is no right of ownership. It is impossible to recognise physical ownership of the atmosphere by private individuals, companies, or countries. Winds, hurricanes, and whirlwinds mix the air masses and carry them around the globe. The circulation of air masses renders recognition of ownership rights as belonging to any entity meaningless.

The situation is less simple when it comes to the right of disposal. Every driver burns annually the amount of oxygen equivalent to the amount consumed by a hundred people. A year of airliner operation is equivalent to the oxygen consumption of ten thousand people. Thermal power plants, heating stations, and production plants consume huge masses of air, at the same time polluting the environment with harmful emissions. There exists a clear need to regulate the relations associated with the disposal of natural atmospheric goods. Many countries have institutional constraints on air, water, and land pollution. Disposal in the atmosphere and the oceans, however, requires development of internationally recognised standards, and the establishment of adequate supra-national institutions.

The first meaningful effort to regulate the use of the Earth's atmosphere was the adoption and ratification of the Kyoto Protocol, although the debate about its benefits and risks continue. In fact, the disputes mostly concern the practical implementation of regulatory functions. Article 6 of the Kyoto Protocol states that, "for the purpose of meeting its commitments under Article 3, any Party included in Annex I may transfer to, or acquire from, any other such Party emission reduction units resulting from projects aimed at reducing anthropogenic emissions by sources or enhancing anthropogenic removals by sinks of greenhouse gases in any sector of the economy." Practical implementation of the idea to sell emission reduction units has yet to be seen in action, but apparently, the idea is not stillborn. Many countries have already expressed mutual interest in co-operation in this field, and are actively working on the mechanisms for implementation of Kyoto agreements. The current situation with the Kyoto Protocol, however, shows that despite the lofty rhetoric, no country wants to sacrifice its national interests. Many countries have not yet ratified the Kyoto Protocol, while the United States and Australia withdrew from the process, saying that the agreements parted from their national interests.

Nevertheless, international treaties are the first step in the establishment of a comprehensive mechanism for the implementation of planetary property. They gradually shape the *institutional infrastructure,* which becomes the basis for the establishment of separate elements constituting the future unified system of appropriation of planetary goods.

When considering the decade-long practice of discussions, negotiations and ratifications of the Kyoto Protocol, one can clearly see the extreme complexity of such processes. If the time needed to reconcile the national and planetary interests in relation to other planetary resources is going to be as long and controversial as the Kyoto process, then planetary disasters, and the exhaustion of the limited energy and physical resources, will come sooner than the regulation and rational use of free goods provided by the natural environment. In order to overcome this contradiction—so that rational solutions could be achieved before the advent of destructive tendencies—it is necessary to accelerate the development and adoption of international legislation, and the whole system of planetary and continental institutions regulating appropriation of planetary resources. We need breakthroughs: in the field of supra-national law; in the development of continental and planetary institutions; and in the determination of the measure of national sovereignty, and general obligations to nature and to coming generations.

Methodologically, the distribution and specification of planetary property rights are given in Table 2. Implementation of the main options of property rights belongs initially to all of humanity. The World Parliament, functioning as a legislative body, has the task of expressing and protecting planetary interests. Administrative functions are performed by the UN and its supra-national committees and commissions. Global economic functions are performed by multinational companies, which already control half of the world's capital and up to 60% of global trade flows and revenues. For resolution of international commercial disputes, it is necessary to create a planetary judicial system, subsystems of which have already been established in the form of the United Nations Security Council and the Permanent Court of Arbitration.

The issues to be resolved will include: limitations on the national civil law; harmonisation of the latter with international law; and elimination of any inconsistencies and conflicting interpretations. An important place in all this work will belong to international civic organisations, such as the green movement, unions of political parties, international trade unions and business associations, and international scientific organisations and creative unions.

Table 2. Distribution (specification) of planetary property rights

| No | Property rights | Appropriating entities ||||||||
| | | Nations (humanity) | Supra-national bodies || | National state ||| International civic organisations |
			World Parliament	UN (world government)	Transnational corporations	National Parliament	Government	National business	
1	Right of ownership	+							
2	Right of use	+			+			+	
3	Right of disposal	+	+	+		+	+		+
4	Income right	+		+	+		+	+	+
5	Sovereign right	+	+			+			
6	Right of security (against illegal use)	+	+			+			+
7	Right of conveyance by inheritance (to future generations)	+	+	+	+	+	+	+	+
8	Right of perpetuity	+	+			+			+
9	Prohibition of use harmful to nature and society	+	+			+			+
10	Liability in the form of penalty	+	+	+		+	+		+
11	The right to restore and protect the violated property rights (availability of institutions)	+	+	+		+	+		+

When speaking about financial resources of the planetary community, it is necessary to address the issue of the *calculation of total global income.*

In order to fight successfully against poverty, and to even out the different levels of poverty in different countries, it would be necessary to ensure measurability of both the poverty rate and the level of development.

POVERTY RATE is an index counting the percentage of population with income below the minimum level deemed to be the poverty threshold. Poverty is the inability to enjoy a minimum standard of life.

The definition of poverty rate is not the same in every country of the world: largely it depends on the definition of poverty itself, which in its turn is determined, among other things, by the standard of living. Not everywhere does it have legislative recognition or an unambiguous legal interpretation. In the United States, the European Union, Asia, Africa, and elsewhere, the term "poverty" has different interpretations, legal status, estimation, and payment policy. Here, we are talking about more than just the various methods of correlating incomes, expenses, changes in price levels, the cost of a minimum essential food basket, and the minimum level of subsistence. Other important aspects include the correlation between the properties of physiological and social dimensions of poverty, the minimum needed for mere survival, and the cost of satisfying the minimum social needs.

The international and global concept of poverty, and calculation of poverty rate, also includes such parameters as availability of certain resources needed for meeting human needs, which is of crucial importance for poverty, and location and concentration of the low-income population on the map of a particular country. This understanding of the *depth* and *intensity* of poverty was suggested already at the end of the twentieth century by an outstanding Indian economist Amartya Sen, who developed the method for measuring the so-called "poverty index".

The concept of the **LEVEL OF DEVELOPMENT** in relation to economic characteristics of the population is quite complex, it covers the data on: the gross national product; per capita national income; the use of natural resources; and organisation and efficiency of production. It also stands in correlation with the *standard of living*, that is, the degree of satisfaction of physical, social, and spiritual needs of the population, as well as availability and affordability of material goods.

The task of achieving measurability of poverty rate and the level of development seems intuitive, but it turns out to be rather difficult when one is comparing countries that are located in different climatic zones, and have different cultural traditions, etc. As a universal measurement of poverty rate or development level, a number of scientists suggested the indicator of the population's economic activity calculated as gross per capita income. The problem of measuring it is closely linked with the problem of calculating global income as a whole, i.e., calculation of the amount of wealth produced by humanity.

The studies suggested that on the face of it, the problem of calculating total world income is not so much a problem of choosing an appropriate method, but rather a technical one; it suffices to calculate the amount of goods produced in different countries, and then add up the resultant values. Since the amount of goods produced in the country represents its gross domestic product (GDP), then all we need to do is add together the GDPs of different countries (Gross National Product (GNP), in fact, is the same GDP, but adjusted for foreign trade operations).

However, even the calculation of GDP itself creates a number of problems. The first one is the choice of the calculation method.

1) If the value-added method is used, GDP is calculated as a sum of values added that are generated in the sectors of the economy.
2) If the expenditures approach is used, GDP is calculated by adding up the spending of the institutional sectors on all consumption goods and services, gross capital formation, and net exports.

When GDP is calculated in any given year, it is measured in prices of that particular year, that is, in current prices. As we know, GDP measured in current prices is called nominal GDP. The increase in nominal GDP can be caused by three factors:

- the increased production of final goods and services;
- the increase in prices;
- the increase in prices and increase in production.

The study has shown, however, that GDP as a measurement of poverty rate and development level has a number of shortcomings:

1) GDP measures everything in monetary units rather than physical units. Therefore, it always has to be adjusted for inflation, and in the case of cross-border comparisons, the price parity has to be taken into account as well.
2) Weakness of GDP as a measure of well-being is connected with its inaccuracy as an indicator of the "real" trend of time. This results from changes in the quality of goods and services. Goods tend to improve over time in a country with advanced technology. Calculation in parity prices does not solve the problem because countries significantly differ in their levels of "average" quality.
3) GDP as a measurement is "blind" to the final use of goods and services. If, in one year, GDP goes up as a result of increased spending on education, and in another, it increases by the same amount due to the rise in cigarette sales, the numbers in both cases will show the same growth.
4) GDP does not say anything about the distribution of goods and services among the population. Countries are very different in this respect. As a result, it becomes impossible to compare the levels of development in these countries.
5. Even though GDP is calculated with respect to both spheres of production—material and non-material—it does not include many of the activities and services that are difficult or impossible to account for. These include the following:

- the work performed by housewives;
- the work of researchers done "for themselves", i.e., not embodied in the form of a finished product (books, samples, etc.);
- barter transactions;
- black-market revenues;
- informal remuneration (for example, tips), etc.

Despite all that, the world income in most cases is measured by adding up the GDPs of different countries.

At the same time, the approach based on adding up the GDPs of different countries has often been criticised, and there are several reasons for that.

First of all, if the total world product "grows" by 10 per cent a year, then, according to classical economic theory, this should reflect the "growth of labour productivity". It is obvious, however, that labour productivity does not increase; money supply is what actually increases, which is not backed by real power. The increase in the money supply leads to increased distortion of the real picture. The world's seven most developed countries account for more than 50 per cent of world GDP. Their banking system annually prints 10% more money than the value of their GDP. The whole set of currencies undergoes a planned inflation of 5% per year. It is another matter that the developed countries redistribute the costs of such inflation between Third World economies.

Second, the degree of variation between the GDP measured by actual and comparable prices from 0.1 to 1.4 for different countries makes one seriously question the correctness of the approach based on the Big Mac Index.

The study has shown that GDP as a measure of total world income is not entirely adequate. It appears that the most suitable method of calculation, based on the data that can be provided by statistics, would be multiplication of the population by per capita income measured in US dollars. The simplest approximation makes it possible to estimate that in 2030, the world income will be over 60 trillion dollars, i.e., it will increase by almost half as compared with the figures at the start of the century. That is the case when using linear function approximation. At the same time, the third-degree polynomial approximation, which has a slightly lower degree of divergence between the calculated and actual data (R^2 equals 0.87 and 0.96, respectively), suggests a more than tenfold increase. In the case of the latter forecast, a reasonable question arises: "Due to what resources?" This is, however, a task for further research.

An attempt has been made to apply retrospective analysis in order to determine the contribution of different groups of countries into the world's "savings box", and describe how the amount of "universal happiness" changes in the course of world income growth. The analysis has shown that the relative place of countries in the structure of world income over the past 15 years remained quite stable. Variance-rank correlation of the time rank, and the rank of share in world income in 2004, equals 0.25, which means that most of the "transitions" happen within the lower ranks. The first three places have not changed at all, and the top ten have also remained fairly stable, with the exception of China, which has been persistently climbing up.

These results seemingly paint a fairly positive picture: during the fifteen-year period, the number of countries that exceeded the level of USD 3,000 per capita has increased; there have become more people living above the poverty line. Upon a closer view, however, it becomes apparent that this positive trend results from the shortcomings in the world income measurement. After all, the dollar is subject to inflation, just like any world currency, which means that these countries have become richer only nominally.

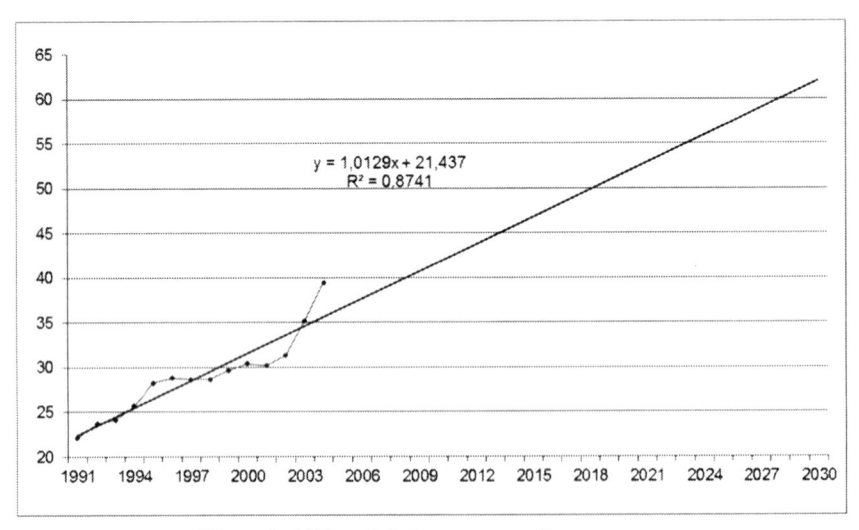

Fig. 4. World income forecast (linear approximation)

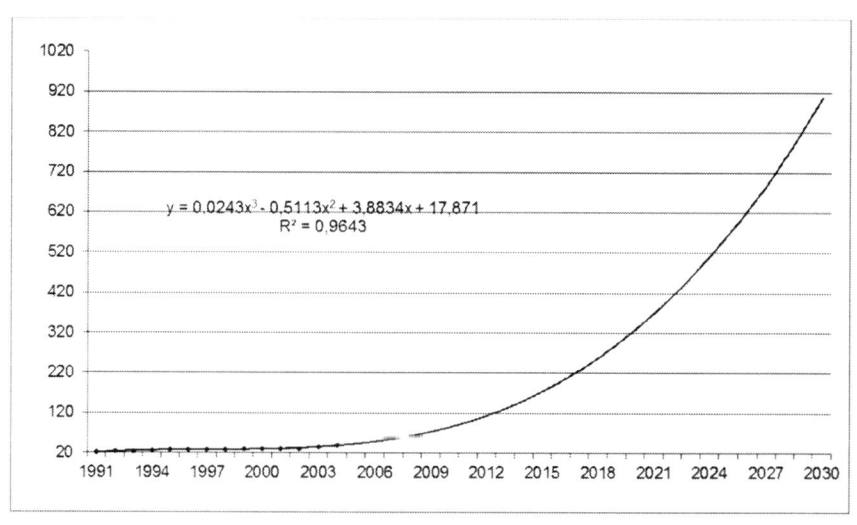

**Fig. 5. World income forecast
(third degree polynomial)**

Alternative approaches to calculating the world product have also been considered.

Perhaps the most famous alternative approach from the standpoint of physical economy was suggested by the American economist Lyndon Hermyle LaRouche. Technological progress, as measured in accordance with changes introduced by Gauss and Riemann into Leibniz's definition of technology (the principle of least action), has a measurable causal relationship with the resultant growth rates of the productive powers of labour and the rates of economic growth. This is essentially what the LaRouche-Riemann method is about.

When calculating the national product, they used the following parameters:

$S/(C + V)$: Productivity (As distinct from "productive powers of labour");
$D/(C + V)$: Expense Ratio;

C/V: Capital-Intensity;
S'/(C + V): Rate of Profit.

Symbol *V* stands for: the portion of total physical-goods output required by all households of the operatives' segment. This is the energy of the system.

Symbol *C* stands for: capital goods consumed by production of physical goods, including costs of the basic economic infrastructure of physical-goods production. This includes: plant and machinery; maintenance of basic economic infrastructure; a materials-in-progress inventory at the level required for maintaining utilisation of capacity; and only that portion of the capital-goods output that was used as energy of the system.

Symbol *S* stands for: gross operating profit (of the particular consolidated agro-industrial enterprise):

$$S = T - (C+V) \qquad (1)$$

where *T* is total physical-goods output (gross product).

Symbol *D* stands for: total overhead expense. This includes consumer goods (of households associated with overhead expense categories of employment of the labour force), plus capital-goods consumed by categories of overhead expense. This is also energy of the system.

Symbol *S'* stands for: net operating profit margin of physical-goods output. (S-D) = S'. This is free energy.

As you know, the strategies for overcoming inequality were outlined in the United Nations Millennium Declaration adopted by Resolution 55/2 of the General Assembly on 8 September 2000. The most important ones among them are the following:

- a policy of duty- and quota-free access for essentially all exports from the least developed countries to their markets;
- implementation of the enhanced programme of debt relief for the heavily indebted poor countries and agreement to cancel all official bilateral debts of those countries in return for their demonstrable commitments to poverty reduction;
- development assistance, especially to countries that are genuinely making an effort to apply their resources to poverty reduction;
- dealing with the debt problems of low- and middle-income developing countries, through various national and international measures designed to make their debt sustainable in the long term.

The study of issues related to the problem of calculating total world income leads us to the following conclusions:

1) The existing statistics and methods do not provide a coherent and consistent picture of the generation and distribution of world income; while the proposed alternative methods either lack statistical data or are based on highly controversial theoretical premises.
2) The level of income per capita can be used as an indicator of the economic activity of the population only with great reservations.

3) UN recommendations are purely declarative; their implementation is often outright impossible or carried out with significant changes and only in relation to those aspects that are interesting for the countries of the Golden Billion (for example, support for certain political regimes).

CHAPTER 8

Industrial and Financial Foundations and Mechanisms of the Planetary Economy

Concept of general economic rent income theory. Rent income characteristics. Infrastructural capital and infrastructural sector of the national economy. Classification of types and forms of rent income. Sources, assessment, and mechanisms of planetary rent appropriation. Types and examples of planetary rent. Mechanisms for managing payments for planetary resource use.

In order to use the planetary ownership institution potential and distribute world income more fairly, in accord with the idea developed as part of the Planetary Project, we must give thought to and develop practical mechanisms of **planetary rent** appropriation for the use of global common resources. Therefore, considerable attention should be paid to developing the concept of sources, assessment, planetary rent appropriation mechanisms, and the general theory of rental income.

As you know, the theory of rent was developed alongside the increased complexity and differentiation of economic activities, and the involvement of new types of resources in the economic process. A new layer of economic relations, associated with appropriation of planetary rent for use of limited planetary resources, is created by: economic globalisation; the rapid development of transnational corporations (TNCs); and the actual domination and often monopolistic position of TNCs on target global markets.

A more modern, more complex, and more diverse system of planetary rent relations makes it possible to generalise the existing concepts of industry-specific types of rent (land, mine, building, information, intellectual, etc.) to develop a general theory of generation, distribution, and appropriation of rental revenues in the modern global economy.

Applying the method of scientific abstraction to the analysis of economic phenomena, we are able to give a generic description of the essential qualitative properties of the phenomenon in question as compared with other phenomena of the same order, and to determine quantitative parameters needed for maintaining its qualitative identity (distinctness). The concept of rent exists alongside other basic types of income, first of all, profits and salaries. The classical division of business resources into labour, capital, and land (a natural resource), was represented in the division of income into wages and salaries, profits, and land (natural resource) rent. The first concepts of rent were formulated through comparisons between these types of income.

During the agrarian stage of economic development, when land was the principal means of production, economists studied the concept of ground rent. Ground rent in the works of A. Smith, D. Ricardo, and K. Marx was defined as revenue received by the landowner (landlord) who rents out the land in exchange for payment. With further development of agrarian relations of ownership and land use, rental payments differentiated into various forms. For the right to use (access) any land, landowners exacted absolute rent. Depending on land productivity and location of the land plot, the landowner extracted differential rent: 1) Additional capital investments that improve the economic fertility of land generate differential rent, and 2) When distributed by the investor, land user and landowner including interest on previously invested capital.

Industrialisation of the economy, and transition to the industrial stage of development, led to the appearance of national investment markets. Inter-industry flows of capital, and inter-industry competition, form prices of production as a sum of industry average production costs and average (equal) profit for capital. The nature and source of rent also experience changes. The owner of the limited resource rents it out for revenue that equals alternative capital investments in banks. Capital value of the limited resource is estimated in accordance with the expected revenue from fixed-term bank deposits for the period when the resource is used. Surplus income over and above average profit becomes the main source of rent.

The transition to a post-industrial society that has occurred in some industrialised countries made the structure of economic activity and priorities in the capital structure more complex. Globalisation and the innovative nature of business create the global market and the inter-country flow of capital. The increased potential of transnational companies, as well as their relations with national states and the international community, shapes the system of planetary property and planetary rent. Ownership of limited planetary resources and renting them out to TNCs, or tenant-countries, forms planetary rent as part of the world's income appropriated by the owners of the resource.

The variety of forms that rent relations take in the modern economy requires more precise determination of the nature, forms of manifestation, sources, and mechanisms of appropriation and distribution of rental income. Theory of rent is best described through its comparison with other forms of income: wages/salaries and profits. This comparative analysis is presented in Table 3.

The comparison of qualitative characteristics of the three main forms of income shows that *rent* is a special type of income. It is received by owners of limited capital resources in the form determined by the type of capital and alternative ways of using these resources. It creates the possibility of surplus profits ranging from the minimum risk-free interest on bank deposits, to the difference between the price to the consumer (demand) and the cost of production (supply).

Seemingly, the concept of rent is no different from return on leased capital. However, significant differences between rent and business profit can be clearly identified through the analysis of: the nature, the type, the method of use in business processes, and the rights of property in different types of capital resources.

The classical division of productive factors into land, labour and capital is no longer sufficient. The emergence and rapid development of human capital theory shows that personal qualities (knowledge, skills, experience, and motivations) can also be turned into capital, and generate additional income for the person, their owner, and the business. The energy and raw material crisis on the planet raised the issue of sufficiency of energy and raw material resources. The theory of natural capital and natural resources has emerged.

Neoclassical theory develops the most abstract (generic) concept of capital as discounted flows of income from productive use of any type of assets in business: material, human and natural. Every capital good can bring profit to its owner if used efficiently. Owners of physical, human, and natural capital receive profit that is no less than average from all possible uses of the capital. Is seems that there is no need for such categories as wages or rent.

Table 3. Comparison of rental incomes with wages/salaries and business profits

No	Socioeconomic parameters	Income of salaried employees (1	Profits (business income) (2	Rent income of owners of resources (3
1	Basic types	1.1. Wages and salaries 1.2. Benefits package 1.3. Investments in human capital	2.1. Accounting income 2.2. Economic profit 2.3. Net profit 2.4. Dividends 2.5. Surplus dividends	3.1. Land rent 3.2. Mining rent 3.3. Intellectual rent 3.4. Social rent 3.5. Information rent 3.6. Infrastructure rent
2	Appropriating economic agents (entities)	Owners of human capital	Owners of tangible assets and financial equities	Owners of limited business resources
3	Objective conditions for generation	Limitedness of specific assets (knowledge, experience, abilities)	Limitedness of investment and factors of production	Limitedness of durable primary resources
4	Sources	4.1. Part of production costs 4.2. Part of profits 4.3. Central and local government budgets	4.1. Accounting profit 4.2. Relative cost savings 4.3. Monopoly on the markets	4.1. Surplus profit 4.2. Monopoly profit 4.3. Excess profit 4.4. Relative cost savings from the use of quality resources
5	Limits of functional sufficiency			
5.1.	Minimum	5.1. Subsistence-level income of a family	5.1. Profit large enough to pay taxes and average dividends	5.1. Risk-free rate of interest on fixed period deposits
5.2.	Normal level	5.2. Sustainable income	5.2. Average return on capital	5.2. Average income from operations related to resource consumption
5.3.	Maximum	5.3. Wealthy income, in accordance with the country's social standards	5.3. Effective income	5.3. Difference between the price to consumer and the cost of production

Such considerations may be logically correct, but, in fact, they do not reflect the special nature of reproduction and circulation of various capital values. The unique qualities of the income received by salaried employees, business income, and rent, are objectively determined by specific qualities of human, natural, and capital resources.

We think that it is essential to distinguish between current and infrastructure capital resources. The traditional division of a firm's capital into fixed and circulating capital should be supplemented with the concept of **infrastructural capital**.

It would be hard to over-estimate the role of infrastructure in modern business development. The availability of infrastructural services, infrastructure costs, and the specific pricing of infrastructure services, in our view, determines the need to generate rental incomes different from profits.

The term "infrastructure" has been used in economic literature since the 1940s. This term was borrowed from the military lexicon, where it designated a logistical network of buildings and installations necessary for the support of military forces. The concept of infrastructure has gradually increased in complexity: first defining the services necessary for the operation of material production (energy, water, transport, communications, etc.); and gradually acquiring its broad interpretation as a network of businesses and services, providing continuous reproduction of goods and essential support for the population.

In the modern context of transition to the innovative type of extended reproduction, it is necessary and sufficient to identify the following subsystems of infrastructure support (see Table 4). Priorities in employing services of infrastructure enterprises are determined by their importance for future competitive positions of the companies.

Important differences in reproduction of infrastructural capital goods are as follows:

1) Significant capital intensity of building an infrastructure facility. For example, construction of a nuclear or hydraulic power plant costs billions of dollars. Construction of roads and bridges, ports and airports, networks of storage facilities, and information networks also requires significant investments and a lot of time. It becomes impractical to build competing (parallel) infrastructure facilities.
2) Long useful lifetime and payback period of infrastructure facilities. Lifetime of buildings, installations, and utility networks averages several decades. Maintenance, repair, and modernisation of these facilities are also specific in nature, which leads to specification of all property rights in these assets.
3) General utility of infrastructure services limits the possibilities of alternative choice and competition among service providers, effectively leading to monopolisation of local markets. Connection to power supply networks and transportation routes, and registration with health and education facilities determine the nature and purpose of infrastructure services.

Table 4. Infrastructure networks of the national economy

No	Subsystems and branches of infrastructural sector	Range of infrastructure goods and resources
1	Innovative infrastructure	Services involving development and use of intelligent products and innovations
1.1	Science and research	Scientific discoveries, research and development, ideas
1.2	Innovations	Product, technology and business innovations
1.3	Venture business	Innovative risk projects
2	Information infrastructure	Services involving access to information and database updates
2.1	Telecommunications	Connection to communication channels
2.2	Databases	International, national, industry-specific, regional and local databases
2.3	Information services	Providing access to databases and accelerated search for useful information
3	Social infrastructure	Services associated with reproduction of human capital
3.1	Healthcare	Preventive, treatment, and health-promoting services
3.2	Education	Educational services, coaching
3.3	Art and culture	Providing access to cultural space, development of creative abilities
4	Institutional infrastructure	Regulation of social relations and management
4.1	Official legislative institutions	Drafting and adopting laws, enforcement of laws, responsibility for violation of laws
4.2	Moral standards and rules of behaviour	Development of moral standards and rules of behaviour, services provided by civic organisations and civic society

4.3	Government administration services	Services provided by federal and regional government departments and offices
4.4	Local government services	Services provided by municipal authorities
5	Market infrastructure	Services to accelerate circulation of goods, capital and labour
5.1	Exchanges	Services to provide acceleration of transactions involving exchange of goods and transaction warranties
5.2	Banks	Services involving acceleration of mutual settlements, accumulation of savings, and selection of investment projects
5.3	Chamber of Commerce and Industry	Services associated with business operations and establishment of business connections
5.4	Companies and agencies providing expertise and consulting services	Services involving expert examination of quality and reliability of business documentation, risk assessment, feasibility of alternatives solutions
6	Logistical infrastructure	Services involving transportation and storage of goods and reserves
6.1	Transportation networks	Transport services, roads, bridges, ports
6.2	Storage facilities	Services involving storage of goods and reserves
6.3	Insurance reserves	Services involving risk assessment and reduction, reserve supplies
7	Economic overheads	Services providing businesses and population with key resources
7.1	Power industry	Providing electric power
7.2	Fuel industry	Providing fuel (oil and oil products, natural gas, peat, wood, etc.)
7.3	Major construction and maintenance	Construction and maintenance services
7.4	Mechanical engineering	Production of machinery and equipment (technological systems)

8	Ecological infrastructure	Services involving environmental protection and ecological balance support
8.1	Purification of atmospheric emissions	Purification of smoke, exhaust fumes, dust collectors, forest reproduction
8.2	Water purification	Sewage treatment plants, water use, protection of water bodies
8.3	Solid industrial and domestic waste disposal	Collection and processing of solid industrial waste and domestic rubbish, disposal and recycling of hazardous waste
8.4	Preservation of soil fertility	Land reclamation and development, balanced fertilisation
8.5	Conservation of biological diversity of plant and animal life	Forest restoration, wildlife conservation
8.6	Monitoring interactions between the society and natural ecosystems	Services of scientific research centres and ecological laboratories for monitoring and assessment of the environment

The mechanism of owning and using the national property is, of course, much more complex than that of private appropriation. This does not mean, however, that public interests and well-being of the majority should be sacrificed in favour of private interests and simplification. Eventually, the historical injustice is recognised and eliminated through political means.

Table 5 shows an approach to classification of rental types by groups of infrastructural resources and forms of appropriation of rental income received.

Table 5. Classification of types and forms of rental income

Forms of generation and appropriation of rental income	Types of rental incomes by sources of infrastructure resources									
	Natural resource rent			Intellectual rent	Innovation rent	Information rent	Social rent	Institutional rent	Energy rent	Transport rent	Contract rent
	Land	Mining	Forest								
Absolute rent	Implementation of exclusive property rights for the resource, payment (price) for access to the resource									
Differential rent	Surplus income over average profit from using resources of higher quality									
Differential rent I, based on relative economic value	Surplus income of the resource owner who provided the user with a resource of higher quality									
Differential rent II, based on effect of investing in improvement of quality of resources	Surplus income of the user who invested capital in improvement of the quality of the resource									
Monopoly rent	Surplus income of the owner of a rare non-renewable resource and product									

We chose the type of resource turned into a relevant kind of operating capital as the basis for identifying industry-specific types of rent. It is possible to specify further the types of rent by a particular resource object, as it is done when classifying various types of natural resource rent (land, mining, forest). Mining rent, in its turn, is captured through field development of various resource types—oil, gas, gold, complex ores, etc.

Kinds of rental income appropriation have already been analysed by the classics through the example of ground rent. These include absolute, differential, and monopoly rents. Forms of rental income appropriation also depend on the type of entity that has ownership of the resource, and the existing system of income distribution. Private owners can capture rent in all its forms in case of a stable institutional system that guarantees the circulation of resources. Firms create resources and appropriate rental incomes in the form of excessive or monopoly surplus profits.

The mechanism of rental income appropriation at the national and planetary levels has its special features. Public facilities are leased to companies or sole proprietors, or operated as a concession. Rental income is included in the lease payments. Part of the rent can be appropriated by the state through tax payments. The issue that has no yet been conclusively developed is participation of the nation's citizens in shared appropriation of rental income, as well as that of inhabitants of the planet; even though the budget and social funds are used to distribute part of the total rental national income among designated families and households.

Economic activity analysis has been based on the premise of necessity and possibility of *alternative choice*. Business skills are manifested not only in choosing combinations of resources for a particular business activity, but also in the choice from the options (alternatives) in attracting any kind of resource. The pressure of market competition, and the desire of business people, determines the need to choose and employ the most efficient resources and their combinations. This leads to rental income generation.

The resource owner's desire to receive the payment of absolute rent is determined by his choice from two possibilities: to lease; or not to lease any (even the worst quality) resource to a business. If the resource is in demand, its owner sets the rental payment at no less than the level of risk-free interest rate on government securities, i.e., at the level of 3%-5% per year on the capital value of the resource. The amount of absolute rent can be calculated using the following formula:

$$R_{abs} = K_{cr} \times N_{rf} \qquad (2)$$

Where

R_{abs} is absolute rent value;
K_{cr} is capital resource value;
N_{rf} is risk-free rate of interest.

Differential rent I can be calculated as a comparison of marginal productivity and profitability of the resource according to the following formula:

$$R_{diff.I} = (P_j - P_{min}) \times Q_j \qquad (3)$$

Where
diff.I stands for differential rent I

P_j is actual value profit from using a unit of the resource;

P_{min} is profit level of the low-priority resource consumer group;

Q_j is production output.

The growth in productivity and profitability of the resource can be used to calculate *differential rent II*, based on additional investments in improving the quality of the resource.

The owner of the resource demands payment of monopoly rent from the tenant when renting out a unique, rare resource used for producing a rare good. A favourable demand-supply situation in the market of high-demand goods allows business people to raise the market price above the price of production. Monopoly rent is paid by buyers of rare goods. It can be calculated using the following formula:

$$R_{mon.} = (P_{cons.} - P_{pr.}) \times Q_j \quad (4)$$

Where, $P_{cons.}$ is price to consumer; $P_{pr.}$ is producer price as a sum of production costs and average profit; Q_j is volume of production and sales of goods.

All forms of extracting rental income exist potentially, but are only implemented in the system of actual relationship between owners and users of resources. If the relevant institutional system, traditions, and payment rates are absent, then, rent may be disregarded and its appropriation maybe be distorted.

Russia, with time, will be able to implement fully its resource potential, and indeed become rich as a country and bring well-being to all of its citizens.

This is subject to: a reasonable estimate of potential rental income; the development and establishment of the institutional infrastructure necessary to regulate relations between owners and users of resources; and constant work on normalisation of practices related to involvement of all types of resources in economic circulation.

Economic science and economic practice mainly focus on reproductive factors and results of operations. Capital and income, labour, and wages, have been comprehensively analysed in qualitative and quantitative aspects, in statics and in dynamics. Less attention has been given to non-reproducible factors and the theory of rent. In the so-called Third World countries, for example, the share of natural resources used for supporting the livelihood of the population is also large. However, the non-equivalent exchange and disparity of prices for raw materials and energy resources do not provide the mechanism needed for recognition, assessment, replacement, and fair distribution of rental income. We think it is necessary to remove this deficiency.

The theory of ground rent emerged and developed in the era of the agrarian economy. Later, the concept of mining rent was introduced. When the list of appropriable environmental assets expanded, the concept of natural resource rent appeared. The existing variety of natural resources and ways of their economic use give rise to a diversity of natural resource rents. Demand for energy resources forms the flows of oil and gas rents, and energy rent in general. Development of ocean resources makes it possible to assess rent from fishing (bio-rent) and transport sea routes. Development of tourism makes it possible to identify recreational rents in locations of mass tourism and recreation.

Development of the planet's atmosphere through rapid development of air transportation used for carrying passengers and cargo, and creation of national and global radio, television and Internet networks, makes it possible to define infrastructure rent for exploration and development of terrestrial space. Consumption of hydrogen and oxygen taken from the air, and pollution of the atmosphere by industries and exhaust emissions, make it important to identify and set the rates of the so-called "oxygen rent", which is reflected in the documents of the Kyoto Protocol.

Finally, humanity has reached the vastness of outer space. Satellite constellations, space communications, and space power engineering increasingly become a usual business environment. In space, however, it would be meaningless to talk about national government property, and national mechanisms of rent appropriation. Flows of solar energy and light, the Earth's field magnetic force, and gravitational forces belong to all humanity. Space resources are truly a universal good belonging to humanity as a whole.

The benefits obtained using planetary goods belong to the world community and should have adequate mechanisms for income appropriation, including mechanisms for natural resource rent appropriation.

Land and mining rents are usually generated and appropriated inside the national economies. For example, OPEC countries, Russia, Norway, Venezuela, and other oil-producing nations extract oil and gas rents, sharing them with transnational companies. Countries that do not have hydrocarbon energy resources have to pay this rent. The international community, as represented by the United Nations at least, still does not get its share of planetary rent.

The same mechanism is used for appropriation of mining rents from development of mineral resources: diamonds, gold, metal ores, rare earth elements, and other resources. At the same time, it is only in the course of history that the Earth's interior has become property of separate national states. The Earth's core, its continental plates, and the vast expanse of the World Ocean cannot be considered national property. These are also objects of planetary property belonging to all humanity.

As mentioned above, the extension of economic activity to space, the use of atmospheric and biospheric goods, and the development of the World Ocean and the Earth's interior makes it possible to argue that a special form of property—***planetary property***—has been formed. Objects of planetary property belong to all humanity. International, supra-national institutions, including the UN and its agencies, as well as global and continental integrated associations, regulate their economic use. Planetary rent represents a type of income received from planetary property use.

Planetary rent is understood as a special type of income from the economic use of planetary resources.

Absolute planetary rent is appropriated by the international community as payment for use of exclusive planetary property. This, in our estimation, includes oxygen rent, payments for excess pollution of the atmosphere and the Word Ocean, and infrastructure rent arising from proceeds of aviation and maritime transport in international space.

Monopoly planetary rent is appropriated by owners of limited planetary resources. Oil, gas, coal, diamonds, platinum, gold, complex ores, rare and valuable species of trees and plants, are limited in area and reserves. In the market situation of demand exceeding supply, monopoly rent arises due to excess price. Most of it is appropriated by economic entities and national states. However, the international community can claim a certain part of monopoly rent, for instance, as contributions to the UN budget or to international targeted funds.

Planetary differential rent I (by location) arises in the internationally recognised airspace and the World Ocean, which are not governed by national government jurisdictions. This, for example, includes extraction of oil and gas from the World Ocean bed in international waters under the license of the United Nations. Profitable sea and air transport routes also represent a source of additional revenue and planetary rent.

Planetary differential rent II derives from major international and continental investment projects and programs. Thus, the European Union gets a share of revenue generated by operation of the pan-European transport system, from energy projects and ecological systems. Transcontinental pipelines and gas networks, information networks and databases can also become sources of planetary rent.

Planetary rent can, therefore, be represented in the following diagram.

PLANETARY RENT			
Absolute rent	Monopoly rent	Differential rent I	Differential rent II

Examples of assets capable of generating planetary rent when used

Earth's atmosphere World ocean Space Fundamental scientific discoveries Global infrastructure	Extractable resources in international zones Limited energy resources Limited mineral resources	International sea and air transport routes Lease of planetary property assets Global infrastructure	Infrastructure rent arising from development of world and continental systems Intellectual rent arising from international innovative systems and projects

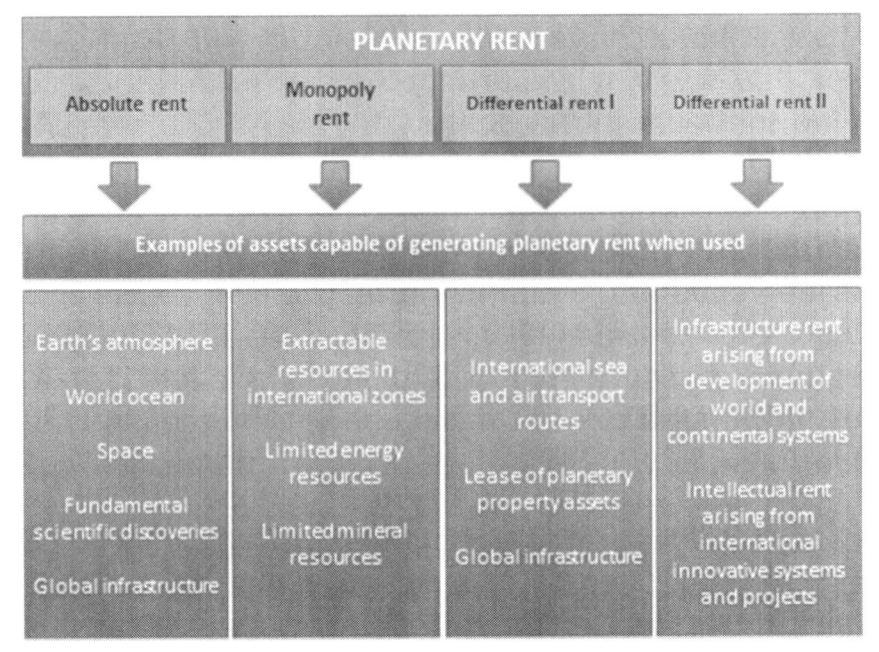

Fig. 6. Kinds and examples of sources of planetary rent

The United Nations Statistical Commission and the World Bank regularly publish GDP data by country. Their data shows that there is excessively large income differentiation across continents and countries of the world. The countries of the Golden Billion appropriate 67%-80% of the world income. It is in the GDP breakdown of developed countries that we should look for rental incomes, i.e., planetary rent is generated in the countries possessing energy resources and raw materials, but it is appropriated through unequal exchange and price disparity by economically strong countries. This means that identification and assessment of planetary rent can be a real source of budget replenishment for the UN, and for increased investment in the development of the world's depressed regions.

A second approach to planetary rent assessment can be based on the analysis of generation and distribution of incomes from use of particular planetary resources. Oil and gas can be considered the most in demand among these resources; all the more so as their world prices are kept at the level sufficient for rent appropriation due to the existing global demand-supply situation.

A more specific mechanism of natural rent appropriation can be observed in those countries that use their oil wealth most rationally. Norway would be a good example. During the 30 years of oil and gas extraction, the nation received over USD 500 billion in revenue, of which more than a third was transferred to the Oil Fund, also known as the fund for future generations. If we regard these contributions to the fund as rent, its level would amount to nearly 40% of the income received. They have accumulated about USD 50,000 or each Norwegian citizen.

To a certain extent, planetary rent is already being collected and accumulated in the United Nations funds, and it is used to finance targeted international programmes. Contributions of member states to the UN budget are determined as a percentage rate, and depend on the level of the country's economic development. Besides, nations participate in financing targeted programmes, such as financial assistance to poor countries, anti-terrorist operations, disaster relief, and others. Decisions to finance joint projects and programmes are taken by national authorities of their own free will, and with due account for the financial soundness of the countries. While preserving the current practice of the UN budgeting and budget implementation, we consider it necessary to develop a mechanism for direct rental payments in return for planetary resource use to the UN budget and its trust funds.

A schematic of assessment and transfer of planetary rent to the income of the United Nations is shown in the following diagram.

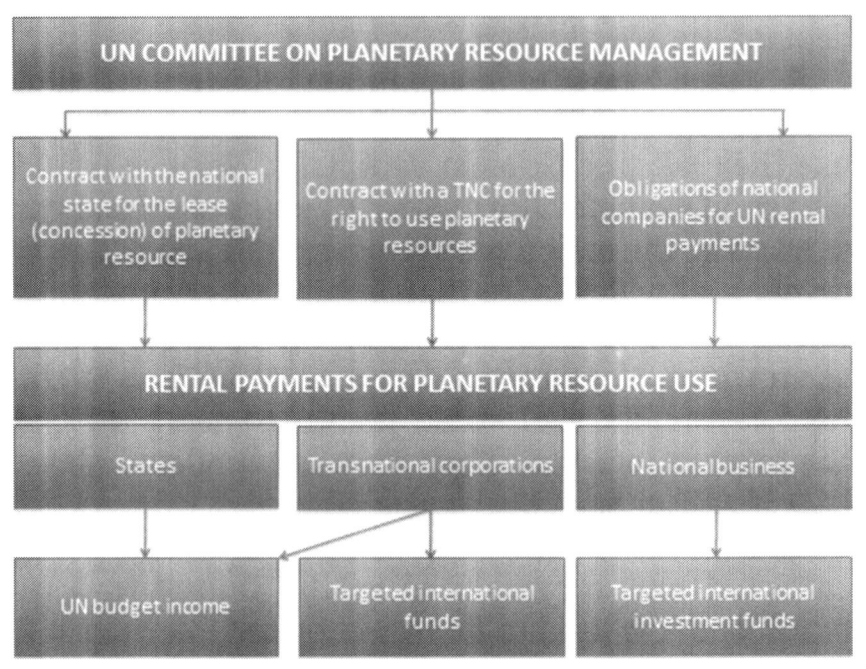

Fig. 7. Mechanism of rental payments for planetary resource use

The rental payment mechanism must be put on an institutional footing. The programme for the reform of the UN should include formalisation of the rights for planetary property in the Charter of the United Nations. Furthermore, a convention on planetary property rights and forms of planetary resource use, should be developed and adopted. Besides, standard agreements (contracts) for the right to use (lease, concession) planetary resources by states, transnational companies, and national companies should be worked out.

The work on assessment of rental incomes and payments for the right to use planetary resources can involve the existing UN agencies and independent international organisations.

The World Intellectual Property Organisation (WIPO), for example, has been developing mechanisms and institutions for evaluation and appropriation of intellectual and innovation rents for the use of fundamental scientific discoveries and the whole system of fundamental science. The World Health Organisation (WHO) regulates issues associated with appropriation of intellectual rent for the use of internationally recognised drugs, and methods of treating global diseases like "bird flu, H5N1". The United Nations Industrial Development Organisation (UNIDO) promotes transfer of high technology, appropriating innovation rent and financing international research projects and alliances.

In fact, a mechanism has been developed for appropriation of rent arising from the use of capital provided by the World Bank, the International Monetary Fund, and other financial institutions. International open-end funds and corporations that finance development of specific planetary resources of the World Ocean, Antarctica, and outer space also look promising. Other international and continental organisations, unions and associations, also have their areas for regulation of revenue streams and rental payments.

There is no doubt that the possibility of attracting additional financial resources will contribute to positive changes in the world economy and international relations.

CHAPTER 9

Planetary Governance Institutions

Necessity to direct integration processes and save the biosphere. Nature of planetary institution. Planetary governance system: objects, processes, functions, goals and objectives. System design principles. Types of planetary governance institutions. Economic mechanism of funding planetary institutions. Infrastructural subsystems of planetary society.

Global human integration, whose purpose is to save the biosphere and create a planetary civilisation based on the principles of justice and harmony, is an endeavour of historic scale and cosmic significance. To be implemented, it will require systemic organisation, planning, procurement, and governance.

First, it implies optimal and effective forms of such organisation, its structuring and functioning, which could be both experience-tested and adequately innovative. Second, it implies resources: financial, information, normative-legal, administrative, and technical. Third, it implies people: human investment, humanitarian capital, scientific and spiritual-moral foundations, intellectual and technological solutions, and leadership initiatives. The human part in this *total rescue operation* is paramount: researchers, analysts, experts, innovators, social activists and administrators, need not be the best representatives of their fields of knowledge and activity, but must unite in the understanding of the gravity of the current world crisis, and the necessity to solve dramatically global problems. The Planetary Project philosophy combines these requirements in the concept of the ***system of planetary governance institutions***.

In institutional theory, the notion of "institution" which economists borrowed from social sciences, has evolved from being a custom, habit or behavioural stereotype (Thorstein Bunde Veblen, John Rogers Commons, Wesley Clair Mitchell), to the concept of "institution" as a complex system of rules, limitations, and forms of inducing compliance (Douglass Cecil North, Redmond Williams). The institutional economic infrastructure is included in the legislation of developed countries, and governmental and non-governmental organisations to ensure compliance with laws and the norms of behaviour.

Today, there is a need to establish more clearly the purpose and function of global institutions. Each of them is meant to **regulate** the international activity of countries and corporations through international legal norms and regulations, and vesting in them the prevalence of the national legislation.

The second mandatory function is to *ensure* favourable conditions for international projects and programmes in various fields. To do this, global institutions must have the necessary resources and mandates.

Finally, the attractiveness of global institutions will increase through the practical development and implementation of major continental and global projects aimed at resolving current global social, environmental, and economic issues, i.e., if they fulfil their *creative and developing* function.

We must now be clear that the Planetary Project philosophy operates the concepts of *international, supra-national, and supra-governmental governing structures* organised in a special way and controlled by international elites. It represents proportionately all *constructive* world cultures, whose mandate related to saving life on planet Earth exceeds the mandate of nation states and existing international associations.

The big issue that anti-globalists, nationalists, and radical conservatives joined by their supporters, or simply ignorant members of the wider public, tend to be concerned about, is why do we need supra-national governing bodies and governance institutions? Will they not usurp world power over nations trying to keep their traditional ethnic identity, and authentic political regimes? Will they not try to impose the type of government that would not serve the interests of one country, or a small group of countries, with political and spiritual values alien to those of the rest of the world?

The answer lies on the surface. It is obvious even if the current world situation is subjected to a quick and superficial analysis. The current national and international governance institutions just cannot cope with the world problems! They are too disunited and bureaucratised, serving national and corporate interests. Some of them are corrupt; others are too ambitious or even hostile to other political systems, ideologies, and cultures. Still others do not have sufficient funding, assets, or adequate administrative experience. There can be a long list of these and other similar inefficiency features of most national and international institutions. One fact is enough to prove the existence of these issues. It is that so far, not every country that participated in the UN conference on sustainable development in Rio de Janeiro in 1992 has formulated or ratified their national sustainable development strategies.

Some people believe that political bodies, government institutions and governance systems, are globalisation's "Achilles heel". In other words, their controversial activity discredits globalisation as a world historical process, and a natural phase in the development of society. Global institutions are mostly criticised for the lack of *openness* of supra-governmental and supra-national bodies, and the blurriness of their *responsibility*. Some are practically powerless, serving as a mere disguise for transnational corporations. Others are, on the contrary, uncontrolled and unaccountable: it is next to impossible to bring them to justice or monitor their actions if they violate human rights. Indeed, from the management point of view, we can hardly talk about fully-fledged global administrative institutions, but rather about creating prerequisites for global infrastructures, regimes, systems, and institutions to emerge. At the same time, they lack integrity and enforcing mechanisms, which makes them inefficient.

It is clear that the unsavoury experience of the inefficiency of current global institutions, and the limited capacity of the market to solve global problems, force us to raise the question of the necessity to perform substantial institutional transformation of society. We believe that we can, and we must, talk seriously about a "new world order" and a "world government" without irony or conspirological references, but rather with a full understanding of the crucial goal of saving life on Earth. Moreover, this is as timely as it ever has been. Therefore, the Planetary Project talks about the need to form a *system of planetary governance bodies*.

The jurisdiction of the planetary governance institutions must include global issues in such spheres as:

- Protection and improvement of the health of the environment;
- Natural resource use and management;
- Demographic dynamics of world nations and asymmetric population growth;
- International relations vis-à-vis territorial and resource disputes, debts, strategic arms and economic co-operation;
- Development of science, education, technical progress, production technologies and information policy;
- All **integration processes** including planetary governance, global problem solving, planetary budget and distribution, *global spiritual synthesis* and ecological education.

United in one infrastructure, these bodies receive institutional status and carry out *functions* directed towards the implementation of planetary governance objectives:

- Monitoring, analysing, and assessing situations, processes, problems and trends;
- Planning structures, processes, and actions;
- Passing laws and creating a normative-legal base;
- Administration, coordination, and regulation;
- Financing and other resource procurement;
- Informing and educating.

The objectives of planetary administration institutions will mostly overlap with the Planetary Project objectives, but they will still be different from the latter in the same way as practice differs from theory, and implementation differs from the original idea. In terms of direction, scale, and implementation time (from strategic to tactical to immediate), the whole range of objectives must:

- Meet the **main goal of planetary governance,** which is global human integration for the purpose of saving the biosphere and creating a noospheric civilisation for future generations;
- Be realistic, scientifically grounded, and compromise-based (the interests of the involved elites must not be ignored);
- Have a sufficient resource base.

Planetary governance objectives are divided into distinct groups according to key directions of solving global problems and uniting humanity. These objectives, whose purpose is to save the planet and create a harmonious civilisation, include environmental, political, economic, cultural, and social objectives.

The planetary governance ***environmental objectives*** will follow from key ***environmental goals*** of alleviating the anthropogenic and technogenic pressure on the planet, saving endangered species of plants and animals, protecting the ozone layer, fresh water, and other non-renewable natural resources.

Environmental objectives associated with planetary governance will comply with the key *ecological goals* of: reducing anthropogenic and technogenic pressure on the planet Earth; saving species of plants and animals from extinction; and protecting the ozone layer, fresh water, and other non-renewable natural resources.

The list of main environmental objectives includes:

- Diagnosing the current state of environmental issues in the world, risk assessment, forecasting natural cataclysms, crisis processes and catastrophes;
- Drafting a united planetary environmental policy, including systemic development of environmental protection legislation and environmental assessment criteria; including sustainable development indicators, as well as product and service environmental quality standards and mandatory environmental certification of all economic entities;
- Developing and launching resource-saving and resource substitution programs;
- Funding innovative technological solutions for biocompatible production and rational use of natural resources, etc. on a priority basis.

The most courageous and determined scientists base their vision of a new world order primarily on global risks. The Russian economist and ecologist, member of the Russian Academy of Sciences, Viktor Danilov-Danilyan, believes that in the twenty-first century, instead of a nation's political structure dictating its environmental policy, the environmental agenda will form the political structure. He transforms here the environmental imperative, making an environmental approach prevail over a political one.

Nikita Moiseev says practically the same thing in his work "Environmental Socialism" (1998): "The end of the century has brought humanity to the point when it becomes a single organism and acquires a common goal that many are not yet aware of: a planetary homeostasis. No country, even the USA, can ensure its own stability doing it alone. Iron curtains disappear by themselves as they are deadly to everyone!" In his writings, Moiseev not only tries to show the bankruptcy of the current dominant system of relations from the point of view of a future human society, but also draws a picture, if sketchy, of a desired social design that would provide the maximum compatibility of individual interest with the interest of society. He calls this type of society *"environmental socialism"*.

Political objectives of planetary governance serve the *political goals* of creating a balance between the integration processes of re-globalisation, and: preserving the national-state sovereignty of countries; reconciling local and global interests; complying with international legal norms; and maximum public participation in the creation of noospheric civilisation.

The key political objectives of planetary institutional infrastructure will include:

- Planning, structuring, and institutionalising planetary governance;
- Creating an internationally recognised and legally bound legislative basis of planetary governance;
- Unification of world political elites according to proportional distribution of power resources for resolving global problems and issues;
- Alleviating international tension on all levels of manifestation, removing the threat of nuclear war, and reduction of weapons of mass destruction;
- Rooting out international and local terrorism, extremism, and genocide.

To improve the planetary *political-legal* subsystem, it would be desirable to combine various international conventions and treaties into a single "International Code" regulating the relationships between states, corporations, communities, and the individual. The UN and its institutions would require more dramatic reforms based on current conditions, as well as goals and visions of harmonious development of the global community.

Resolving the *economic issues* of planetary governance is meant to ensure the achievement of the fundamental *economic goal* of creating a biocompatible system of production, distribution, consumption, disposal, and reproduction. The foremost economic objectives include:

- Ensuring the financial basis and functioning mechanisms of planetary governance institutions;
- Encouraging innovations, and formal and technical sciences for the creation of economic technological infrastructure that meets the standards of the Sixth Techno-economic Paradigm;
- Creating and implementing an energy sector based on alternative sources of energy;
- Building resource-saving industry based on resource substitution technologies;
- Opening and stimulating new points and zones of economic growth, including creative economies, especially in Third World countries, to develop their internal markets, increase their GDP, and improve their standard of living.

There is a lot of criticism of the International Monetary Fund, the World Bank, and the World Trade Organisation. What are the ways of transforming them into genuinely global market institutions independent of political interests in line with the "unipolar world order?" This question needs to be discussed and resolved. A number of other issues have emerged relating to global transportation network regulation, and creating anti-crisis reserves on the continents. In other words, there is an urgent need to form a planetary logistics infrastructure.

Planetary governance **cultural objectives** should be oriented towards the main **cultural goal** of developing planetary consciousness and a planetary agent: integral people and *WE-humanity*. The product of planetary governance cultural policy should be a new—bio-centric—*attitude to the world* unifying all of its spiritual-practical aspects. Hence, the fundamental cultural objectives can be formulated as follows:

- Ensuring cross-cultural co-operation of all constructive public forces to save life on Earth;
- Developing and implementing a system of ecological education of people starting with an early age;
- Developing a universal bio-centric ideology, ethics, and morality on compromise-based global spiritual synthesis;
- Popularising bio-centric and environmental values with all possible means of information and propaganda;
- Saving traditional cultures, ethnic groups and their historic heritage from extinction;
- Rooting out totalitarian, authoritarian, and destructive sects and cults;
- Eradicating illiteracy and backwardness.

The planetary ***innovation*** subsystem will be responsible for overcoming manufacturing property barriers, ensure access to new technologies and beneficial business types for developing countries. It is necessary to expand scientific programmes and research projects within continental communities or the world as whole. Developing science and innovations on a world scale requires a high level of education, which entails global social infrastructure development. Educational projects and programmes must evolve from international aid-funded worker training programmes provided to developing countries, to setting up international universities on different continents, which would have the best educational human and material resources. The main thing is that scholars, specialists, and managers graduating from these universities would be sent to their countries to solve their countries' problems. Otherwise, we would not be able to overcome the proverbial "brain drain" from developing to developed countries.

The **social objectives** of planetary governance derive from the systemic **social goal** of organising and maintaining a world design that is just towards people, and harmonious towards nature. When we reviewed the Concept of Sustainable Development, we established the organic and irremovable relationship between the environment, economy, politics, science, culture, and social issues, problems, and regularities. Therefore, planetary governance social objectives are not less important and significant than the ones listed before them. Moreover, solutions to other planetary transformation objectives will be condensed in the social field, because resolving all these problems will benefit, along with nature, the *individual person* as an element of the biosphere. The following social objectives can be identified:

- Investing human rights with the status of international legislation with compliance mandatory for everyone;
- Developing and implementing a single system of assessing the quality of life;
- Rooting out all forms of social, racial and cultural discrimination, and forced exploitation;
- Solving global health problems including, and especially, mass diseases and pandemics;

- Developing and carrying out an efficient food policy;
- Developing civil society institutions and increasing their role in politics, social life, global human integration, and planetary governance processes through using civil rights;
- Creating and implementing effective programs of social protection and rehabilitation of the most vulnerable social groups;
- Creating additional mechanisms and forms of social mobility for people across the world.

We have now outlined the most important and general planetary governance objectives, which could even be called planetary governance development vectors. They have to be concrete; they must be put on the relevant scientific-methodological, normative-legal, and spiritual-ideological basis, and supplied with the necessary resources already at the planetary governance institution operation stage. Obviously, this will require detailed study, planning, and justification.

To form a planetary governance system as a single and integrated infrastructure, we must:

- Design, model and structure planetary governance institutions based on the experience of international global institutions;
- Define their mandate, and develop and implement a mechanism of vesting them with an appropriate mandate;
- Staff them;
- Set up public oversight and regulations bodies.

It is also obvious that the united planetary governance infrastructure must follow systemic organisation principles, including:

- Priority order, responsiveness and efficiency;
- Accessibility, openness and democracy;
- Optimal balance of centralisation and dispersity;
- Interconnectedness, network co-operation and synergy;
- Legitimacy and mandate;
- Adequate resources;
- Reliable funding.

We must reiterate here that, according to the Planetary Project, planetary governance institutions must meet the needs of all countries, with the needs of developing countries receiving special attention.

It is also important that the process of creating a single planetary governance system must be organised and carried out comprehensively and consistently. This does not mean that these reforms must take decades: the current crisis-ridden humanity just does not have time for that. The experience of developed and some developing countries, and many international organisations demonstrates that in large-scale reforming efforts the success does not depend on the amount of time spent on them so much as on their *management quality* and *motivation*.

As far as planetary governance institution types, the Planetary Project identifies four basic types of institutions that will be able to address planetary governance directions, goals, and specific objectives.

The general structure of this typology includes the following:

1. Spiritual-ideological institutions
1.1. The World Academy of Sciences
1.2. The World Information and Education Space
1.3. The World Dialogue of Churches

2. Political institutions
2.1. A modernised United Nations
2.2. The World Parliament
2.3. Continental Parliaments (Euro-parliament, etc.)
2.4. Planetary political parties and social movements

3. Economic institutions
3.1. Planetary Property Institution
3.2. The United Planetary Development Budget
3.3. A system of planetary and continental development programmes

4. Supra-national governing institutions
4.1. The Planetary Council
4.2. The Security Council
4.3. Regional Councils for Economic and Social Development

Separately, we would like to present the economic mechanism of funding planetary institutions:

Table 6. Economic mechanism of funding planetary institutions

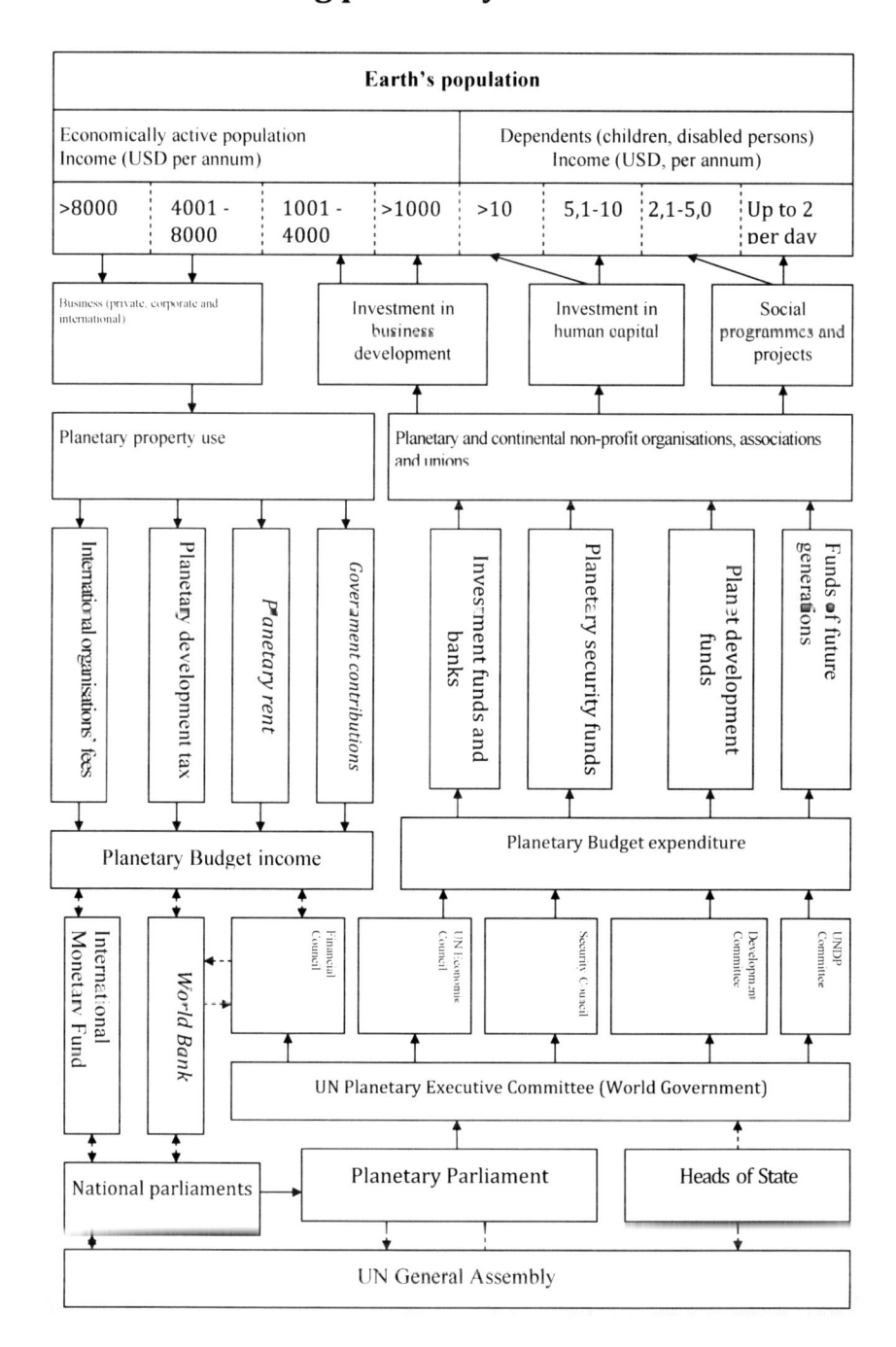

Earth's population							
Economically active population Income (USD per annum)				Dependents (children, disabled persons) Income (USD, per annum)			
>8000	4001 - 8000	1001 - 4000	>1000	>10	5,1-10	2,1-5,0	Up to 2 per day

- Business (private, corporate and international)
- Investment in business development
- Investment in human capital
- Social programmes and projects

Planetary property use

Planetary and continental non-profit organisations, associations and unions

- International organisations' fees
- Planetary development tax
- Planetary rent
- Government contributions
- Investment funds and banks
- Planetary security funds
- Planet development funds
- Funds of future generations

Planetary Budget income — **Planetary Budget expenditure**

- International Monetary Fund
- World Bank
- Financial Council
- UN Economic Council
- Security Council
- Development Committee
- UNDP Committee

UN Planetary Executive Committee (World Government)

National parliaments — Planetary Parliament — Heads of State

UN General Assembly

The Planetary Project concept of *infrastructure* can also mean basic social life subsystems and various spheres of life in society, in our case—planetary society.

Infrastructure studies traditionally concern improvements in three sectors: production, market, and social infrastructures. In post-industrial society, infrastructural activity has undergone more detailed differentiation. Research literature provides at least eight infrastructure sectors.

1) **Production infrastructure** includes services of supplying the population and business with energy, fuel, water, production equipment, and capital construction, and maintenance.
2) **Social infrastructure** ensures reproduction of human potential and capital through vocational training and healthcare.
3) **Market infrastructure** encourages turnover of goods, money and capital; and includes exchanges, banks, and insurance services.
4) **Institutional infrastructure** enables the regulation of relations between economic players, and facilitates their interaction through law making and law enforcement, and maintaining and developing business ethics and social responsibility.
5) **Logistics infrastructure** provides transportation, storing goods in warehouses, and creating reserves.
6) **Information infrastructure** provides communication channels, building databases and providing access to them, and telecommunications.

7) **Innovation infrastructure** includes creative activities, such as science, innovations and venture business.
8) **Environmental infrastructure** is formed to protect the environment and life-subsistence systems.

This infrastructural complex is emerging in economically developed countries. Seriously modernised and adequately funded, this infrastructure is required at the planetary level as well. As we already pointed out, planetary infrastructure features must be useful and accessible to all countries, corporations, and the economically active population. It is vitally important today to meet nations' infrastructural needs.

Infrastructural reforms will inevitably raise the question of the new roles of international organisations. If people have realised that, if multiple development issues are resolved in a comprehensive manner, there inevitably arises a question about the necessity to integrate nations on a new global basis. Humanity is objectively uniting in the face of a planetary collapse. Integration factors have so far been caused by economic issues; whereas today, two major directions, *environmental* and *social*, have strengthened the objective basis of integration.

These factors require a much higher unification level of the world community. These are not just related problems; they are interconnected and interdependent. One can confidently say that social-environmental-economic factors have emerged as the basis of integration. They form a unity that has an advantage over previous factors in that it integrates the interests of countries at different development levels and with different strategic interests. Each country finds its own interest in the pool of reasons causing nations to co-operate.

In a very general way, we can suppose that primarily developed countries pursue economic and environmental interests. Countries lagging behind in their development are more interested in co-operating in bridging the wealth gap. We cannot say that the interests of developed and developing countries do not overlap, because then there would be no sense in talking about a single integration basis, but these interests manifest themselves with varying degrees of intensity. It would be naïve to hope that contemporary states would not primarily pursue their national interests. Pursuing these interests, they must consider the interests of their partners in achieving common goals and make reasonable concessions. Concerning developed countries, they combine environmental and economic interests quite well. Initially, the third—social—aspect was less prominent in their agenda. Two things are worth pointing out here: the first one is that paradoxically, developed countries will not be able to find an economic solution to environmental problems. Industrial civilisation has put humanity on the brink of an environmental catastrophe. It is clear, of course, that the lion's share of guilt rests on the shoulders of leaders of this civilisation development direction. However, if these countries abandon this course, they stand to lose out, and make an enormous step back in their standard of living.

From a common sense perspective, those responsible for the situation that does not satisfy anyone have to rectify it. However, in reality, they are not able to improve radically the situation. They do not have sufficient resources for that. Moreover, despite the fact that developed countries strive to convince the world of the opposite, they are the main block in the implementation of a development strategy commonly referred to as sustainable development.

To give you proof of the above, one has to remember the origins of the Concept of Sustainable Development. Americans were the first in this area. First, they started to work on their environment, but having seen that the problem could not be solved within one country, they initiated an international environmental movement. They were the first to realise that the main instrument of ensuring their own environmental security was to co-operate with other countries. Environmental security is considered one of the most important parts of US national security strategy. Americans believe the world environment crisis, deriving from environmental degradation and the upset biosphere sustainability, presents no lesser threat than military ones.

They quickly realised that the world would not follow the requisite path if confronted by the environmental threat alone. The wealth gap is rising as an associated social problem that is equally dangerous. That approach was the only correct one from the sustainable development perspective. However, science is affected by both internal development logic and social needs.

It is difficult to say what the main reason is of scientific development, but in this case, we can suppose that developed countries may be interested in easing international social tension, but this is not exactly part of their national interests. It is only recently that social tension has started to be associated with threats to the world in the context of international tension and waves of terrorism. Initially, when the Concept of Sustainable Development was just being made, this problem was presented as affecting the majority of the world's population, and it convinced people that poverty was a threat to the global environment. Moreover, a large group of scholars and politicians then (and now) viewed overpopulation in developing countries to be the main cause of an approaching catastrophe. They tried to argue that it was the reason for the shortage of natural resources for humanity. Of course, this problem should not be ignored, but to put it centre-stage would not be correct either.

Practically in all spheres of current world development, developed countries are trying to put a major part of responsibility for solving planetary problems on the rest of the world. Nobody is deceived today by the formally high level of expenditure on the part of industrialised countries on implementing many international sustainable development programmes. This is because the expected outcome of joint solutions to global human problems is much greater for them than for developing countries, or even transitional economy nations.

The second important point, which increases the interest of developed countries in ecologising economic relations, derives from their dominating position in terms of forces of production. The fact is that, by pursuing an active policy to increase the environmental factor share in practical policies of all nations, they do not forget to strengthen their economic positions in the world economy. It is no coincidence then that the Declaration on Environment and Development, adopted in Rio de Janeiro in 1992, included a provision that to fight the degradation of the environment, nations must co-operate in creating a favourable and open international economic system, which would lead to economic growth and sustainable development across the world.

Developed countries strengthened their active participation in globalising processes by a powerful environmental argument; although there is no direct link between development and the current globalisation model.

On the contrary, there is an obvious interest that industrialised countries have in maintaining their leading position in the world community. Here, developed countries' hegemonic tendencies manifest themselves once again. Meanwhile, logic requires at least, equality between participants of the process of preventing a global cataclysm. Moreover, a question may arise about changes and revision of the status of some nations in resolving global problems in the context of their contribution to the worsening of environmental conditions, and to the improvement and maintaining of the environment at a stable level. This frightens industrialised countries; they fear losing, in the end, the status of being the world's leading nations, which is so important for them.

Currently, ecologisation strengthens the position of industrialised nations. This is because the expected re-orientation of the world community to environmental effects will help those countries keep their long-term leading roles, which firstly, can produce ecologically friendly products; and secondly, can give and sell machinery with minimum impact on the environment. The faster the ecologising process of the world economy will be, the stronger the position will be of those countries that are at the cutting edge of scientific-technical revolution. This gives advantages primarily to developed countries, which now possess resource-saving and ecologically efficient technologies, the sale of which will strengthen their leading global market status.

Existing interrelations and interdependences between countries of the world have already brought us to the realisation of the necessity to form a single administrative centre, both at the level of the entire community, and at the regional and national levels. Numerous scholarly discussions about the need to create a world government are now entering the implementation dimension, for which the Planetary Project is ready to act as a catalyst.

CHAPTER 10

Concept of Managed Harmony

Concept underlying ideas. Managed harmony, planetary world order and noospheric civilisation. Planetary anti-crisis management. Differences between the Concept of Managed Harmony and the Concept of Sustainable Development. Managed Harmony results criteria: methods and calculation formulas. Environmental Sphere Development Index. Economic Sphere Development Index. Driving forces of this new way of development.

As we said earlier, the Concept of Sustainable Development has already been popularised and developed for several years. However, it has not shown sufficient effectiveness in its practical implementation and resulting macropolitical, macroeconomic, and macrosocial changes that would make a genuine contribution to solving global problems, especially preventing a global environmental catastrophe.

Chapter 3 of this book outlines fundamental systemic critique of the Concept of Sustainable Development from the Planetary Project perspective.

The complex dynamic and interrelation of biospheric evolutionary processes and civilisation is normally referred to as the system "nature – society – person". Understanding it brings us to the conclusion that the Concept of Sustainable Development does not address many parts of this system and its diachronic and asymmetric processes, which are characterised by a different degree of intensiveness in different regions of the world and different communities. Analysis and criticism of the Concept of Sustainable Development has brought us to a review of a number of tenets of the theory, and a realisation of the necessity to considerably modernise it and further develop its correct ideas. This is how we developed our own *concept of managed harmony*, which can underlie the paradigm of *planetary world order* and *noospheric civilisation*.

We can say that the Concept of Managed Harmony implies looking at world processes and problems from slightly different theoretical and methodological perspectives compared to those of the Concept of Sustainable Development; our view is the view of social scientists and economists.

The **Concept of Managed Harmony** underlies the Planetary Project philosophy; and the **Concept of Sustainable Development** largely inspires a new vision of the global crisis and humanity's alternative prospects. What do they have in common? In common are the Concept of Sustainable Development key principles that we share and assimilate in the context of our assessment of the current world situation, namely:

- The world, as we know it today, is on the brink of destruction caused by the anthropogenic factor objectified by the current civilisation activity;

- Civilisation itself is at a deadlock and negates itself; it recognises its deep crisis nature and is not satisfied with the fruits of its prior development;
- People are now facing a complex but urgent problem of global choice;
- Global problem solutions must be science based and take into account objective laws of nature and society;
- Economic growth must be limited, production and consumption modified, but it can only be done without harming national-economic and political interests of individual countries to avoid provoking a world war;
- Mankind must follow the path of progress by meeting its needs without harming nature;
- Economic growth has objectively become the source and genetic mechanism of global problems, but it is not possible to stop it by conventional means.

Unlike the Concept of Sustainable Development, the *Concept of Managed Harmony* has:

- Alternative understanding of the process of development and its modern requirements;
- Identifying development driving forces;
- Specific solutions in terms of harmonious development management schemes, mechanisms, and techniques.

Seeing a clear picture of the current systemic civilisation crisis, the threat of a Third World War and an environmental catastrophe, and the total risks caused by unresolved global problems, we deem it necessary to launch immediately the process of global human integration to prevent a planetary collapse, save the biosphere, and build a just world order.

The ultimate goal of this process is the creation of a noospheric civilisation based on resource substitution production, creative economy and biocompatible culture, with *WE-humanity* and *the integrated person* as its agents. The strategic prospect is revealing human cosmic potential, and implementing people's planetary mission to explore outer space actively.

Managed harmony will be the paradigm of advancement in these directions, and at the same time the form of existence for post-crisis humanity and the planetary community. In the framework of the Planetary Project, *Managed Harmony* will be the paradigm of moving in these directions and, simultaneously, a form of existence for post-crisis humanity and the planetary community.

The name itself makes it clear that our concept of planetary development purposefully and consciously emphasises and strengthens the following key points of civilisation development:

- Goal-orientedness, integration and synchronicity;
- Comprehensive and systemic character;
- Centralised manageability;
- Balance, co-ordination and regulation.

When developing any social development concept, its authors inevitably face the question of what development model they can see unfolding in human history. The answer to this question largely determines the meaning we can put into both the

Concept of Sustainable Development and the *Concept of Managed Harmony*. Moreover, modern social science, especially western sociology, has largely abandoned the idea of development by substituting it with the concept of social change.

In disputes over the meaning of history, particularly the *problem of social and civilisation development*, we profess a positive, if fundamentally critical, position. We recognise the existence and objective character of personal and social development as an inalienable and fundamental feature of anthropo-sociogenesis. The current historical stage is when civilisation has come up the closest to the abyss of self-destruction together with the entire planetary biosphere. We believe that, at this stage, growth and development processes cannot be left unmanaged any longer, as they have been until now.

The most important aspects of positive historical development results are: economic, scientific-technical, social-political, and cultural. They are meant to benefit the individual and society. However, it has happened only partially and selectively; whereas negative consequences of unrestrained economic growth have proved to be universal. These include: the excessive anthropogenic pressure on the biosphere; barbaric exploitation and exhaustion of a whole range of natural resources; and the production and accumulation of weapons of mass destruction. Directly or indirectly, they harm the entire nature, including humans; they put under question the existence of life itself, hastening its imminent death even with the current pace of global problems.

When we talk about "development", we mean: a positive philosophical category of a qualitative increase in the system; improving the interrelation and interaction of its elements and subsystems responsible for the system's further functioning; and reproducing its sustainable evolution on the path to perfection.

Thus, we cannot really talk about any development of society and civilisation if we do not meet the key condition for any further development of the human species on this planet. This key condition is solving global problems, and saving the biosphere as a natural habitat of humans and other living species. This is impossible without global human integration, and the creation of a biocompatible economy and noospheric culture.

As the essential, vitally important objective of humanity is to save itself and solve global problems, humanity must, in essence, transform public development into anti-crisis management through the use initially of available planetary resources, and transform existing global governance institutions into *the system of planetary governance institutions.* This would entail creating new effective instruments for solving global problems.

Planetary crisis management is a transitional stage from the current systemic crisis of the global world, to *managed harmony* of a new planetary world. We understand world development harmonisation quite clearly as a centralised and purposeful process which implies:

- an active role of contemporary humanity especially of its progressively minded public, constructive civil society institutions, scientists and public figures, as well as spiritual and political elites;

- comprehensive development and implementation of effective economic, political-legal, technological, information-communication, and cultural instruments of global problem solving;
- optimising the use of natural resources, transition to natural resource-saving and resource-substitution production, consumption, disposal and waste management;
- construction of an integral creative economic system based on the re-distribution of planetary rent income, and other planetary asset liquidity (including regulation and compensation of economic growth);
- providing financial-economic and other resources for the system of planetary governance institutions formed in part through reforming and modifying existing global institutions (e.g., the UN), but largely by creating qualitatively new bodies;
- improving the health of the environment, reconstructing damaged ecosystems, reviving plant and animal species that are now on the brink of extinction;
- consistent and systemic approach to the Sixth Techno-economic paradigm using large-scale innovation policy, and mass implementation of breakthrough technologies.

The Concept of Managed Harmony implies: activating people as constructive planetary process agents; their evolutionary involvement in correcting historical mistakes; and therapy of their "development diseases" that cause suffering to the environment, which is the biosphere where they belong. As an anti-crisis manager of their own destiny, modern people should not wait for the right moment or the mercy of the higher forces, the cosmos, or providence. The moment is here; and we have neither the luxury nor right to leave our history unmanaged.

It is already in the phase of planetary anti-crisis management that we must start solving the problems of harmonious world design and public development. This must be done on a systematic basis in practically all spheres of the economy, environment, and social policy. From the macro-level of global problems, we must move to the micro-level of the individual as the end consumer of re-globalised society wealth. From the Planetary Project and the Concept of Managed Harmony perspectives, we propose modernising and augmenting UN statistical indexes. A social harmony indicator will be introduced based on the assessment of both the development levels of different social spheres, and the gap between them.

The proposed social harmony criterion must include three blocks: social, environmental, and economic. Each block must have relevant third-level indicators. To evaluate social harmony, we must have required information. Currently, the UN's international statistics provide most global development data. However, this data is not sufficient to assess the quality of life and development harmony. For example, some important quality of life indicators are missing, such as:

- People's cultural and moral level;
- People's satisfaction level with living conditions nationwide (including the country's image assessment);

- People's satisfaction level with living conditions regionally;
- People's satisfaction level with living conditions locally;
- People's satisfaction level with socio-psychological and economic conditions at the microlevel (in the workplace at companies and organisations, and in the family);
- People's satisfaction level with future prospects, social stability, etc.

Based on these blocks, there are social, economic, and environmental indexes, which are further divided into specific indicator sub-indexes.

Sub-indexes are calculated according to the following methodology:

$$J_n = \frac{\hat{y} - y_{min}}{y_{max} - y_{min}} \qquad (5)$$

Where, J_n is the subindex of indicator n;

y, y_{min}, y_{max} is a factual, minimum and maximum value of a quality, respectively;

$$\hat{y} = \begin{cases} \hat{y} = y, y \leq y_{max} \\ \hat{y} = y_{max}, y > y_{max} \end{cases}$$

$\hat{y}$ is the value used in calculations.

Thus, the exceedance of the factual indicator value over the reference one is ignored, because no compensation of low figures for some indicators with super high values of other indicators must take place. Besides, indicators should be put on an ascending scale, for example, from 0 to 1, where 0 is the worst value, while 1 is the reference value.

We suggest the following formula be used to calculate indexes for each sphere (social, environmental, and economic):

$$Ij = \sqrt[n]{J_1 \times J_2 \times ... \times J_n} \qquad (6)$$

We suggest the following formula be used to calculate an integral social harmony indicator:

$$SGDRI = \sqrt[3]{I_1 \times I_2 \times I_3} \qquad (7),$$

Where, *SGDRI* is a social harmony indicator;
I_1, I_2, I_3 are social, environmental, and economic indexes, respectively.

In integral social reproduction indicator calculations, we must use the geometrical mean of its constituent parts (both for the integral indicator and indexes). In this case, the larger gap between constituent elements will yield a lower result value, which manifests social disharmony. Whereas, greater values for one of the constituent parts will equally compensate lower values for another one or other ones, when the geometrical mean is applied. It means that using the geometrical mean allows us not only to assess development, but also to evaluate proportional, harmonious development.

Calculation methodology for individual indexes and sub-indexes looks like this.

Social Sphere Development Index (SSDI).

SSDI includes:

- Life Expectancy Sub-index calculated as expected length of life at birth;
- Education Level Sub-index calculated as an aggregated adult literacy index (two thirds) and a total number of learners at first, second, and third level educational institutions (one third);
- Individual Income Equitability Coefficient (IIEC).

We propose that UN Human Development Index calculation methodology be used to calculate Life Expectancy and Education Level Sub-indexes, i.e., according to the following formula:

$$J_n = \frac{y - y_{min}}{y_{max} - y_{min}} \quad (8)$$

Where, J_n is the sub-index for indicator n;
y, y_{min}, y_{max} are factual, minimum and maximum values for a quality, respectively.

To build sub-indexes, fixed maximum and minimum values have been set (y_{min}, y_{max}):

- Life expectancy at birth: 25 and 85 years;
- Adult literacy (age 15 years and older): 0% and 100%;
- Total number of learners: 0% and 100%.

Concerning IIEC, differentiation has a much deeper impact on social development and does not confine itself to income re-evaluation. This is an extremely important end orientation and social policy effectiveness indicator. Therefore, income differentiation must be calculated as an SDI separate category.

For this purpose, IIEC has been introduced in the Social Harmony Index social block as a separate component (along with life expectancy and education level indicators).

According to the theorem, a geometrical mean cannot exceed an arithmetic mean. Besides, the more a quality varies, *the lower its geometrical mean value will be compared with its arithmetic mean value.* Vice versa, the arithmetic and geometrical means coincide at zero dispersion (with zero standard deviation), i.e., with absolute income parity for the entire population. Thus, the geometrical mean carries some information about the variability of quality.

In this regard, we suggest a new income differentiation indicator calculated as the ratio of a geometrical mean and an arithmetic mean of incomes *(individual income equitability coefficient):*

$$IIEI = \frac{\prod_i x_i^{a_i}}{\sum_i a_i \times x_i} \quad ; \quad \sum a_i = 1 \qquad (9)$$

Where, x_i is the income of population group i; a_i is the share of group i in the total population.

Values for this indicator vary between 0 (in the event of absolute income inequality) and 1 (in the event of absolute income equality across the whole population). Thus, there is no need to create an additional IIEI-based sub-index as we can use IIEI to calculate SDI.

Formula (7) is used for selective data. When income distribution approaches the lognormal law, we can easily demonstrate that for the general totality this coefficient moves to the value:

$$IIEC = \frac{Me(x)}{M(x)} = e^{-\frac{\sigma^2}{2}} \qquad (10)$$

Where, *Me(x)* is distribution median (it is equal to the geometrical mean value in lognormal distribution);

M(x) is the mathematical expectation of income value;

σ^2 is the income logarithm dispersion.

By comparing coefficient values in (9) and (10), we can indirectly assess the correspondence of the empirical distribution to the lognormal law.

The proposed IIEI has some advantages over existing differentiation indicators:

1) Unlike quantile or fund coefficients, it takes account of information about the entire distribution (as does, in fact, the Gini coefficient).
2) Unlike the Gini Coefficient, the IIEI scale is not sensitive to the fact that quantile data is used in calculations, whereas, when we, for example, evaluate a Gini Coefficient with deciles, we can easily show that its scale covers the interval of 0÷0.9, and with quantiles the interval of 0÷0.8, etc. Therefore, to assess a Gini Coefficient

correctly (especially for high values), we would need to use quite detailed initial data (e.g., percentiles).
3) The methodology of calculating IIEI is simpler than that of the Gini Coefficient. Calculation results are quite satisfactory if decile data is used.

Environment Sphere Development Index (ESDI)

The environmental block is based on the Environmental Sustainability Index (ESI) calculated by Yale and Columbia Universities, USA. It uses 76 variables, grouped in 21 indicators, which, in their turn, compose 5 components: "Environmental Systems", "Reducing Environmental Stresses", "Reducing Human Vulnerability", "Social and Institutional Capacity", and "Global Stewardship".

Two ESI components are used to calculate ESDI as environmental subindexes:

- "Environmental Systems" has the following five indicators: "Air Quality", "Water Quality", "Water Quantity", "Biodiversity", and "Land";
- "Reducing Environmental Stresses" has the following six indicators: "Reducing Air Pollution", "Reducing Ecosystem Stress", "Reducing Population Stress", "Reducing Waste & Consumption Pressures", "Reducing Water Stress", and "Natural Resource Management".

Each indicator, constituting the above sub-indexes, consists of variables. Thirty-eight variables are used to calculate the two components (sub-indexes) presented above.

ESDI calculation is based on the Environmental Sustainability Index calculation methodology, with the only difference that the two above components were chosen out of the five that are the most important and relevant to society's environmental development level. The fact is that the "Environmental Systems" component reflects the state of the environment in all its spheres, whereas the "Reducing Environmental Stresses" reflects changing levels of human pressure on the environment.

Since ESDI includes many diverse indicators, we should approach responsibly the issue of normalising and standardising data. To do that, all initial data (variables) is tested for distribution normality and is modified, if necessary (e.g., logarithmically), which removes distribution asymmetry and remainder heteroscedasticity. Then the modified sets are standardised according to the following formula:

$$z = \frac{x - \bar{x}}{\sigma} \qquad (11)$$

Where, z are standardised variable values;
x is a factual variable value;
$\bar{x}$ is a mean variable value in sampling;
σ is the standard variable deviation.

The above formula is used if higher variable values correspond to a more favourable state of the environment (e.g., biodiversity, fertility, etc.). If lower variable values are environmentally better (e.g., amount of emissions), the numerator uses an inverse subtraction, i.e., the factual variable value is subtracted from the mean variable value.

Further, some indicators have a simple arithmetic mean of the standardised variables it includes.

Sub-indexes are calculated as the simple arithmetic mean of indicators, converted into a normal distribution function (in this case, the range of subindex variation is 0÷1).

Finally, to calculate an ESDI index value, we find a geometrical mean value of two subindexes: "Environmental System" and "Reducing Ecosystem Stress".

Economic Sphere Development Index (ESDI)

We only included one indicator—a per capita GDP—in the economic block when calculating a HSD Index. The Per Capita GDP Indicator is not only considered a final economic indicator, but also as a variable that reflects society development areas unaccounted in other blocks. Meanwhile, the per capita GDP arithmetic mean value variable is not an optimum one for international comparison, just as the "patient's mean temperature" is not the best indicator for a hospital!

First, it is easy to demonstrate that it does not depend on dispersion, which is one of the most important distribution characteristics.

Second, it is possible to show that it is strongly affected by fluctuations in the right-hand side of the distribution, i.e., an income increase of the richest minority quite strongly affects the per capita income of the whole population.

Third, this variable can hardly be considered a mean one, if we consider the fact that over half of the population (up to 75%) makes less than the "mean" level.

In light of this, we must change the calculation methodology for a mean per capita income, so that it contains income differentiation data.

Our studies have showed that population income distribution follows the lognormal law in all countries. Therefore, we must use the mean income logarithm, corresponding to the geometrical mean.

Thus, it would be logical to presume that the mean income variable could be calculated using the arithmetic mean income logarithm exponent, which would correspond to the income geometrical mean, because:

$$\overline{\ln x} = \sum_i a_i \times \ln x_i = \sum_i \ln x_i^{a_i} = \ln \prod_i x_i^{a_i} \; ; \quad \sum a_i = 1 \qquad (12)$$

Where, $e^{\overline{\ln x}} = \prod x_i^{a_i}$ is the income geometrical mean of the entire population.

The Per Capita GDP Sub-index calculation is carried out based on the UN methodology for HDI. Generally, the UN income index is calculated according to the following formula:

$$W(y) = \frac{\lg y - \lg y_{min}}{\lg y_{max} - \lg y_{min}} \qquad (13)$$

Where:
y is the arithmetic mean GDP per capita;
y_{min} is the minimum GDP level taken to be USD 100;

y_{max} is the maximum GDP level taken to be USD 40,000.

We use an income geometrical mean; therefore, we set the lowest and highest values to be USD 100 and USD 36,000, respectively. The highest value corresponds to the arithmetic mean value of USD 40,000 (according to the UN methodology) and IIEI to be 0.900, which is part of SDI. Thus, the Per Capita GDP Sub-index is calculated as follows:

$$J_n = \frac{\lg(y) - \lg(100)}{\lg(36000) - \lg(100)} \qquad (13)$$

In the end, this subindex will equal ESDI, because it has no other economic subindexes.

So, what are harmonious development and managed harmony from the Planetary Project perspective? They mean a programme of comprehensive and practical changes in all interrelationships and interdependences of the system «person – society – nature». They are aimed at saving and improving the health of the biosphere; and then building the relations necessary for people to return to the environment more than they take out, to save its balance, and to maintain planetary life reproduction. However, unlike the Concept of Sustainable Development, we insist on the necessity to solve all major global problems, not just those affecting the environment. A suitable financial and economic base should be in place to introduce real and radical changes: policy and education on their own are not sufficient. If it is to be effective, harmonising management should have a solid foundation in the economic instruments. In other words, their objective sustainability quality will depend on the level and influence of normative-legal, administrative, cultural, and information management instruments.

Using the concept of *"harmony"* in our socio-economic construction and historical-civilisation modelling, we are completely aware of the risk of being accused of idealism or even utopianism, at least by sceptics and pessimists. Nevertheless, we think that this notion is sufficiently scientific and theoretically sound to use as a basis for a social development theory. Moreover, it meets the criteria and reflects the nature the Planetary Project because, as a philosophical category, harmony implies consonance and balance of diverse and even opposing elements as *many in one.*

The word "harmony" is of Greek origin, and it carries the idea of integral wholeness of all living things in the cosmos. This can be possible only due to the internal reasonable order that is capable of being grasped by the human mind. Harmony keeps things in wise agreement in the world. This agreement is accessible to human understanding, and is the opposite of *chaos.*

The dialectical relationship of *chaos, cosmos, and harmony* in the philosophical tradition of Ancient Greece from Heraclitus and Pythagoras to Aristotle and Nicomachus, described *systematicity* and *manageability* vs. *accidentalness* and *shapelessness* as development stages of nature and society. Later, harmony started to be applied to characterising and evaluating regularities, commensurate combinations, consistent dynamics, and managed systems. It is also important that the concept of harmony include the idea of the identity of thinking and being, at least in the sense that the orderliness of thinking is possible due the orderliness of nature.

In our view, to apply the concept of "harmony" to social reality is relevant if only due to: the existence of such institutional mechanisms of enforcing social order through human activity as *education, morality,* and *law;* as well as to such macrosocial mechanisms as democratisation, progress, and cross-cultural relations. At the same time, it is clear that to describe the whole civilisation context as harmonious is quite problematic. This inevitably poses a question about: the substrate and agent of history; the role of people and social groups of various types, and the organisational structure in it; the linearity and vectors of historical development; and about progress and regress. We do not deny historical plurality as a scholarly position either from ideological or methodological points of view. However, we say today that the time of this plural diversity is over. We are living through the stage when humanity must either take the path leading to the abyss of self-destruction, or to integration mobilisation and systemic development management and growth transformation. There may not be another cycle of history after this one.

Concerning our understanding of social driving forces and managed harmony administrators, we would hesitate to pass categorical judgment about the entire *humanity* when our civilisation faces the most comprehensive crisis it has ever faced. This notion seems problematic to us now due to the lack of unity and solidarity in people today.

At the current stage of the systemic civilisation crisis and the deepening of global problems, from the Planetary Project perspective, we see the anti-crisis management potential in the elites alone: national, regional, continental, and international elites. By the term *elites*, we do not mean specific small or closed club-like organisations, but the best representatives of communities, organised by professional, party, cultural or any other principle. It is important that they would clearly understand global problems, risks, and threats that humanity faces today. They believe in the necessity to save nature, people, and society by all acceptable modernising means, breakthrough technologies, and legal and economic instruments. They realise that humanity must unite to be able to achieve this goal.

Indeed, elites formed by this principle (to be more exact, existing elites, especially scholarly communities) can act as drivers of a new–*managed*– type of global development. What is left is to integrate themselves and to give them a clear systemic vision of planetary resources and the mechanisms of their use, all of which is the goal of the *Planetary Project*. The problem is that they are often critical of such a complex, contradictory, and problem-ridden construct as "humanity".

According to anthropologists, historians, and sociologies, Homo sapiens is characterised by features that not only considerably differentiate it from other living organisms in terms of life sustenance and behaviour patterns, but also seriously impede its integration at the level of its kind. For instance, determining qualification of a *human population* can vary, which, according to the notable Russian historian Lev Gumilyov, can sometimes be viewed as a social entity, while in other contexts as an ethnos. He also noted a core feature of any ethnos (just as any other type of a human collective) is to unite based on being in opposition to non-members of their group. This opposition is so deep-seated and stereotypical, that it covered both the conscious and subconscious motives, actions and behaviour patterns of most people. It manifests itself in the worldview, culture, art, ideology, social, and political practices. It is activated when humans need to defend their territory, and when they want to establish "their" identity, often protecting their irrational and symbolic *fantasies*, removed both from the common sense and from any instinct. This factor, coupled with heightened sexuality, typical of any primate, stimulates the expansiveness of humanity, which greatly exceeds the aggression level of any other mammals.

Meanwhile, human psychic organisation has intellectual (reasonable-rational), artistic, moral-ethical and spiritual components, which, together, constitute the basis for communication, co-operation, generating meaning and social goods for all people. Only due to such *cloud categories* as "universal human values", "world culture", "international practices", and the "collective intelligence", we have a legitimate and moral right to raise the question of humanity as the united planetary phenomenon.

In other words, only registered, constructive and centripetal trends in human interaction enable us to admit the possibility of human integration into a real single humanity. The entire historical process has proven this, especially its current global stage that may be viewed both in terms of systemic problems and crises, and in terms of a dialogue of *civilisations*.

Unfortunately, we can talk about "humanity" in its biological sense rather than in its political, social, or cultural senses. **Humanity** is a phenomenon that can realise its potential only at the planetary level. It is yet to be born, and faces the threat of its own demise. There are very many prerequisites but only one chance for it to happen. This is what is needed to realise that chance:

- A united mobilising planetary integration ideology;
- A correct, balanced, compromise-based strategy for all participants;
- Effective instruments of communication, organisation, and management;
- Sufficient financial, legal, and political resources;
- A well-adjusted system of administrative institutions;
- High technologies for all project infrastructures;
- Monitoring and regulation at all stages.

We believe that integrating our contemporaries into a full-fledged humanity as a planetary (in the future: cosmic) agent, capable of saving themselves and their habitat, is quite possible even at the current civilisation development level with all its flaws. All we need to do is apply **planetary goodwill** based on: a systemic understanding of the crisis; biological and spiritual solidarity; an ontological relationship with all forms of organic life; and on natural survival and procreation needs.

Planetary ethics strives to combine these objectives, understanding them, and transforming them into an integration motivation at the spiritual synthesis level.

Planetary ethics must lay the foundations for the worldview of a *modern anti-crisis person*, then of an integration person as a *managed harmony agent*, and, in end, of a *planetary person*, actively exploring outer space.

CHAPTER 11

Planetary Ethics

Necessity to change fundamentally public consciousness. Unified mobilisation anti-crisis integration ideology and planetary ethics. Universalism and compromise-based character. Planetary ethics problems and application areas, external and internal objectives. Planetary ethics direction and goal. Its complimentary character vis-à-vis world religions and constructive spiritual teachings. Global spiritual synthesis.

Saving the biosphere and laying the foundations of a noospheric civilisation are integral and interrelated processes. This is explained by the fact that the goals of self-preservation and further creative development equally require global human integration as their basic condition. No nation, however technically and morally developed it may be, can fulfill these global goals alone.

Transition from the current systemic crisis of the global world to planetary anti-crisis management of transitional humanity, and later to managed harmony of the planetary world and noospheric civilisation with the prospects of space exploration, is the most large-scale project in our common history; commensurate, perhaps, only with the emergence of Homo sapiens. Only this step can give people a chance to save themselves and all organic life. It will require concentration of all reasonable, progressive forces of people: starting with the elites, this process must involve masses of people in all countries of the world.

We must be very careful when formulating motivation to participate in global human integration, and creating a single economy and global governing institutions, i.e., to establish a *new world order*, however good this movement might be. We understand quite well that there is a certain risk of being misunderstood. Self-preservation should ideally be *voluntary,* even when such an endeavour as the collective salvation of life on Earth is the most important endeavour of any that could be considered. This is the case at least for its drivers, leaders, and people making strategic decisions in their communities. Of course, we mean here representatives of the elites who could be able to take an active part in planetary anti-crisis management; those who share the values of the Planetary Project and the Concept of Managed Harmony and could lead their loyal groups.

The voluntary character of participating in the Planetary Project implies, first, that people perceive its ideas and values through profound understanding, comprehensive examination, and strong personal conviction. Such strong negative motivations as fear and anxiety about the present and the future should be complimented by positive mobilisation stimuli such as common sense, creative and innovation impulse, inspiration, and even business interest.

It seems so simple: it is equally obvious that global problems are in their most drastic stage, nature and civilisation are under threat of perishing, and that we need to do something to save the biosphere and make people's life harmonious from social and environmental perspectives. Basic instincts and moral-ethical principles must work here: they have been tested by centuries of human history. However, collision and conflict start as soon as it comes to collective action to carry out world integration, redistribution of spheres of influence, power dispersion, and reconciling local and planetary interests.

In principle, it is quite easy to put them into economic, property, and financial categories and resolve them. It is enough to find and activate necessary resources, financial means and political-legal mechanisms. It is much more difficult to deal with conflicts and collisions that have to do with mentality, subjective cultural differences, psychology, religion, and morality.

In *everyday life,* the archetypes and stereotypes, sacred symbols and prejudices, ideals and self-identification complexes of socio-historical organisms act as overt or covert reference points. These socio-historical bodies include national, ethnic, cultural or social groups, ranging from traditionalists to sect followers, and from party members to football fans. Rational methodology of raising awareness or persuasion is not always effective in these cases; appeals to obvious truth fail if we do not know specific communication codes of group identity, and cannot use them.

The beginning of the third millennium of human history is witnessing the deterioration of traditional problems and the emergence of new ones, threatening the existence of life on Earth. Some of these problems are: social stratification; impoverishment and chronic undernourishment that plague a sixth of all humanity; a reluctance to understand each other; dramatic clashes of cultures and civilisations, and the resulting international terrorism. In their basis lies not only increasing economic social-economic differentiation, but also a different understanding of the fundamental values that determine the way of life and social well-being of nations populating this planet. For example, most people do not see sufficient reason for global human unification. Moreover, they believe that global human integration will rob them of their independence, the right for which they have only within their closed communities (countries), and bury their traditional identity forever.

These phobias are created and fuelled by political radicals of all shades and colours, as well as Nazis, nationalists, and ultra-right conservatives: all those whom the famous twentieth century philosopher of science, Karl Popper, called *enemies of open society*. In this context, we must argue our position both rationally and ethically stating that, at the stage of planetary anti-crisis management, we will only deal with economic integration aimed at creating a united distribution system, and program funding of global problem solving sourced from planetary rent income. Economic integration will not affect negatively either national sovereignty or cultural diversity, just as technological integration has only enriched them.

In the same way, most national governments do not want to abandon their national interests for the sake of global ones. Our answer will be that any private, narrow, local interests are too feeble in the face of global risks and threats. These include for instance: an approaching environmental catastrophe; a technogenic or financial collapse; and the threat of a Third World War, which in estimations, would be the last bold-type full stop on human history. No national, regional, clan, or corporate interests, will not be significant if they harm universal, planetary interests. They will simply not be satisfied, or if they are, the effect will not be long-lived. Nuclear powers should especially understand this.

The same is true about nations that deny universal human values and human rights. As a rule, this is an indicator of the fact that in those countries, the *private individual* has incommensurably limited rights dramatically removed from the classical ideals of civil society. Nevertheless, to find a way to agreement and peace we must thoroughly analyse civilisation differences in national cultures, behaviour norms, customs and traditions, and other informal institutions.

We are entering the realm of ethical, moral and ideological issues, ultimately of a value-symbolic character. Hence, the need for **planetary ethics**, capable of laying a foundation of a new worldview meeting the goals of planetary anti-crisis management and future managed harmony.

A monumental task faces humanity as part of the Planetary Project: to create conditions for fundamental changes in public consciousness, mass beliefs, national mentality, and finally, the *people's self-identification.* In other words, it is necessary to persuade leading scientists, politicians, economists, and social activists, as well as leaders of ethnic-cultural movements and churches to shift from words to action in solving global problems, saving the biosphere, and integrating humanity. They must be equipped with necessary information and communication instruments to disseminate Planetary Project ideas among their followers, and later among the wider public.

We need a *united mobilisation anti-crisis integration ideology.* At the initial stage of the planetary "rescue operation" it will work as an instrument of enlightenment and propaganda to involve people in integration processes, new production, and economic models, co-operation and consumption, as well as motivation and behaviour. Later, it will have to perform *a paradigm shift* in the modern belief system taking it from: a crisis to an anti-crisis phase; then to biocentric, compatible with managed harmony strategy; and then to the phase of planetary self-identification contributing to the fulfillment of humanity's space mission. The planetary type of thinking is possible not only due to a leap in science and technology and the dominance of rationalism of the Sixth Techno-economic Paradigm, but also due to *a global spiritual synthesis* that needs to be carried out through the joint efforts of all constructive social forces of the modern world.

To develop, launch, and assimilate a single mobilisation anti-crisis integration ideology, which is in line with Planetary Project objectives, and make it truly influential, it must contain more than scientific arguments, utilitarian-practical schemes, programmes of action and solutions in the fields economy, politics, law, ecology, and social reform. It is not enough to have information alone, however logically flawless it might be.

To transform consciousness significantly, judgement, motivation, and interest, it is not enough to involve only rational reasoning; especially when it comes to making choices and accepting limits. It requires deeper psychological influence. In this regard, we are fully aware of the significance of the figurative, emotional-psychological, moral-ethical and spiritual components of human decision-making motivation. Even ultimately proving to be *irrational*, this side of human motivation plays, perhaps, a bigger role than the rational side. It is in the nature of man: thousands of years of human evolution have not made him a fully rational being. This is not strange; it is normal and natural, since the basic motivation–*the motivation to live*–incorporates instincts, impulses and desires that play as big a role as reason.

However, here as well, things are much more complicated than they seem: the problem is that instinct must be spiritualised to the same extent that an action could be stimulated by motivation. Various studies in psychology, philosophy, and human behaviour sociology have yielded the same conclusion about the necessity for an action to have *sufficient reasons*. The notion of such sufficient reasons is backed by an act of will, and expressed in the form of motivation; it is then necessarily checked against the value "compass" of a person or group. The dominant status of *value* for human activity is explained by the fact that values (as objectified or subjectified desires), normally, underlie motivation, decision-making, and active behaviour.

One of the most important civilisation aspects is the legal basis of economic relations. The fact that different nations have different cultures and moral values usually means that they will have different methods of carrying out economic activity. German sociologist Max Weber was the first to notice and appreciate this interdependence. He tied economic ethics with a dominant religious tradition.

Any human activity requires understanding and motivation. Collective activity, especially, needs them because it is based on the common vision of goals, objectives and means that are adequate and optimal for their implementation. Experience shows that success is guaranteed for deeply understood and adequately motivated activity that has gone through the actor's internal critical filters and personal value system. The requirement that results are realistic is secondary.

Thus, it becomes clear that the Planetary Project dissemination, public awareness and communication objectives can be effectively resolved; and they can lead to needed worldview transformations only if they are justified and warranted from a spiritual-value perspective. In other words, to be convincing even to the elites, to claim loyalty and become a cause to fight for, Planetary Project *mobilisation anti-crisis integration ideology* must operate equally by facts, figures, values, spiritual principles and moral-ethical categories. **Planetary ethics** is in charge of creating an axiological basis of the Planetary Project.

Developing and substantiating planetary ethics is a primary objective as part of developing and promoting the Planetary Project. This responsible work will have fundamental significance for the Project's popularity and success, because we have to win the hearts and minds of future supporters of the great mission of saving the biosphere, global human unification, and creating integral humanity in the form of noospheric civilisation. Planetary ethics does not exist yet; it has yet to be created. We have a clear understanding of its necessity, and vision of its applications, key external and internal objectives, as well as of the basic points of reference and axiomatic articulation.

We have an intuitive understanding of the source of planetary ethics as a truly unifying, universal force based on compromise vis-à-vis multiple value systems that belong to various nations, and characterise different languages, cultures, religions, and rational and mystical constructive teachings. We refer to the source and universalism ability of planetary ethics as ***global spiritual synthesis***.

Accepting values and meanings of the Concept of Sustainable Development (especially when it concerns the interdependence of the environment and economy), we still have to admit that biocentric and global problem-solving ethics must be broader and more decisive than the disparate postulates of the Concept of Sustainable Development. Planetary ethics must be systemic, universal, biocompatible, practical and realistic; but it also has to incorporate diverse cultural and civilisation spiritual experience. For planetary ethics to be able to do that, we must cast an impartial and responsible look at the problematic situation that the Concept of Sustainable Development first found itself in, and the current situation with Planetary Project, the Concept of Managed Harmony and future planetary ethics.

We mean here the problems that act as a sort of "supplement" to objective global problems. In its turn, it results from global processes reflecting in specific socio-cultural mentalities, which assess differently and demonstrate a different attitude to nature, life, integration, justice, human rights, social development, etc.

Such issues facing planetary ethics could be referred to as cultural-psychological and social-ethical. The following are the biggest among them:

- global world exists, whereas neither global community nor global consciousness exists;
- no spiritual-ethical and value grounds for integration models, environment protection practices or joint resource management have yet been developed; by the way, no universal or compromise-based models exist in principle;
- universal human values and human rights do not enjoy universal respect and instead of being shared face unconstructive criticism and resistance from some cultures and ideologies;
- biocentric, vitality, and environmental values are not accepted on a global scale or in all ideological forms; on the contrary, they are discredited and devalued under the guise of pseudo-spiritual interpretations;
- destructive cults are widespread, popular, and influential in many countries, while authoritarian and totalitarian sects, extremist, and militaristic ideologies threaten human life,

health, rights, and mental health as well as the integrity and quality of the ecosystems, and plant and animal life.

The above and other general and private problems cover the planetary ethics application area. We must solve these problems by changing constructively people's worldview and mentality, and by acting flexibly in the communication space between civilisations. Hence, we have planetary ethics external and internal objectives.

Planetary ethics ***external objectives*** will be directed at the public; they will deal with contradictions of mass consciousness, individual mentality, and cultural issues, their conflicts and paradoxes. They may include:

- Contributing to institutional understanding (through education, public awareness and religion), and spiritualisation of world objectives of saving the biosphere, global problem solving, and attainment of social justice and harmonious development;
- Creating a compromise-based model of global human integration and its universal spiritual-ethical justification;
- Moral-ethical justification of limiting economic, needs and population growth;
- Propagating bio-centric, vitality and environmental values and motives in the life of society and the individual, their rehabilitation, and basing them in culture;

- Constructing noospheric priority ranking in accordance with value-symbolic codes of the most influential world cultures and religions;
- Creating a new value-symbolic code of planetary consciousness, and the self-identification initially of the anti-crisis person and later of the *integral person* as a planetary agent.

In addition to the above large-scale strategic external objectives, planetary ethics will deal with smaller, tactical "field tasks", but they are not less important or timely because of that. They include, for example:

- Driving military values out of socialisation mechanisms and ethically positive cultural archetypes;
- Moral "cleansing" of politics;
- Ecological education at early stages of personal development, etc.

Planetary ethics **internal objectives** will involve the formation, development, self-development and self-justification of planetary ethics. In this regard, we must formulate our own axiological axioms and postulates, generate principles and values, norms and symbols, and formulate hypotheses. It is clear that the central reference framework should include the values of life, naturalness and harmony. At the Planetary Project's initial stage, the most important internal objectives of planetary ethics can be represented in the following statements:

- Clear formulation of planetary environmental imperative;

- Clarification of the essence, origin, content, structure and purpose of the phenomenon of *spirituality* as human ontological quality;
- Development of the ideas of panpsychism and holism interpreting the world of nature and people as a single living organism;
- Review of the categories of development, progress, harmony in relation to society, bio-centric consciousness, history; and a comparative civilisation analysis in the spirit of the Planetary Project;
- Revealing the internal potential of planetary ethics for further psychological and ethical human evolution.

The draft formulation of a ***planetary environmental imperative*** could be the following: any systemic social activity (including at the level of the world community and national economies), which influences nature and its processes, and people and their relations, must be based on ecosystem inviolability, interests of integrating humanity, and their strict enforcement. In this connection, the only civilisation that is acceptable and justifiable is the one whose key values would be *life* in all its productive-symbiotic manifestations, and the protection of ecosystem equilibrium and reproduction. This civilisation includes humans as well as diverse plant and animal life, natural resources, and the ecosystem.

It is clear, however, that postulating the values and principles of planetary ethics should be the collective law-making activity of all global integration players; with their rights, interests and values being honoured if they serve the ultimate goals of saving the biosphere, and implementing the idea of managed social harmony.

The planetary ethics ***direction*** is dynamic and evolutionary (this is its main innovative difference from traditional, self-absorbed kinds of ethics): it is meant to ensure that people consistently pass through stages of their already *managed history* from current civilisation's anti-crisis mobilisation to opening planetary possibilities, and realising their cosmic potential as part of a noospheric biocompatible civilisation they build themselves.

The planetary ethics *goal* stays constant at all foreseeable stages; it is to harmonise people through systemic and stable synchronization of reasonable-rational and imaginative-intuitive qualities of their soul as spiritual faculties. We view the dynamics of planetary ethics in the Planetary Project as a transition from the effect of paradigm shift and elite integration mobilisation, to the effect of creating a new mass ideology for the Earth's population. It is important to note that neither the direction nor the objectives of planetary ethics contradict world religions and constructive spiritual teachings, which is confirmed by Planetary Project research.

It is important to note that many scholars believe that major faiths have a lot in common despite their apparent differences. To start with, this similarity concerns basic truths. All religions teach us to be good and just; they condemn vices and show us their path to salvation. Major religions are also united in teaching that people are brothers. This understanding naturally follows from the idea of one God. However, all religions apply the idea of human brotherhood primarily to their own followers. This can be explained by the fact that religious associations focus on the external side of their faith rather than on their basic core. To achieve peace and conciliation we must consistently emphasise what unites us rather than what separates us as different nations, cultures, and civilisations.

The planetary ethics project contradicts neither current ethics scholarship nor basic ethics research questions. On the contrary, we are ready to be engaged in researching, for example, human nature from the points of view of the Planetary Project and the Concept of Managed Harmony. The objective is that it is most important to reconcile personal interests and needs with recognising a person's planetary responsibility as an integral part of nature. People can find this accord in the spirit as the supersensible basis of their existence.

Moreover, the planetary ethics project is an integral part of the whole reform line of the philosophical discipline that emerged in the early twentieth century due to the criticism of the *normative paradigm* by the founder of European analytic philosophy, George Edward Moore. His movement started with classicism, went through meta-ethics and descriptive empirical ethics to end up as applied ethics, which now looks more like an expanding family of special ethics ranging from bioethics to deontological, to political and journalism ethics. The essence of these transformations is in the ethical discourse naturally drifting from research to explanation and transformation, and from beholding to vigorous action. From being an abstract theoretical discipline, ethics is becoming practical. It is adapting increasingly to real moral-ethical, spiritual, value and behavioural problems of living people. It is trying to resolve concrete contradictions, dilemmas, conflicts and collisions involved in social practices. Modern ethics is entering the tension space filled with the divergent interests of people and social groups, and their values and actions, as well as ideologies generated by social institutions. By doing this, it reveals its historicity and follows the general logic of civilisation development. In this sense, it is becoming increasingly humanistic and rational.

We have already said that we believe global spiritual synthesis to be the source of comprehensive systemic planetary ethics. Now, we must explain what we mean by that. Global spiritual synthesis has three basic meanings in the philosophy of the Planetary Project.

Firstly, *global spiritual synthesis* is a colossal potential of affirmation, understanding, image-based, and rational interpretation of basic biocompatible values including life, nature, love, creation, kinship, solidarity and justice contained in all constructive religions, sciences, mystic systems and teachings. We must only reveal this potential, systematise it, translate it into a modern language, and make it universally understandable and familiar. We believe strongly that *all that is the most important and valuable* for us today, all that is capable of helping people unite and together save the planet and themselves, was already formulated thousands of years ago. Like pearls in their tightly closed shells lying on the bottom of the sea, we can find needed symbols, values and meanings in a multitude of sacred texts, spiritual revelations, metaphysical treatises, scientific theories and novels. It is high time we collected them.

Secondly, by the notion of global spiritual synthesis, we understand the future global work of Planetary Project supporters aimed at finding, extracting, and the comparative analysis of precious meanings of global spiritual experience. Planetary ethics does not need it for collection or decoration: we expect that collected in a certain correct sequence, these clues will be able to crack any cultural code. In other words, we need such universal argumentation that could be capable of involving into the Planetary Project even the most reserved and conservative leaders of communities that have not joined globalisation.

Thirdly, global spiritual synthesis has an equally important objective finally to put the house in order in terms of defining **spirituality** itself. It is time to formulate a contradiction-free, concrete, and positive definition of this most enigmatic quality of human nature, which holds the key to its understanding. We must turn the concept of spirituality into a scientific category stripping it of the narratives of individual religions, occult dogmas and the pressure of various "scientific" theories and ideologies.

Indeed, the concept of spirituality is commonplace in social sciences, political ideologies, religious teachings, occult systems and moral codes. It is commonplace in ethics, everyday discourse, professional communication, and education. Religious worship, literature and journalism have made it a mere truism that does not excite in people any expectation of real meaning or definiteness. In social sciences and humanities, the notion of spirituality tends to be used as a repressive concept alluding to an undifferentiated cultural context. Its positive meaning remains unclarified, as if it were secondary. The notion just "works" in various contexts usually ethically tense and polarised, whereas its own meaning remains essentially unfixed. However, any appearance of spirituality in humanitarian reasoning, discussions or texts legitimately transforms it into a research question raising the issue of its relevance to scientific thinking, philosophic tradition, logical acceptability, and ontological tenability.

Genetically deriving from *spirit*, the concept of spirituality is likely to be: firstly, one of the most ancient thought forms, which emerged in the period of animism; and secondly, be quite developed and logically and methodologically impeccable, as it belongs inherently to human sciences. Is it the case in reality?

Wherever the question about spirituality has ever been raised *in concrete* rather than about something that hides behind this word, there have been a lot of valuable guesses rather than fixed ideas, and symbols and hints rather than thoughts. However, intuitive methods of essential or, in philosophical terms, *eidetic treatment* have yielded the clearest understanding of spirituality, whose experience has tried to rid itself of narrative constraints of any level. Such largely intermediate but very useful intuitions of spirituality have included, for example, revelations regarding its personal character, attitude to behaviour and activity and closeness to but not full identity with *animativeness*.

Cultural history, including philosophy, religion, and science, has always operated the concept of spirit as part of its ethical-political context. This fact has caused the inertia with which spirituality has acquired socio-cultural category features, and become so attractive to various ideologies. However, this movement has confined spirituality to sociological empirical and relativist interpretations of the historical processes, psychologism and opportunistic moralising. You can see this picture in such popular twentieth century movements as Marxism, scientism, and Frankfurt School theories. It seems that they describe spirituality quite convincingly as a certain socio-philosophical concept connected in a systemic way to socialisation mechanisms, and the category of the way of life. However, this technique of supplying the concept with status, and "registering its domicile" within the more or less clear-cut discursive framework, does not add it reflexiveness, or make it more plausible philosophically.

Search for spirituality has unexpectedly found its place at the confluence of sociology, economics, and Max Weber's historical analysis. Max Weber was the only European thinker to be able to oppose Marx successfully, and overturn Marx's key historical materialism claim. In his famous work *Protestant Ethic and the Spirit of Capitalism*, he saw spiritualisation in the Puritan economic motivation to produce and accrue capital. Moreover, Weber was able to rise from "ideological motivation" of behaviour to the level of *activity basis*, when the latter became an ontological category (even more so, because historically, it was an activity truly changing the image and soul of civilisation). Weber's spirituality determines human material practice, but does not result from it as deriving from life-sustaining activity. Weber's theory, therefore, requires thorough philosophical treatment. However, he also understood that the universal semantic and communication monopoly for the actual word "spirituality" belonged to religion, primarily the church, and, we might add, pseudo-idealistic and conditional-mystical teachings (e.g., theosophy), which are often called by the same name – "spiritual systems".

If we scrutinised spirituality for the fragments of positive ontological understanding of it, which are fearfully widespread across various theories, teachings and paradigms, we would seem to be able to sketch a portrait of spirituality made up of these obscure and hardly visible features. Intuition alone can guide us on this way.

Accepting the existence of spirituality's possible content makes us presume that this notion may not be just mere abstraction and an empty category, but have some concrete meaning. It is understood not as some empirically verified phenomenality, but as something that can be given intuitively as *supersensible*. It exists in the world as something we call beautiful or reasonable; and in our conscience as wonderful confidence that there is some higher being whose existence is incommensurable with human existence. Nevertheless, only if we accept it, we can establish the basis for evaluating and understanding our life, the categories of good and evil, beauty and ugliness, truth and lies, and justice and lawlessness.

Spiritual intuition is based on an unconditional internal (not necessarily completely understood, or conceptually thought through, or theoretically verified) acceptance of the absolute existence of some source of, say, being and the unequivocal acceptance of good and evil as absolute fundamentals and forces that would be inherent in being.

Psychology and philosophical-anthropological science normally treats such an unconventional and non-relativistic postulating of good and evil as sources of existence and forces as "naïve", and brands those who have this kind of experience as historically or theoretically immature. The fact is that it is often difficult to explain the roots and basis of this "naïve" (in reality–direct) experience of *being, good, and evil* and the confidence that it exists.

To conclude this section, we can say that the attractiveness and high potential of planetary ethics are based on the fact that it will not stop developing, even when it reaches the state of being a coherent and functional system, applicable to solving motivational-psychological problems of planetary anti-crisis management. Having experienced the first success in saving the biosphere, and establishing the noospheric civilisation foundations, it will create a new cultural-anthropologic type of person, the *integral person*, and a new bio-socio-historical evolutionary agent, *WE-humanity*, destined to realise the cosmic potential of planet Earth. Alongside innovation science and the breakthrough technologies of the Sixth Techno-economic Paradigm, planetary ethics will create the worldview of the *Future*.

Humanity needs *meaning* for its existence as much as an individual needs it. At least, all constructive religions and spiritual systems teach this. To the same degree, however, human development needs a purpose and goal. Such a global goal can be overcoming chaos in the world in all its manifestations: from the micro-level of wars, and meso-level of threats coming from outer space, to the mega-level of the increasing entropy of matter. The question whether this victory over chaos can be achieved is an open one, at least from a scientific point of view. From a moral-ethical perspective, this goal is ultimately beautiful and exalted.

CHAPTER 12

Planetary Project Implementation Results

Avenues of Planetary Project further development: economic-technical, environmental, political-legal and social-ethical. Planetary Project implementation logic. Re-globalisation. WE-humanity as a planetary agent. A new evolutionary scenario and the architecture of the future. Innovation development programs and space. From Homo sapiens to Homo spaciens.

The last chapter of this monograph, which is the first overview of the Planetary Project in book form, will be dedicated to the expected results of implementing the project's key ideas. Obviously, we are now offering a working hypothesis. The Concept of Managed Harmony and the hypothetical future architecture model will be amended and corrected later, but it will already be possible within the Planetary Project philosophy framework. Right now, we must formulate a general vision of *a new evolutionary scenario.* United humanity must become its agent, as it has been able to put its history under control and induce it with rational and humanistic vectors of development.

According to the logic of the Planetary Project, the following conditions are necessary in order to find a way out of the systemic crisis facing current civilisation, to solve global problems, and to save the biosphere including humans. Below, we will describe them as three stages of a planetary agent's self-expression, which starts with the Planetary Project ideas, and is carried out as the project's implementation unfolds.

1) Further development of fundamental ideas of the Planetary Project follows key directions of its future implementation: economical-technical, environmental, political-legal, and social-ethical.

The *economic-technical direction* will include such issues as: the organisation and optimisation of production; natural resource saving technologies; resource saving and resource replacement; economic growth transformation; economical consumption and biocompatible waste disposal; and production forces and taxation management. This will create the basis of a new economic policy and the system of planetary governance institutions, investing in innovations and encouraging the implementation of Sixth Techno-economic Paradigm breakthrough technologies. The strategic goal of this work will consist of developing an integral resource saving economic model based on high production technologies, strict environmental control, and a mechanism of proportional distribution and biocompatible consumption. As a result, an entirely new economic system in quality, costs and efficiency must be developed that would be capable of not only meeting the current needs of society, but also providing solutions to the world's global problems: political, environmental, social, and demographic.

The ***environmental direction*** of the development of the Planetary Project ideas must achieve the goal of creating a total system of environmental control of economic activity, first at the national level and then at the level of the integral planetary economy. Besides its regulatory role, it will fulfil the functions of proactive planning, final approval, certification and licensing of resource consuming activity, including granting permissions or imposing bans, as well as consultation and coordination in economic management. Initial objectives to be solved as part of the environmental part of the Planetary Project include: taking stock and qualification of global problems from an environmental perspective; actualised resource consumption assessment; and the development of comprehensive recommendations for economic reform planning directed towards planetary resource use, and benefiting from planetary rent possibilities. Parallel to this, work must be carried out to prevent environmental catastrophes and crises in particular natural zones, and to save disappearing soils, flora and fauna belonging to the ecosystems affected by excessive anthropo-socio-technogenic damage.

The goal of the ***political-legal direction*** of planetary research is to create an infrastructural system of planetary governance institutions. For this to occur: normative-legal issues of a new world order must be resolved; politological and sociological analysis of opportunities associated with the implementation of new administrative-political practices must be carried out; and the prognosis of mechanisms of integral power adaptation and development must be formulated. It is of vital importance that the following should be observed: the principles of national-state sovereignty of countries; mutually acceptable balance of their interests; peculiarities of national political cultures; dispersion of power; and parity of rights.

The following philosophical-pedagogical, information-enlightenment and propagandistic objectives must be addressed within the framework of the ***social-ethical direction***: the Planetary Project must receive a reliable spiritual-ethical justification and be adapted to effective communication, promotion and acceptance as a mobilisation ideology. The goal here is to win the confidence and support, encouraging involvement and active participation, first of the world's elites and then, with their help, of all people of the world. Achieving social-ethical objectives furthering the ideas of the Planetary Project promises to have a long-term and multimodal effect. This is because it will influence the formation of new socialisation mechanisms as well as upbringing and education systems.

It is important that the whole activity aimed at developing the Planetary Project fundamental ideas should be conducted through collaborative and unanimous efforts of the best theoreticians and practitioners, scientists, and business people, politicians and public figures, spiritual leaders and law-makers. These people should be united by a common understanding of the critical situation modern humanity finds itself in, and the need to find a way out of it, save the life of the planet, and should ensure that future generations have healthy and worthy prospects. These people's co-operation must result in the transformation of the Planetary Project into a universal system of a new integral biocentric and noosphere-oriented worldview. Its most important applied aspect must include a step-by-step concrete programme of preventing an approaching world collapse, which can occur unless we relieve considerably the athropo-socio-technogenic pressure on the environment and prevent resource wars.

2) The ruling elites receive a scientific-practical contradiction-free scheme, based on the Planetary Project ideas, which resembles a detailed business plan, or a program of actions in the "road map" form. The elites begin to co-operate actively to create integral innovation economy and mechanisms of generating financial means from the use of planetary resources and their targeted distribution, to develop a planetary governance institution infrastructure, and to solve global problems. Having accepted the Planetary Project innovation reforming ideas, and having received the algorithms and methodology of required action, the world elites unite around the ideas of global self-preservation and start a mechanism of **planetary anti-crisis management**. Its goal is to take the world out of the profound systemic crisis, thwarting the threats of environmental, military, and technogenic character, alleviating global economic, political and social conflicts, improving the health of the environment, and normalising society.

The anti-crisis stage can be quite long and labour-intensive, and require not only resources and a technological leap, but also the breaking of century-old stereotypes, standard transformation and interest re-orientation. Initially, this reforming movement is expected to spread from several continental and regional zones, which are currently characterised by a high level of economic and technical, development. This polycentrism will stimulate the development of a joint and compromise-based planetary anti-crisis management format, and ensure an alternative scenario of global human integration we call *re-globalisation*.

It is worthwhile pointing out that already at this stage of breaking the *stereotypical thinking patterns*, a new type of consciousness, both public and personal, and, of course, a new type of carrier must start to emerge: a collective carrier—the *planetary mega-community*; and an individual carrier—*the integral person*. Let us emphasise that at the re-globalisation stage, transitional from a systemic crisis to *managed harmony*, we just see the beginning of the drastic transformation of society and the individual, rather than its end. Therefore, we tend to talk about transitional mega-social and socio-anthropological human types in terms of their organisation and self-organisation, and cognition, and behaviour.

3) The result of the successful phase of planetary crisis management will save the world from anthropo-technogenic risk factors, and improve the health of the environment and society. The result of this will be that nations of the world guided by their elites will naturally unite. The Planetary Project integration scenario is much more realistic than all that preceded it because it corresponds to the Planetary Project logic.

Some people believe that the logic of historical development tends to enlarge social organisation forms, ensuring their complexity and development from the pre-historic totemic clan to the technocratic civilisation. Smaller, less significant, culture-specific forms of social phenomena give way to larger social forms, by assimilating, modifying or receiving a cultural-symbolic status. This does not contradict the integral macro-economic context.

Global communication resources are powerful drivers of *integration processes.* They enable unlimited information possibilities and contacts, ranging from private correspondence to working from home and e-commerce. In this sense, the information-financial space was integrated a long time ago. The economic objectivity of integration is that, having started in more industrially developed countries, it soon spread to different level economies and markets. It concerns not only the flow of goods whose sale could benefit only one country, but also quite objective processes involving large populations in poorer Third World countries, labour migration, and transborder capital movement.

It is important that scientific and political innovations, as well as new cultural and even language trends, possess equal mobility as the economic ones. One can think that this is the way that only progress and fashion manifest themselves. It would be correct, but only partially: only the surface of a process looks like this. The process's core is in the fact that human cognitive, worldview, and purpose, shifts take place in this manner. The common goal orientation is the most natural and successful integration motivation of all.

The Planetary Project integration scenario is much more realistic than all that preceded it. This is because it is based on the principles of common threats and challenges, activity and ownership, social justice, civilisation and ethical universalism; while the existing ways of life, cultures and religions (unless they contradict planetary goals) are preserved on a compromise basis.

The mega-community finds itself quite capable of implementing the **Concept of Managed Harmony** having brought the world into a safe and balanced state by the efforts and resources of an integrated economy, and planetary institution infrastructure. Just to remind you, it is the name we used for a mature Planetary Project phase that implies a maximally balanced and symmetrical type of social development, which involves an ideal interaction between people and nature, ensuring their joint stable homeostasis. Managed harmony can be considered the most valuable achievement of post-crisis humanity. It needs to be cherished and maintained by joint effort. It can generate intentions and ideas for further progress by itself.

All necessary conditions for the formation of *a noospheric civilisation* finally emerge when there is a type of social development such as managed harmony, which has an ideal symbiosis of people and nature. Let us remind you that in our view, the prerequisites have started to emerge even now, at the time of global crisis. They might have actually started to emerge even before, in the eighteenth and nineteenth centuries. However, it is at the anti-crisis planetary management stage that they have actualised and flourished in the period of managed harmony.

At that time, the process of systemic integration of nations of the world will be finalised, and we will be able to talk, not just about a mega-community, but also about a planetary *WE-humanity* as a planetary agent of world history and a creator of noospheric civilisation. This is a fundamentally new type of socio-cultural, civil, intellectual, and spiritual organisation of people, when their integration has become absolutely natural and organic. WE-humanity is essentially a qualitatively different product of evolution, the result of *managed development*, and biosocial super-species. As a planetary organic super-system, WE-humanity possesses internal interrelations organised at a higher level than any known type of human communities. It is becoming possible because WE-humanity is equally a *super-population* and a single *macro-organism*. We see the WE-humanity genesis as a permanent creative process based on synergy and symbiosis.

Philosophers and historians have thought of **noospheric humanity** at different periods, and within different intellectual traditions: from Vernadsky and the Russian cosmists, to Jaspers and European existentialists, and from Pierre Teilhard de Chardin to Nikita Moiseev. Today, this is a popular interdisciplinary topic studied at the junction of ecology, sociology, globalism, philosophy of history, and ethics. It is worth noting that, speaking conditionally, *noospheric anthropology* works on united humanity issues, critiques etatisme, and has an original interpretation of globalisation.

Of all its ideas, we are interested in the following ones in the context of the Planetary Project:

- The noospheric humanity planetary community does not equal the State. Government institutions are secondary and auxiliary vis-à-vis a strong

system of open and dynamic civil self-government institutions.
- Natural as well as spiritual foundations are available for the real unity of humanity. They are objective in equal degree. In combination, they are called humanity or humaneness. This is, in clear form, a *biosocial* phenomenon, the product of evolution and history.
- The ideal unity of humanity can be actualised under certain conditions. It is now contained as potential in the spiritual experience of the world's nations, in *value-symbolic universalisms*. According to synergetic worldview principles, images of the remotest future have already been registered by the *spiritual practices* of our ancestors. Evidence of this is the artefact of various origins: from religious literature to prophetic science-fiction writing.
- The pre-historic period of humanity saw the first objectified rudiments and early forms of human integration. There are grounds to believe that the actual principle of social organisation of our ancestors into totemic clans, and then into tribes, was a giant leap forward in their life, and their response to the threat of self-destruction. According to the most original anthropo-sociogenesis versions, the entire species of prehominids, predecessors of people, found themselves on the brink of death because they killed each other, driven by sexual aggression. To harness it, taboos or prehistoric bans emerged that laid the foundation of conscious behaviour regulation and subordination, totem clans, mythological consciousness, language, and

labour. However, besides integration effects, the early forms of social organisation kick-started disintegration mechanisms based on the friend-foe identification. This indicated the fundamental ambivalence of both human conscience and all its objectifications.

- A possible noospheric unity is not prone to the risks of "universal equality" in its absolute expression, as integration critics fear. The latter is not possible due to some objective reasons and regularities of both a natural and social kind. People can be equal only in the eyes of the written law, i.e., legal norms and the so-called unwritten law, i.e., moral norms. It is clear, though, that society should compensate for the natural inequality of people in some accepted forms. The more harmoniously society is structured, the more effectively it will perform such compensation tasks.
- The implementation of any integration programme, including the noospheric project, must not rely on illegal violence and discriminatory, segregating, and narrowly oriented ideology. History shows us that such projects, having essentially annexationist character, have failed (Alexander the Great's *Oecumene*, the Holy Roman Empire, the Golden Horde, the Third Reich, and the USSR).
- We can only apply the term noospheric to poly-social and poly-political humanity combined, based on reasonableness and humanistic spirituality; which boosts the probability of the unlimited existence of the Earth biosphere.

By becoming a new planetary species, WE-humanity restarts world history implementing a rationally managed evolutionary scenario at the junction of humaneness and bio-centrism. The anthropogenic factor reveals itself as a productive driver of evolution: by entering into a co-creation with nature, noospheric people fulfil the mission of protectors and stewards of organic life, because, having learned the lessons of their predecessors, they see their own benefit in the welfare of their habitat. They set their new strategic and tactical objectives in line with the requirements of biocompatibility, while the microcosm and the macrocosm are becoming the vectors of human intensive and extensive development. The interests of the planet remain a priority.

The following directions have become the core of all innovation scientific-technical programmes including basic and applied Research and Development, natural sciences and humanities experimentation, which together, are called "projects of the future". Below are their large thematic categories:

- nanotechnologies
- microelectronics
- robotechnics
- material studies
- energy
- transport
- the creative economy
- biotechnologies
- genetic engineering
- anthropology
- cybernetics and the artificial intelligence
- space
- synergisms and futurology

These high technology applications have been the highest rated development avenues in terms of impact on all spheres of human activity. They are based on high consumer demand, government support, and multiple applied and basic research findings. Despite the early twenty-first century crisis in some science-consuming industries, research activity has not stopped; it has even expanded. The successful implementation of these scientific studies can generate a new technological leap in the development of humanity and solve some pressing socio-economic problems at the global level.

Scientific-technical progress and outstanding feats of engineering are primarily associated with **nanotechnology**, which is the most innovative field of science and technology. Some people call nanotechnology as twenty-first century chemistry. According to the creators of nanotechnology, their essence is in the ability to rebuild cell structure, or create new cells, by manipulating atoms. This enables scientists to create organisms and substances that have incredible qualities. Nanotechnology breakthrough will be possible when we are able to construct nanorobots that would undertake tasks to change molecular structure, and nanocomputers that would operate nanorobots. According to some scientists, nanotechnology can: increase computer productivity; encourage the production of new materials with required qualities; reproduce live organic tissue; and bring about radical physical and chemical developments capable of changing the course of civilisation.

According to some forecasts, nanorobots will transform Homo sapiens as a biosocial species into a fundamentally new organism and life form—a *Nano sapiens*, a cyberman. Nanorobots will be able to resolve the conflict between people and nature, because they will be able to create artificial sources of energy that will rid us of resource dependence, and the environment of destructive human interference. For example, nanocomposite membranes will even resolve the problem of the deficit of drinking water.

Nanotechnology experts identify three main development stages of this field of knowledge and activity. The first stage of passive nanostructures is already over. Now, we are going through the second stage of evolutionary nanotechnology, which is expected to continue until 2020. It is characterised by the development of *active nanostructures* and a *system of nanosystems*. They imply the creation of: nanoelectronic, photonic, and nanobiotechnology components; as well as medical products and equipment, neuroelectronic interfaces, and nanoelectromechanical systems.

The role of nanobiotechnology is increasing in the pharmaceutical (up to 23%), cosmetics, and food industries. Tomorrow, nanotechnology will be used in 100% of computer and radioelectronic equipment, up to 85% in home appliances, and up to 21% in automobiles. This will enable engineers to make a transition to operated nanosystem self-assembly, creating 3D networks, nanorobots, etc.

After 2020, we expect to enter a third nanotechnology period referred to as the stage of "molecular nanosystems" or of "radical nanotechnology". They include molecular devices, atom design, and so on. The molecular manufacturing of macroscopic objects will become possible. According to http://9000innovations.ru, a considerable leap is expected in: the development, manufacturing and sale of nanotechnology research and special equipment; nanoelectromechanical systems for the nanoelectronic industry; and bionanotechnology for the medical, cosmetics, and food industries. A nanotechnology revolution is right around the corner!

Microelectronics is one of the most dynamically developing directions of world science; the microelectronic industry is a leading part of any national economy. American researchers are working on a microcomputer 1mm^3 in size, which signals microelectronics turning to nanoelectronics. Today's mainstream electronics and informatics research is focused on developing high capacity computers; new communication and international computer networks; and integrating different communication systems.

Unlike several other fields of knowledge, including technical sciences, **microelectronics** is dynamically changing in its quality. More than any other applied sciences, it is considered capable of working wonders: even now, 90% of all innovations in solid-state physics derive to various degrees from microelectronics.

The industry's future is believed to involve the implementation and use of nanomaterials that enable the reduction in size of microchips and transistors for computer chips. The prime material is graphene; the width of a graphene band may be smaller than one atom. Graphene has been shown to remain stable and to conduct electricity when broken into fragments of less than a few nanometres. The strong hydrogen-hydrogen link keeps graphene's honeycomb cell structure even when silicon oxidises. Therefore, nanotechnology is expected to set the future microelectronics trends. The last several decades have seen microelectronics and the related fields of solid-state physics, chemistry and mathematics, change social life more drastically than any other field of science or technology.

The future of **robotechnics** is directly linked to new materials, including nanomaterials, nanotechnology, and artificial intelligence. The industry promises a transfer of some type of work from humans to robots, especially in the areas where even now, robots are clearly superior. It is true, for example, when exploring spaces that are difficult to reach, and working in emergency and hazardous conditions. Some people believe that today's machines demonstrate quite complex behaviour, which could even be considered intelligent; and they continue to learn. The programmed intelligence is getting increasingly complex; machines are acquiring more and more different functions and autonomy. Intelligent robots will be indispensable in such spheres as identifying and ensuring safety, providing security and surveillance, searching and predicting, and carrying out complex scientific experiments.

General Motors in the US and Honda in Japan, are the two leading robot manufacturers, including androids. They claim that robots will work alongside humans in the home, manufacturing, warehouses, hospitals, or other places. In the near future, designers and producers of intelligent robots are going to be focused on expanding robot autonomy and sensitivity. Intelligent machines must be able to work as far away from the operator as possible, or without any operator at all.

Robotics history shows that progress in the field has never been or will ever be a linear one: the industry is bracing for a breakthrough in the next few years that will forever change the life of humanity.

In the ***energy sector***, alternative sources of energy have for several years been the world's main research area; and they are still the main area today. These alternative sources of energy must be able to meet the long-term energy needs of humanity. Current energy solutions cannot ensure sustainable energy supply due to their high costs and insufficient capacity. The key energy innovation projects include:

- developing new sources of energy that would have the capacity of existing sources of energy;
- reducing alternative energy costs to a competitive level;
- creating transportation means that would use alternative energy-based fuel, including electricity, solar power, alcohol, hydrogen, and reprocessed waste.

Energy innovations are moving towards both superconducting materials including superconducting turbogenerators and transformers, and thermonuclear fusion. For example, minimal size devices for charging electric cars are already manufactured. Radical solutions transforming thermal energy to electricity are also worked on; they will ensure that energy sources are economical, simple to use, reliable, and long lasting. Transmission solutions are potentially the most promising in this regard.

The twenty-first-century's most important trend—**the alternative energy sector**—is actively expanding its share of the market at the expense of the cave technologies of burning fossil fuel. Renewable sources of energy—nuclear and solar power—are expected to have a bigger share than shale gas. The period of giant nuclear power plants is ending; the world is bracing itself for a new type of nuclear power: small size, renewable, and safe. The future belongs to 50 to 100 tonne units charged for 8 to 10 years and over. The cost of energy they will produce is far lower than the electric power generated by burning coal, oil, or gas. This is despite the fact that, according to the World Economic Forum and the CNBC expert publication, the demand for energy is expected to rise by 41% by the year 2035 compared to the current level; as much as 95% of it is expected to come from developing countries. India will be the biggest energy importer and consumer. Brazil, Mexico, South Africa, Nigeria, Egypt, Turkey, Saudi Arabia, Iran, Thailand, and Indonesia will also increase their shares in the world energy market by 2040.

As far as shale gas is concerned, the USA and Canada will remain the leaders of the industry, while China will substantially boost its shale gas production as well. Europe will increase shale gas and liquefied gas consumption.

The decreased cost of hydrogen-based fuels will boost the development of environmentally compatible sources of energy: renewable sources based on recycling household waste into gas will also continue to develop. Serious success awaits wind farms, because the cost of producing wind generated energy per 1 kW is reducing, despite the fact that they are being equipped with large turbogenerators of up to 600 kW, instead of the 400 kW ones used only recently. Wind farm have also become more efficient, and stand the chance to become an integral part of a balanced energy business.

We can expect a revolution in the energy storage device, the battery in terms of its size and functionality. This will encourage automobile producers to shift to mass manufacturing electric cars.

It is quite possible that a "cloud" energy system will emerge, in which large power stations will be replaced by small power units working on renewable energy sources and solar power. They will be united into a large virtual system if need be. This system can include space solar stations capable of transforming sunrays into shortwave electromagnetic radiation to send focused energy flows to terrestrial industrial current converters.

Concerning *future materials* to be used in industry and the home, we could point out engineering ceramics including the above graphene, carbon fibre-reinforced plastics, amorphous alloys, and composite and self-healing materials. A boom is expected for analogous and alternate materials causing them to decrease in price, and to be used widely. *Silecene* is hailed as a substitute for graphene. This silicon atom layer a hydrocarbon atom wide has superconductor properties and extra flexibility, and is completely compatible with modern, silicon-based electronics. We can also mention the following recently developed materials: *aerogel* is the best thermal insulator and absorbent material to date; and *ferrofluid* or "liquid metal" capable of changing its shape under the influence of a magnetic field, is used in the automobile industry, and is expected to be used in astronomy and medicine.

The main research direction in developing new composite materials is creating a group of thermoplastic molecular composites, ceramics, plastics and amorphous alloys that are resistant to high temperatures, and that have low weight. New materials will be used in the aviation and automobile industries. To resolve global issues, including environmental protection, researchers are working on high-grade ceramics with improved qualities to produce machines that have high efficiency, do not harm the environment, and work on different types of fuel.

What is **new in materials** is that they have pre-programmed qualities that the materials never had before, or could be generated through specific exposure. So, for example, the 2020s are expected to see the appearance of contact lenses capable of accessing the Internet. Lenses and glasses with Internet access will be able to project for the user virtual reality coupled with fast face recognition, and automatic translation between languages.

There are predictions that in the near future we can expect the development of programmed matter: computers will set the shape of new materials. Microchips already exist the size of a pinhead that can regroup very fast when exposed to an electric discharge, i.e., practically by the push of a button. Claytronics is an important programmed matter development area It deals with creating nanorobots that could make contact with each other and produce 3D objects the user could interact with.

"Green technologies" minimally affecting the environment have recently started playing an increasingly significant part in new material development. The same requirements are applied to the new materials themselves in terms of their use, disposal, and recycling. They rely on exhausting the full life cycle of a material, and the integrity of its functional chain. Additive technologies have a great potential whose purpose is to produce a specific item by gradual building it layer after layer. Additive technologies are a powerful lever of increasing productivity and simultaneously reducing labour consumption by almost 30-40 times.

Transportation development is closely connected to innovative solutions in energy, new materials, software, artificial intelligence, and telecommunications. The key transportation problem today is that it lags behind information technology, which slows down trade: you can choose and buy products within hours or minutes but have to wait for days or weeks to get them. Moreover, combustion engines pollute the environment. Therefore, breakthrough transportation solutions will address these issues.

The time is not far away when new original **means of transportation** will be mass-produced. Many already have prototypes, including a car working on compressed air, driverless or autonomous cars, extra-small personal cars, and solar-powered buses. Monorail, string railway and pneumatic solutions, hold great potential for cargo transportation. Pneumatic transportation deserves a few extra comments. The concept implies transporting goods and people inside a tube with the speed of slightly over 1220 km/h, which is close to supersonic speed, and promises to be the most ambitious alternative to land, rail, water and air transport. The idea uses pneumatic tube advantages to minimise turbulence and maximise speed. Americans are already discussing constructing a "hyperloop".

The aviation industry is going to follow an environmental-friendly path as well: new generation jets will use electricity, take off vertically, and reach supersonic speed. Giant flying machines are being designed that would use liquid hydrogen, and that would be capable of reaching a speed of up to 6,400 km/h, and cover distances of up to 20,000 km without refuelling. Four-wing planes are going to break the supersonic barrier, and take off from a strip of less than 700 metres; silent propeller planes will use biofuel to fly.

Hybrid types of transportation will spread widely carrying both passengers and goods: a *ground effect train* hovering over the ground on an air cushion; a *flying motorcycle,* a hybrid of a quadcopter, and an ordinary motorcycle; a flying car; and a flying boat.

Genetic engineering and **biotechnologies** are the most dynamically developing research areas. Applying research findings will encourage substantial progress in medicine, healthcare, agriculture, and food production. The global community is viewing genetic engineering as a means to fight starvation and diseases. The main genetic engineering innovation projects include:

- studying and deciphering human genetic information, and the genetic material of plants and animals;
- creating new medicine for diseases previously considered to be incurable;
- creating more productive and disease resistant crops including cereals, fruits and vegetables.

Nanotechnologies, computers and software will aid biotechnologies and genetic engineering. They will radically transform agricultural technologies, the food industry, as well as the pharmaceutical and medical industries. These changes will make it possible to overcome infectious bacterial and virus diseases, inherited defects, and the so-called "diseases of civilisation". Later, they will boost the personal transformation of people, and greatly contribute to the human ability to manage matter. Even now, scientists use special nanoparticles in medicine as carriers of the biologically active molecules of medical substances. They have found that this helps to overcome effectively barriers in the body that these substances are not capable of overcoming on their own. This changes the effect and effectiveness of a medicine.

The main global medical innovation projects include:

- developing new types of medicine to treat diseases that are hard to treat with today's methods (cardiovascular disorders, AIDS, the oncological diseases, old age dementia, etc.);
- using genomics to treat diabetes, cardiovascular diseases, improving resistance to antibiotics, brain disorders and infectious diseases;

- creating artificial organs for surgical transplantation.

American scholar and inventor Ray Kurzweil talked about genetics, nanotechnologies, informatics, cybernetics and cognitive technologies as the most influential disciplines of the near future. In his futurological bestsellers, *The Age of Intelligent Machines* (1990), *The Age of Spiritual Machines* (1998), and *The Singularity Is Near--When Humans Transcend Biology* (2005). His prediction is that by 2040, the human body will have been able to take any shape comprised by a great number of nanotechnological devices, which are of higher quality than natural ones (essentially spare parts or biological "nanolego" pieces). Technologies will be used that will extend the productive part of human life. DNA samples will enable us to revive many plant and animal species.

Food and industrial issues will be resolved with a "universal replicator", a mega-device capable of creating anything from anything, including from waste. The traditional industries of manufacturing and agriculture will get rid of needs; human labour will be dramatically transformed as well. The arts will flourish accompanied by a boom in entertainment, research, and other development practices.

Artificial intelligence is one of the most intense, exciting, and controversial issues in science and social research, because it has an ethical dimension and it defies prediction.

The futurologist and trans-humanitarian Hans Moravec made interesting predictions based on this involvement robotics. Some of them, which he discussed in his book *Mind Children* (1988), are already finding validation.

Indeed, the 2010s saw the development of robots whose intellectual abilities are identical to those of a lizard. Some models, for instance iRobot, fit the description; they perform household chores and associated tasks without human guidance. According to Moravec's logic, robots will possess the intellectual abilities of a highly developed primate around the year 2040. They will be able to identify simple technical and household problems, and set and perform tasks without human commands. Moravec made this prognosis following the emergence of the first drones with innovative solutions. Approximately, by the mid-twenty-first century, people will be able to upload their brain into the computer. Therefore, after 2040, robots' intellectual abilities will reach the human level and later surpass it.

According to Ray Kurzweil, the other influential futurologist whom we have already mentioned above, personal computers will reach the human brain computing capability even earlier – by 2020. Ten years later, artificial intelligence and human intelligence will be fully synthesised when nanodevices are implanted into the human brain, and transmit needed signals to and from brain cells. When this is implemented, people will not need to learn or get education in the traditional sense. Thus, the ultimate shift to the cyborgisation or human *singularity* will take place.

Next, ***space*** will become the human development horizon. WE-humanity's super goals will be connected with it in the future. **Space** research is a much wider area than the stereotypical ideas of it as basic research or orbital space flights. Even today, it includes a number of sub-research areas; with time, their number and scope will only increase.

The most important "Earth-related" space task is protecting the planet from the meteorite threat. It has two aspects: looking for and observing small space bodies, and finding technical solutions to their deviation in case it presents a threat to the Earth.

A separate task is to find organic life and other civilisations in space: radio astronomy and infrared astronomy deal with it by looking for radio signals from the far reaches of the Universe, and sending radio signals to various galaxies. Space flights to the Moon, Mars, and Venus, pursue the same goal of finding traces of living organisms. Comprehensive study is planned of Jupiter's satellites.

Associated with the above is the research of the genesis and history of planets, the Solar System, galaxies, and the accessible part of the Universe: this is the domain of astro-archeology. It is believed that planet research is akin to investigating the origins of life. Venus is located at the internal rim of the zone of life; Mars, on the outer one, and Earth is in the middle. To understand the difference between these planets is to make another step in finding life outside the Solar System.

The direction of cosmic studies that is the most utilitarian has to do with earthly needs, interests and activities. These are meteorology, satellite communication, and media communications (in future – the Internet from space), and the energy sector.

Space exploration, however, holds the keys to the future: it includes human protection and life-sustenance in the unusual conditions of airless space and weightlessness, adaptability to different atmospheres, and readiness to make long voyages on spacecraft, etc. Finding galaxies and planets suitable for human life and their colonisation are not only science-fiction themes, but also the focus of scientific research. There is reason to believe that these intellectual efforts will greatly increase both in terms of quantity and quality, and needed solutions will be found when people make a leap forward in their development here on Earth. We cannot exclude the possibility that having transformed and revealed their rational-spiritual and socio-biological potential, humanity will extend its life beyond the life cycle of its planet and will need new living space.

It is interesting that a qualitative leap forward in all the most important scientific-technical areas of contemporary knowledge, and in the high-tech industry, which are closely interconnected, will take place at about the same time: between 2020 and 2045, or 2050. For philosophers, physicists, sociologists, futurologists, and science-fiction writers, including Vernor Winge and Raymond Kurzweil, this great historic moment is called technological singularity.

Technological singularity is a point in the future when the evolution of human intelligence will accelerate due to nanotechnologies, biotechnologies and artificial intelligence, to such a degree that a significantly faster brain with new thinking qualities will emerge. This will mean that a new type of civilisation is born. People and the world around them can change beyond recognition. However, to live to this moment, however close it might look, we must make sure our planet is still alive.

Concluding the predictions of the above human technical victories and achievements, future breakthroughs, and unprecedented changes in human life, we must say that they can materialise only if we start solving global problems, and save right now the biosphere, and the world we live in. This implies the necessity to implement the Planetary Project, taking humanity from the current systemic crisis through anti-crisis planetary management to a balanced type of development, managed harmony, when humanity will enter a truly qualitatively different period of its history.

Thus, what synergy effect can people and nature expect from the Planetary Project when it is successfully implemented in a comprehensive manner? What can become possible and realistic on the new— *planetary*—financial-economic basis through an infrastructural system of planetary governance? **A future world** would be: without wars, starvation, pandemics, poverty, environmental and economic crises and degradation; a world of flourishing nature, a rich diversity of plants and animals, and renewable resources; a world of healthy and happy people living and developing in harmony with the environment, and exploring the unending cosmos.

The future world will belong to a new humanity who has corrected the defects and flaws of human nature on the way from the global world to the planetary one, from chaos to harmony, from the faceless objectivity of anonymous historical forces, to the practice of planetary historical management; from a disunited world population to a united WE-humanity; from futurophobia to an active and rational creation of the future, and from *Homo sapiens* to *Homo spaciens*.

Why and how is it all possible? Why is it not a utopia? Because we have most things we need to achieve it: instincts, potential, experience, reason, spirituality, and technologies. What is left to do is to combine everything into one pool, and launch, and later, to tune, improve, monitor and keep. We can only hypothesise how many years or decades it will take us to cover the historical journey of preservation laid out in the Planetary Project.

CONCLUSIONS

The minimum task we have to fulfil today is to survive and meet our obligation to future generations and mother Earth. Therefore, the self-preservation instinct is taking on an obvious and undisputable spiritual dimension and justification—even *sacredness*, if you will. By saving ourselves, we are saving the world. We cannot save ourselves unless we save the whole world, improve the environment, and totally restructure our life. Nobody can be exempt from this obligation. Exclusiveness and selectness are no more than an illusion in the case; it is deceptive and harmful.

However, it is in human nature that having set the minimum task, we immediately go on to set a maximum task. Minimum is simply not enough for us. It is not enough just to survive; we want to *live*. With quality, substance, and fullness. Better than yesterday. Better than any time in the past. Evolution has invested us with the need to develop. Possibly, we already have the needs and purpose of a new species greatly superior to us. Last century, Homo sapiens showed signs of an emerging Homo spaciens. To reach that state, humans must go through the transitional stage of Homo integralis, a *united and integral human*, whose existence is a condition and possibility of achieving the subsequent, more complex, and perfect forms of man.

Today, we, as Homo sapiens, have practically reached the abyss of self-destruction; we must understand that we cannot continue to live off the achievements of our ancestors. We have all but run out of this handicap. We must earn our own value in the history of the world by correcting our mistakes. No nation, however highly developed or powerful it might be, is capable of doing it on its own. At least because the global world has become very small and fragile, where bad things can be done alone, but good things only together. The global world, as we know it today, is not a limit or a dead end; it is not a mistake or a verdict. It is just a milestone on the path to a *planetary world*, in which human life and nature should come to balance and harmony. This world, *in which there will not be "others"* is not possible unless people take a conscious and voluntary decision to unite based on the need to survive today, and save their common home for the future.

In order to do that, we must become real humanity. This is important, because there are still some doubts whether people populating the Earth constitute single humanity. Indeed, they do not have the solidarity and common vision regarding at least the most important issues in their life and destiny. Humanity is not an arithmetic set of representatives of one species, united by common external features. Humanity is a phenomenon based on the common origin and common existence, purpose, rationality, spirituality, needs, and orientations. It is worth becoming humanity to experience the synergy of the effects real integration provides. They include the collective reason, intellectual resources, spiritual experience, universal human values and rights. It is also important that we cannot become humanity unless we are consciously oriented towards a common goal, a common vision of the future, and strive to achieve the desired image. These things can only be structured within a *planetary dimension*, as this monograph has tried to illustrate.

It is very important that the current *anti-crisis understanding of humanity* would not have any dominating phantasms. None of the existing concepts of humanity and civilisation paradigms can be considered satisfactory, because they are helpless during the global civilisation crisis. Their deficiency lies in the fact that they focus only on one or a limited number of values, relationships and trends (whether they are "rights and freedoms", "consumption", "retribution after death", "victory of ideas" (or any other things), and completely ignore objective necessity. This objective necessity has three dimensions today: in the form of natural laws (a biospheric-environmental dimension); the self-preservation instinct (a biosocial dimension); and economic reasons (a social-historical dimension).

It is clear that any new civilisation paradigm or any anti-crisis programme or integration model must equally take into account these necessities and skilfully operate them, making them mutually compatible. Indeed, as we pointed out in several sections of this book, it is only possible to resolve global issues, including environmental problems, if we have adequate economic resources and effective mechanisms. The main thing is that it is quite realistic, because we find funding sources for re-globalisation and integration measures, environmental protection and reconstruction projects, and the creation of an innovative economic system, and the just distribution mechanism that would not harm any national economies! Intellectual resources, alienated intellectual economic effects, and intellectual rent mechanisms will come first. The task of consolidating raw materials and global infrastructure networks will follow.

To fulfil this task, we must have necessary preconditions, including changes in the worldview of the national elites, the mobilisation of the political will, and the compromise-based co-ordination of interests directed at the common goal of human survival.

Why is it not a utopia? Why is it possible to save the biosphere and civilisation today, despite the world's deep systemic crisis and global problems? Why is global human unification, the basic condition of survival of life on Earth, realistic on a planetary scale? In our view, these are not rhetorical questions anymore; they can receive a direct and categorically positive answer for several objective reasons that have been defined, described and substantiated on the pages of this monograph. All we need to do now is to sum them up saying that the current moment of history is a unique one, because it presents a whole range of possibilities to institutionalise human unity. We are convinced that the global community is ready to move from potentiality to effective action. Firstly, this is because there are sufficient material, technological, infrastructural, and information-communication integration platforms. Secondly, because there are prerequisites enough to implement humanity's key concepts, i.e., such comprehensive conditions allowing people to integrate into an ultimate planetary community, synergistically much more powerful than any individual nation and their arbitrary associations. There are three such concepts: motivational, rational, and prospective.

The *motivational concept* implies that people consciously or accidentally unite in a situation characterised by a high probability of the radical change or elimination of the traditional order of existence. Mythological and religious literature and spiritual traditions call this situation Doomsday, the Judgement Day, the completion of the universal divine cycle, etc.

Today, it manifests itself as an environmental and social crisis, global problems and threats, and the approaching depletion of the most important human sustenance: resources. Understanding these crisis conditions can integrate humanity based on global security and the self-preservation instinct. We have already said that the self-preservation instinct is enough to ensure global human unification, transform the existing world order, and launch a planetary mobilisation movement. We would just have to spiritualise this instinct in light of our responsibility towards the generation to come, and all living things with which we have an inherent relationship as part of the common biosphere. Surviving, improving the environment, caring for the future, and raising the standard of living and of the environment, are strong motives to overcome the legal-cultural constraints of individual nations, and to form a united planetary civilisation.

The rational concept of humanity implies the emergence of humanity as a rational and moral supra-organism that enters into co-evolution with nature, and which is responsible for its activity. To achieve this goal, we must ensure that our thinking and self-awareness reach the level of *universalism*, characteristic of global human identity. It is clear, though, that it must be extra-ideological and supra-national. It must be planetary, i.e., noospheric.

What makes it possible to form and disseminate this type of identity? There are several factors at work here. First, never in history has a private person been so sovereign, valuable, and responsible as they are now. The dramatic events of the twentieth century and current global problems have prepared us to accept the ideas of global human integration and saving the world as a common and unified effort.

Second, never have science and religion, rational and mystical types of thinking, been so close both striving for the compromise and synthesis of universal truths and values. Today, they are quite capable of a creative symbiosis for the sake of ensuring the future. Third, undoubtedly, contemporary intellectual universalism is based on global interaction made possible by the high level of technology, communication, and transportation.

The *prospective concept* of humanity is characterised by the fact that the existential questions, "who are we?" and "where do we come from?" are addressed through the questions "what are we doing?" and "where are we going?" The unifying factor here includes the united vision of global creative prospects and the joint effort of their systemic realisation. The innovative character of current civilisation acts as the prerequisite of this. The innovations, however, should be redirected from addressing narrow goals of making immediate profit to achieving global historical goals connected with building a new economic system, which would be resource and energy consuming, nature saving, and recycling oriented. Key technological innovations must include alternative renewable energy sources, improving the health of the biosphere, and space exploration. Thus, the prospective concept transforms the task of restricting consumption into that of expanding our capacity as a planetary species to sustain and reproduce *development* without harming the environment. Immanent humanity is moving towards transcendental humanity, and planetary agent is moving towards cosmic agent. Humanity, being the agent of this kind, reveals and expands the world and the Universe in infinitely small and large phenomenality directions. This process started in the previous century; the task of the current age is to invest it with the new meaning of planetary-cosmic prospects.

Therefore, based on the prerequisites of all of the above concepts, we have a truly historic chance to achieve maximum unity of people in a non-violent way, when they unite to make up the world where there will be no "others".

It is characteristic that emerging and finding response in different parts of the world, the purpose of the Planetary Project has found its final form in Dubai. Today's Dubai is not only one of the world's capitals, an ultra-modern city with a powerful infrastructure, and a high standard of living; it is a real image of the future, an amazingly friendly and comfortable place, where people from many countries, religions, and cultures live together under the warm sun of the Arabian Peninsula. In Dubai, it is felt that the balance of people and nature is found, and that people are able and willing to receive gifts from above, and enjoy the fruits of their labour in peace and agreement with each other.

Some people believe that the Islamic world is treating globalisation with caution, seeing the risks of levelling the national cultural diversity of non-Anglo-Saxon civilisations. In practice, today's Muslim community is not only well-informed of the multiplicity of globalist scenarios, but understands the inevitability and objectivity of integration processes, and is trying to find realistic global integration alternatives. According to Eastern nations, globalisation must not be restricted to material gain from commercial activity, but encompass the moral-ethical and enlightenment aspects of human existence. In this regard, the re-globalisation thrust of the Planetary Project ideology could be organically integrated in the cultural, ideological, and value universe of the Arab world and in appropriate paradigms of looking at the world based on the Islamic worldview.

Modern Eastern nations cannot be accused of the lack of modernising intentions: the United Arab Emirates, to name just one country, places great value in education, basic and experimental research, high technologies and such benefits of civilisation as the rights of nations to self-determination, their own language and values, as well as cross-cultural communication and inter-denominational dialogue. A close look at Dubai life shows that the United Arab

Emirates welcomes constructive innovative ideas not only in formal, technical, and natural sciences, but also in the humanitarian dimension of human thinking and interaction. This country's example demonstrates that the enlightened Muslim community is open to the world and does not resist progress, but only insists on the principles of pluralism, partnership, and equality for all its participants. It means that the East is not only ready to be engaged in forming a new civilisation of a *planetary type*, but become a leader of this most large-scale process in human history. Then the metaphor of a *new axis time* can be realised with maximum concreteness: just like 500 years B.C. a modern-type civilisation started to spread from the East across the world, tomorrow the East will become the land where a new *planetary civilisation*, the civilisation of the future, will emerge and start its East to West journey.

The author of this monograph is completely aware of the fact that the book presents more questions than gives answers, and provides more food for discussion than validated evidence. It is fundamentally important that, by presenting Planetary Project ideas, we invite to a dialogue all those who represent constructive and creative forces of the world community. There is a need for the collective synergy of technological, economic, political-legal, and cross-cultural platforms of global human unification. The process of involving national and transnational elites in the integration process is especially timely in the run up to the World Expo 2020, to be held in Dubai in 2020, whose motto is "Connecting Minds, Creating the Future". The Planetary Project is ready not only to become a scientific and spiritual anti-crisis movement of the contemporary world, but also to serve as a platform of cross-cultural communication, dialogue of civilisations, and discussion of the formation of a post-globalist, multi-polar world, freed from superpower domination. Publication of this monograph itself marks a further development of the Planetary Project as an instrument of mobilising the collective intellect of our contemporaries united by a search of ways to solve global problems, and harmonise world development.